FREEDOM FROM WORK

CULTURE AND ECONOMIC LIFE

FREEDOM FROM WORK

Embracing Financial Self-Help
in the United States and Argentina

DANIEL FRIDMAN

STANFORD UNIVERSITY PRESS
STANFORD, CALIFORNIA

Stanford University Press
Stanford, California

©2017 by the Board of Trustees of the Leland Stanford Junior University. All rights reserved.

No part of this book may be reproduced or transmitted in any form or by any means, electronic or mechanical, including photocopying and recording, or in any information storage or retrieval system without the prior written permission of Stanford University Press.

Printed in the United States of America on acid-free, archival-quality paper

Library of Congress Cataloging-in-Publication Data available upon request.

ISBN 978-0-8047-9826-6 (cloth)
ISBN 978-1-5036-0025-6 (paperback)
ISBN 978-1-5036-0026-3 (electronic)

Cover photo: iStock.
Text design by Bruce Lundquist
Typeset at Stanford University Press in 10/14 Minion Pro

Contents

Acknowledgments

In the years since I started working on the research for this book I have lived in four different cities and have been fortunate to receive the support, guidance, and encouragement of many friends and colleagues.

First of all, I want to thank the members and leaders of financial self-help groups in New York and in Argentina, who let me join them in their activities and learn from their lives. This book would not exist without their openness, generosity, good will, and eagerness to teach me. To preserve anonymity, I am not using their real names. But they know who they are, and I am grateful to them.

This project started at Columbia University. I was fortunate to receive the extraordinary guidance of Gil Eyal, who continues to influence my sociological thinking in ways that I discover every day. Gil has an admirable ability and precision to detect where arguments can be strengthened or enriched, and I am deeply indebted for his generous feedback. Diane Vaughan has been an intellectual inspiration and a more than generous and supportive colleague, mentor, and friend. I also want to thank Bill McAllister, Josh Whitford, David Stark, and Peter Bearman. Charles Tilly, who guided me in the very first steps of this project, sadly passed away before I could tell him my fieldwork stories. Chuck was a role model of intellectual commitment, egalitarianism, and generosity with students that I hope to emulate. An extraordinary group of colleagues, including Delia Baldassarri, Ernesto Castañeda, Brandon County, Nancy Davenport, Marissa King, Jennifer Kondo, Dan Lainer-Vos, David Madden, Denise Milstein, Rasmus Nielsen, Emine Onculer, Gustavo Onto, Pilar Opazo, Onur Ozgode, Natasha Rossi, Uri Schwed, Randa Serhan, Mattias Smangs, Natacha Stevanovic, Zsuzsanna Vargha, Mari Webel, and Steve Wills, provided emotional support, intellectual conversation, and substantial feedback throughout my time in New York. The Mellon Interdisciplinary Fellows Program at the

Institute for Social and Economic Research and Policy was the perfect place to start discussing my findings with a vibrant group of scholars and putting ideas on paper. I shared an office with Harel Shapira back in 2008, where he helped me clarify incipient ideas about my fieldwork. By a stroke of fortune, his office is next to mine at the University of Texas, where we continue talking sociology every day.

I want to acknowledge the support of various institutions. A Lazarsfeld Fellowship from the Department of Sociology at Columbia University allowed me to take the time to conduct ethnographic research in Argentina. In addition, the Institute of Latin American Studies at Columbia provided financial assistance for travel in Argentina. I also thank the Lozano Long Institute of Latin American Studies and the Department of Sociology at the University of Texas at Austin, the Centro de Estudios Sociales de la Economía at the Universidad Nacional de San Martín, and the University of Victoria for their support. A University of Texas at Austin Subvention Grant awarded by the Office of the President provided financial support for the compilation of the index. I also thank Cashflow Technologies, Inc. for allowing me to use some of their trademarked images in this book.

I presented chapters of this book to various audiences whose questions, comments, and criticisms helped shape and refine its arguments: the Instituto Gino Germani (Universidad de Buenos Aires), the Instituto de Altos Estudios Sociales (Universidad Nacional de San Martín, Argentina), the Programa de Estudios del Consumo y los Mercados (Universidad Diego Portales, Chile), the Workshop on Ethnographies of Neoliberal Governmentalities (University of Victoria, Canada), the University of Victoria Latin American Research Group, the Seminario Permanente de Sociología Económica (UBA-UNSAM, Argentina), the Capitalizing on Performativity Symposium (École de Mines ParisTech, France), and the Jornadas de Sociología at Universidad Nacional de General Sarmiento, Argentina, as well as the ASA, ESS, ISA, and SASE meetings. I am grateful to organizers, discussants, and audiences in all of these forums, especially to Tomás Ariztia, Howard Becker, Michelle Brady, Ana Castellani, Eve Chiapello, Liliana Doganova, Marion Fourcade, Kieran Healy, Federico Lorenc Valcarce, Andrew Leyshon, Javier Lezaun, Mariana Luzzi, Fabian Muniesa, and Nicolás Viotti.

I have also benefitted from the insightful feedback of several colleagues who read different versions of the manuscript or individual chapters. I am grateful to Gabriel Abend, Michelle Brady, Peter Miller, Sharmila Rudrappa, Uri

Schwed, Zsuzsanna Vargha, and two anonymous reviewers. The students of my seminar on development, markets, and society at UT Austin kindly suggested using a session for a workshop on the near-completed manuscript. I thank Julio Gutierrez, Sam Tabory, and Victoria Wilson for a lively session and especially Nino Bariola for his detailed feedback. Caity Collins worked with great care in fixing many weird sentences that worked well in my mind but not in real English. She went above and beyond, providing feedback on substantial issues of presentation and argument that helped make this book better. Noel Norcross and Katie Jensen provided additional editing for some chapters, and Laura Palomino assisted with interview transcriptions.

At several points of this long road, many other colleagues and friends shared their support, encouragement, and wisdom with me (and in some cases coffee, wine, beer, or *asado*), and I am thankful to them: Emiliano Álvarez, Sam Binkley, Ariel Budnik, William Carroll, Rob Crosnoe, Matías Dewey, Melina Furman, Adrián Franco, Neil Gross, Charlie Hale, Mariana Heredia, Ken-Hou Lin, Raúl Madrid, Héctor Mazzei, José Ossandon, Gabriela Polit, Teresa Principato, Lucas Rubinich, Daromir Rudnyckyj, Susanna Sharpe, David Sheinin, Vanesa Schittner, Elaine de Silveira Leite, Fred Wherry, Ariel Wilkis, Christine Williams, Viviana Zelizer, and the members of the *Apuntes del CECYP* group. Three fellow Argentine sociologists deserve special recognition. I saw Javier Auyero for the first time when he presented his inspiring ethnographic research in a massive intro class at the University of Buenos Aires. As a first-year undergraduate student, I could never imagine at the time that two decades later he would be my colleague at the University of Texas, a mentor, a friend, and a neighbor. Not only did he read a few versions of the manuscript, he also patiently answered my excessive questions about it. Claudio Benzecry was there from start to finish. From the early days in New York to our long cross-country phone conversations, he has always been a patient and generous friend and colleague. Gastón Beltrán, amazing sociologist and even better friend, tragically passed away before he could see this book in print. I'm not alone in missing him, and his friendship, generosity, and intelligence.

My manuscript found an ideal home in the *Culture and Economic Life* series at Stanford University Press. I am thankful to acquisitions editor Jenny Gavacs, who shared her enthusiasm for the project and offered many suggestions to improve the writing, and to the editorial team at Stanford, especially James Holt, Emily Smith, and David Horne. Series editors Fred Wherry, Jenn Lena, and Greta Hsu have been incredibly supportive throughout the process.

Throughout the years in which I have lived far from Buenos Aires, Sara Szyber regularly reminded me of how tough it is to have her son abroad and rarely failed to tell me that I never call and never write (independently of the actual frequency, of course, but she may have a point). This book is also a product of her great efforts in so many ways. My sister, Analía, and her family, Javier, Tamara, and Melina, miss no chance to show me how much they love me and how much they believe in me. They are always there. I also thank Paty Avilés and César Zazueta for their love and unconditional support, and Myrna and Jay Brock, my family in Texas. To all my family, *gracias!* Words are not enough to express how important Pilar Zazueta has been throughout the process of research, writing, and rewriting of this book. She stoically stood more talk about financial self-help than any human being ever should. She read over drafts and sat with me and the manuscript at the crucial crossroads in which I needed someone to unblock me. But most important (and this is particularly where words could never do justice), she makes my life joyful every day. In the middle of all this, our daughter, Leonora, clearly demonstrated that there is always more love to give.

FREEDOM FROM WORK

Introduction

GUILLERMO IS THIRTY-SIX and sells books in a little booth he owns in Parque Alvear, a park in Buenos Aires famous for its lively outdoor market of used books, magazines, and CDs, not very far from the neighborhood I grew up in. He sees himself as a small entrepreneur who hopes to one day open a regular bookshop and eventually make enough money to live off of investments. This long-term project is something relatively new in his life. Just a couple of years ago, he had no bank account and barely thought about business or investing. Guillermo attributes these new concerns to an important change in his outlook on life and money: "If you feel guilty about having money, you're not going to be able to advance financially. . . . You have to feel that it's right. You need to allow yourself to do it. And to allow yourself, you need to solve those issues in you that don't allow you to do it," he told me during a long conversation in 2007.

Guillermo only got into the used-book business after years of moving between various menial jobs. His father left when Guillermo was a kid, and his mother worked as a cook: "It was enough for the roof, and that's it. . . . Imagine the salary of a cook. We would pay the rent and keep enough for the bus, and then we would sew our clothes, send the shoes to the cobbler. . . ." Guillermo dropped out of high school when he was fifteen, and took a job in a factory, where he painted doors and windows. The working conditions were so terrible that he promised himself that he would never return to this sort of degrading work again. Guillermo then cycled through a series of odd jobs: he worked in construction for some time, then painted apartments, and later sold homemade t-shirts, jewelry, and posters in Buenos Aires' street markets and at beach resorts along the Argentine coast. A few years later, he started helping his brother, who was already a book vendor in the same park where Guillermo now has his shop.

Despite having dropped out of school, Guillermo has always been a curious and avid reader. While working with his brother at the bookstand, he observed how one particular book kept flying off the shelves: the financial self-help bestseller *Rich Dad, Poor Dad: What the Rich Teach Their Kids About Money That the Poor and Middle Class Do Not!* He purposefully ignored it: "For two years, I had the book and I sold it, but I didn't pay attention to it. I would look at the book and say, 'These are the ones who think about money and nothing but money, and they don't give a shit about people.'" His rejection of the book was rooted in his family's left-leaning politics, which prompted him to see capitalism as evil, as the "poison of peoples." Reluctantly, but taken by curiosity, he finally decided to crack open the cover, and was quickly intrigued. Reading this book prompted Guillermo to not only see economic prosperity in a new light, but also connect his finances with other spheres of his personal improvement. "Behind the issue of money were many of my issues, about how I saw all that. I realized that I had to change myself if I wanted to reach goals. If I didn't change, I would just hinder myself. I was already working on my personal history, my life experiences, but now they seemed connected with economic progress, prosperity, abundance; all those things are related," Guillermo recalled. His immediate feeling as he read his first financial self-help book was of regret: "I had lost so much time. . . . At first I thought, 'What if I had started earlier?' But then I realized that I was meant to read it at that moment."

A few months after he read *Rich Dad, Poor Dad*, learned more from various financial self-help books, and tried out small innovations in the business, Guillermo's working relationship with his brother began to suffer. For instance, on the recommendations found in *Rich Dad*, Guillermo started keeping better track of his business and personal expenses, recording every expense in detail, regardless of how small it was. His brother, who didn't want to be "a slave to numbers," rejected the practice. Guillermo eventually decided to dissolve their partnership and start his own bookshop in the park: "I used to have this prejudice that business and investing was a matter for sharks and backstabbers. When I split with my brother, I was then able to try ideas out and put things that I was learning into practice."

Guillermo told me that the first lesson he took from *Rich Dad* was that he was unlikely to rise above the social circle that he frequented. His friends at that point were mainly bohemian artists—musicians, painters, writers, actors—in addition to some people from the used-bookselling business. For Guillermo, his circle of friends was partly responsible for his until-then-unquestioned view that money was bad and capitalism was evil. In an effort to meet new people, he did some online research and found a local forum of fans of *Rich Dad*. Among other things, forum members organized informal meetings to play Cash-flow, a board game designed by Robert Kiyosaki, the author of the best-seller. Guillermo purchased a homemade imitation of the game on the Argentine version of eBay (MercadoLibre) and played with his wife, Sandra, but they soon realized that it was not so easy and that they needed an experienced player to guide them. So he and Sandra invited people from the online forum to play with them in their home. The success of the event—ten people showed up, including an experienced player who brought an extra board—led them to organize two more games in coffee shops in Buenos Aires. Guillermo started meeting other forum members from all walks of life. While they may not all have had similar backgrounds, they were concerned with similar issues. They were all trying to become financially successful; they were all influenced by the same book; and they were all interested in meeting "like-minded" people. They were trying to master a new language and interpret their lives through a common lens.

As part of his quest to meet new people and be exposed to new experiences, Guillermo eventually attended a talk about foreign exchange trading in the house of another forum member. When he returned home, he wrote a long post in the forum that is worth reproducing in its entirety. In more than one way, Guillermo's post encapsulates what this book is about:

> The lecture was truly very instructive . . . because even someone like me, who didn't understand anything about the topic when he arrived, left the lecture with a much clearer *understanding of the basic principles*. I'm not going to tell you that I'm already a trader—not at all. But at least now I know the meaning of leverage, lot, pip, spread, pairs, broker, and several other terms about which I didn't have the remotest idea before. Now if someone says pip, I know he's talking about ten dollars and not about the sound used in the media when an insult is censored.
>
> Joking aside, what I took from the talk as the major "asset" is that I *connected with real people* who, like you and me, are afraid, or for whom it's not easy to become an investor—people who *want to overcome this fear*, who *search for knowledge* and invest their time in acquiring it, who take seriously the idea of *having your money work for you*, and who do things to make that happen. They don't

wait for it to occur randomly, but rather *seek to be the architects of their own lives*. After all the information and tools that this [online] community is making available to us, now more than ever the decision is ours.

To finish, I want to urge you to maintain the enthusiasm that we evidently have. That enthusiasm, with the right direction, can be like the wind that blows the sails of our ship, which will make it sail faster towards the port of our desired *financial freedom* (and the personal realization, transcendence, happiness, love, peace, fulfillment, and other things that come with it), knowing that we have to identify very clearly the destination we want to reach and the price we are willing to pay. Otherwise, the wind will be useless.

Guillermo continues to seek to transform himself into an investor. He wants to achieve *financial freedom*—a term that will be central throughout this book. In his post, he is quite clear that the project of financial freedom is not easy and that it demands a lot of effort. Guillermo now understands and embraces newly acquired language and technical tools of finance. The language and expertise of foreign exchange trading, which he ignored before the lecture, did not automatically make him a trader. But he now sees himself as a more competent person in the financial realm, a person who does not confuse a financial term like *pip* with a noise. This process of learning and self-transformation, the post reveals, is not experienced in isolation. Guillermo is happy to have come in contact with other people with concerns and objectives similar to his—in fact, he sees this as the major asset he gained from the event. Reading a book that tells you who you should be if you want to be financially successful is one thing, but meeting and interacting with several "like-minded" people is quite different because it provides the hopeful, enthusiastic social environment that such a vital project demands. Guillermo also knows that learning a few technical terms or even mastering the inner workings of global financial trading is important but not enough to lead to financial freedom. The individual has to overcome the fears and weaknesses that prevent him or her from becoming financially free.

Guillermo also hints at the idea that the ultimate goal lies beyond merely amassing money. Financial freedom does not belong to the economic sphere only; he ties it to realization, transcendence, and fulfillment. Acquiring the strength, knowledge, and discipline to have your money work for you is meant to provide the crucial individual autonomy without which one simply cannot be the architect of one's life. Guillermo says that the decision to become financially free is fully in the hands of the individual. Like the books that inspired him, Guillermo explicitly dismisses any factor other than himself to explain the eventual outcome of his financial endeavors. Financial freedom, I learned over two years of fieldwork, is two things at once: first, not having to work for one's income; second, an internal condition of the self, one in which the individual overcomes his or her deep fear of taking economic risks.

Producing the Neoliberal Self

This book delves into the world of financial self-help: a set of discourses, practices, techniques, interactions, and objects through which people make sense of and attempt to transform their financial planning and behavior, their social positions, their goals, and their selves. This is an analysis of a social world inspired by best-selling books that encourage their readers to become rich by transforming themselves. As Guillermo's story suggests, changing oneself into someone with the right conditions to become rich is not a simple process. Most financial self-help books do not provide simple formulas to "get rich quick" but rather suggest to readers that there might be something fundamentally wrong with the core of who they are as a person, and that they have to endure a long and challenging self-transformation to correct it.

Financial self-help is an instance of the *production of capitalist economic subjects* in contemporary post-industrial societies. My interest in this production can be traced back to Max Weber's interest in the emergence of the modern subject and of capitalist economic action. In *The Protestant Ethic and the Spirit of Capitalism* (2002b), as well as in his work on world religions, Weber examined the conditions under which rational capitalist economic action appeared. For Weber, economic action in capitalism did not simply reflect material economic conditions, although those conditions certainly mattered, but was deeply connected to the ethical orientations and beliefs of subjects. In the case of the protestant ethic, belief in the uncertainty of religious salvation provided the motivation for the kind of rational, methodic economic calculation that distinguishes modern capitalism. Weber also considered technical abilities and accounting devices (such as double entry bookkeeping) as central in making new forms of economic action in early capitalism possible. One can calculate more rationally if specific tools have been invented and made widely available.

We are now in a very different time from the early modern period Weber analyzed. For Weber, the ethical tribulations around the salvation of European protestant believers only provided the early impetus for action, but once capitalism flourished, "the religious roots were beginning to die and give way to utilitarian earthly concerns" (Weber 2002a:118; see also Wherry 2014:421–22), and economic action became purely instrumental, disengaged from religious motivations. Yet this book suggests that ethical ends, although not necessarily religious, are still crucial to understanding how and why people today engage in specific forms of economic action, self-transformation, and calculation. The way Guillermo connects a mundane technical seminar on foreign exchange trading to transcendent desires for freedom and personal realization is an indication of this. I argue in this book that, as Weber suggested more than a century ago, both ethical motivations on how one ought to conduct and shape oneself *and* technical tools for calculation are at the core of contemporary capitalist economic action.

We find in Weber an early inspiration for an analysis of the intersection between ethical ends and technical tools in configuring economic actors (Weber 2002a:366). Two more recent theoretical frameworks have analyzed, in different but also intersecting ways, how actors are made in contemporary societies: *governmentality* and *economic performativity*. Both of these frameworks are in many ways indebted to Weber's focus on the conduct of life (Callon 1998:23; Gordon 1987; Mennicken and Miller 2014:19; Power 2011:42; Steiner 2008; Szakolczai 1998:1405). In my analysis of financial self-help I bring together these two theories, which while different have important affinities.

Governmentality and Technologies of the Self

Financial self-help is first and foremost a set of *technologies of the self*, a term coined by Michel Foucault (1988:18) to refer to techniques that "permit individuals to effect by their own means or with the help of others a certain number of operations on their own bodies and souls, thoughts, conduct, and way of being, so as to transform themselves in order to attain a certain state of happiness, purity, wisdom, perfection, or immortality." In other words, Foucault identified as technologies of the self the many ways in which individuals turn themselves into targets of their own self-transformation. While Foucault himself explored technologies of the self mostly in Greco-Roman cultures and early Christianity, his definition is abstract enough to leave open what specific desirable condition individuals may aspire to reach. Throughout history, these technologies have aided individuals in achieving a variety of such states. For example, renouncing sexual pleasure or practicing Christian confession are techniques that have been used to get closer to a desired state of purity. Contemporary financial self-help defines one particular condition as desirable: financial freedom. Financial freedom does not simply involve having lots of money. Readers of financial self-help are told that they will only be able to get money once they have transformed themselves into individuals who *actively* strive for *freedom*.

The exhortation to become free and entrepreneurial makes financial self-help a set of techniques of the self aimed at the creation of *neoliberal* selves. The terms *neoliberal* and *neoliberalism* have been the source of much confusion in the social sciences and humanities as well as in public discourse, so it is important to clarify what I mean here by neoliberalism and what it means in relation to financial self-help. First, a great deal of the confusion results from overuse: the neoliberal label has been attached to an increasing variety of phenomena and with little or no explanation of its meaning and content. This overuse blurs its specific properties and particular effects while crediting almost any novel social phenomenon in contemporary times to neoliberalism (Flew 2014). Second, the term *neoliberalism* "is most frequently employed by those who are critical of the free-market phenomena to which it refers" (Boas and Gans-Morse 2009:140), becoming "an all-purpose denunciatory category" (Flew 2014:51). The problem with this is not only that neoliberalism as a term has become a shortcut for "bad" and "undesirable," but also that it is increasingly used with the assumption that readers will understand what it means. Recent literature has tried to spell out the varied meanings and empirical uses of neoliberalism. While there are several typologies of neoliberalism available,[1] Wendy Larner's (2000) seminal classification is still useful to distinguish three broad understandings of the term. First, neoliberalism can be understood as a more or less defined set of policies applied by governments in different countries since the 1970s to decrease state intervention in the economy, including reducing welfare programs, balancing budgets, deregulating markets, and privatizing previously public services. Second, neoliberalism can be characterized as an ideology upon which those policies have been based, and which promotes individualism and free markets. While each of these two visions grasps something important about neoliberalism, they are also limited if one wants to identify and understand more profound economic, social, and political changes in contemporary societies. While the latter makes neoliberalism appear as a unitary, coherent, and consistent ideological or philosophical doctrine, the former prevents us from grasping the effects and groundings of those policies and ideologies beyond the sphere of state programs. The third major understanding of neoliberalism, and the one that largely informs the analysis of this book, is neoliberalism as *governmentality*.

First put forward by Michel Foucault, the idea of governmentality encapsulates a set of scattered concerns about the rationalities and techniques deployed in the activity of governing (Rose, O'Malley, and Valverde 2006; Dean 1999). It is important to highlight that governing here is not limited to the state, but rather designates both the grand and mundane efforts of *conducting the conduct* of people. In a series of lectures in the late 1970s, Foucault (2008) examined twentieth-century neoliberalism as an interrogation into the "art of government." More than a set of well-defined policies or a coherent philosophical doctrine, Foucault framed neoliberalism as a practical rationality of government with the paradoxical intention of not governing too much (Foucault 2008:13). While we can surely find typical neoliberal ideas (free markets, individualism, property rights) and typical neoliberal policies (deregulation, tariff reduction, austere fiscal policy, privatization), for Foucault and other scholars who analyzed contemporary societies following his concepts, what truly distinguishes neoliberalism is an approach to the art of government in which the priority is governing "from a distance" (Barry, Osborne, and Rose 1996; Miller and Rose 2008; Rose 1996).[2] Neoliberalism is generally an attempt to deploy market mechanisms not simply as a system of distribution of goods and services but as a governmental principle that can be applied to any sphere of life. Neoliberalism is the art of governing through the free choices of autonomous individuals who feel responsible for themselves. The "retreat" of the state under neoliberalism, for example, is not simply a retreat, but also "a positive technique of government" (Barry, Osborne, and Rose 1996:11). Neoliberalism promotes spaces of individual autonomy so that the state has to intervene less directly. The freedom and autonomous choice accorded to individuals by neoliberalism is therefore not a reduction of "government" but rather a rearticulation of governmental techniques that puts more emphasis on individual self-governing (Dardot and Laval 2014).

Viewing neoliberalism as governmentality allows us to grasp changes in contemporary societies that have been subtle yet profound. Foucault (2008) identified as one of the most salient features of neoliberalism the notion that individuals should become "entrepreneurs of themselves." By using markets as a governmental technique, neoliberalism prompts individuals to construct themselves as autonomous and free subjects who are able to compete. For Foucault, neoliberalism (particularly in its American version) understands individuals as enterprise units engaged in the accumulation and maximization of what economists such as Gary Becker called "human capital." Their relation to themselves is seen as equivalent to that of an entrepreneur to his or her business, assets, and capital, demanding strategy, calculation, risk, and innovation.[3] Thus, neoliberal rule seeks to create spaces of individual autonomy and to promote individuals' self-understanding as autonomous entrepreneurs of themselves. As Graham Burchell (1996:29) notes, neoliberal forms of governing "encourage the governed to adopt a certain entrepreneurial form of practical relationship to themselves as a condition of their effectiveness and of the effectiveness to this form of government." In sum, neoliberalism as a governmentality promotes the notion that individuals should be autonomous entrepreneurs of themselves, fully responsible for what they can or cannot achieve (Miller and Rose 1990; Rose 1996, 1999). This explains why technologies of the self are particularly important for neoliberalism.[4]

Financial self-help advocates and provides techniques to furnish exactly this free and entrepreneurial subject of neoliberalism. However, financial self-help products are not produced or promoted by any state agency. They are popular market products, even global best-sellers in their own right, like Guillermo's *Rich Dad, Poor Dad* that flew off the shelves of his humble bookstand in Parque Alvear. This shows the pervasiveness of neoliberalism, beyond a centralized policy framework or a coherent top-down ideology, as a widespread set of practical techniques of self-government, of technologies to know oneself and operate on oneself that do not originate in a clear center of power. The production of neoliberal selves occurring in the world of financial self-help is not a top-down process of grand policy carried out by institutions, but rather something that happens every day, in self-organized groups, with the aid of colorful, best-selling books and other practical resources. Users voluntarily purchase and use them not as part of any government program, but as a way of dealing with the strains and difficulties that they find in their own economic lives. Many of these difficulties originate in the structural changes that the global expansion of neoliberalism prompted, particularly the changes in labor markets that have weakened job stability. Nevertheless, financial self-help enthusiasts learn that economic structures are not to blame for their economic difficulties, or for that vague feeling of having to work too much for very little reward. Placing the blame outside the self goes against the entrepreneurial and free spirit that they ought to cultivate if they wish to be financially successful. Readers are told that they have to search deep within themselves to break free from a dependent spirit inherited from welfare society, which relies on the security and guidance of institutions (welfare agencies, the state, corporate employers), and focus on cultivating their entrepreneurial qualities and striving for freedom. Indeed, the fact that they voluntarily adhere to the project of financial self-help is seen as part of a growing entrepreneurial spirit. They are not waiting for their problems to solve themselves magically: they are taking action. As Guillermo says in his forum post, they "want to be the architects of their own lives."

Economic Performativity and Calculative Tools

Shaping the free and entrepreneurial self of neoliberalism is not only a process of changing one's will, feelings, and desires but also a *technical* transformation. In the world of financial self-help, an indispensable tool if one wants to achieve financial freedom is *financial intelligence*. Financial self-help resources exhort users to educate themselves financially. People do not only have to desire financial freedom, they also have to acquire the technical tools that will make such a goal attainable. Guillermo, for example, had to reframe his deeply held resistance to making money and, among other things, stop feeling guilty about it; he had to revisit his relationship to money and to himself, his fears and preconceptions. But he also started to cultivate new tools for calculating. By reading, playing games like Cashflow, and attending workshops practitioners learn to calculate in new ways. They change how they classify income and expenses, assets and liabilities, and how they calculate risk and returns of investment. They even learn the technical and legal intricacies of evaluating real estate or stock market deals. In very practical ways, they try to turn themselves into market actors that calculate for the maximization of revenue from financial investments and the minimization of their own labor.

In order to understand this *technical* self-transformation that financial self-help entails, I have relied on the literature on *economic performativity*, which gives calculation and the material tools associated with it a central place in explaining how markets and market actors are configured. The concept of economic performativity, first introduced by sociologist Michel Callon (1998) as part of an expansion of Actor-Network Theory into economic sociology, has been particularly fruitful in explaining how markets and economic action are shaped by economic expertise.[5] The main idea of performativity is, simply put, that the field of economics does not (just) study the economy, it actually performs it. From this perspective, economic models and theories are not mere reflections of a reality outside of them; they have the power to make the economy work in ways that are similar to those originally predicted by such models and theories. In other words, economic expertise contributes to making the world it studies (MacKenzie, Muniesa, and Siu 2007; Mitchell 2005; Muniesa 2014). This is also true about the frequent protagonist of economic action according to economics: the individual who rationally calculates in order to maximize benefits and minimize cost, also known as the *homo economicus*. In this sense, the homo economicus (or any form of economic action that can be assumed and modeled in economic theories) is neither a natural occurrence nor the fiction that sociologists have tried to expose for years. For Callon (1998), the fact that the homo economicus is not natural does not mean that it does not exist: distinguishable forms of action and calculation, such as the homo economicus, can in fact be produced. Callon asserts that the rejection of the homo economicus as a fiction prevented sociologists from investigating the processes through which market actors are actually configured and formatted. The challenge is not to prove that the homo economicus is an unrealistic simplification, but rather to understand the processes through which people acquire the tools that make them similar—although with varying distances from the ideal—to what economists treat as a reality.

This notion of economic performativity has brought attention to the role of calculative tools in shaping economic actors (MacKenzie 2009). For Callon, the homo economicus is essentially a form of calculation. That calculation is not a purely mental process; it involves collaboration between humans and nonhuman actors. Callon calls this collaboration "calculative agencies," the assemblage of humans and calculative tools that makes up the *real* homo economicus. Formulas, accounting tools, balance sheets, lists, computers, and various forms of expertise (most notably economics) are regarded as "prostheses" through which people become calculative market actors. The performativity approach helps us understand the role of technical expertise and material tools in the production of economic actors. Economic action is an achievement that is not the result of the right "mindset" of a stand-alone actor, but of the right assemblage of calculative tools.

To be sure, when one thinks of economic expertise, financial gurus who publish how-to-get-rich best-sellers are not the first to come to mind. Yet they are economists in their own way. Callon has called attention to the importance for the notion of economic performativity of expertise that may not be immediately classified as "economics." He calls these experts "economists in-the-wild," who complement "confined economists" (Callon 2007:336). Callon emphasizes the role of formulas, statements, experiments, and techniques produced by non-academic economists in shaping the economic world. In fact, the idea of performativity to a large extent blurs the boundaries between theoretical and practical economists. The distinction between theory and technique is more a matter of establishing hierarchies than a true difference in types of production (Callon 2007:333). Several "lower-status" forms of expertise—lower when contrasted to academic economics—have a crucial role in shaping economic actors. For Callon (2007:333), "a host of professions, competencies and non-humans are necessary for academic economics to be successful. Each of these parties 'makes' economics." Financial gurus and the resources and technologies that they promote are part of the network of calculative agencies that produces economic actors. Financial self-help is a vehicle by which economic concepts, language, and techniques reach mass audiences unlikely to have direct contact with more legitimate forms of economic expertise. A best-selling book that is probably never assigned in a university classroom and would never appear in the reading lists of professional economists introduced Guillermo and many others to a realm of economic calculation they had no idea existed.

Creating Economic Subjects: The Intersection of Calculative Tools and the Self

As a theory concerned almost exclusively with the relation between economic expertise and markets, economic performativity helps us understand how economic actors are shaped by calculative tools *as actors in markets*, but it says little about how this role relates to those actors' subjectivity. Economic performativity is based on Actor-Network Theory (ANT), a theory that has prompted scholars to take seriously the significance of nonhumans (such as technologies or nature) in stabilizing and altering the social world, warning us of the dangers of invocations of "culture" or "society" as disembedded from the material world (Latour 1988). For ANT, action is not only human, but rather distributed in networks of humans and nonhumans (Latour 2007; Preda 1999). Therefore, nonhuman calculative tools are as much the protagonists of economic action as humans are. Yet because of this theoretical approach, economic performativity does not probe into the significance of humans as actors who reflect about who they are and who they want to be. In considering the shaping of economic actors, economic performativity focuses on how assemblages of humans and nonhumans are equipped with relevant technical powers of calculation, but does not consider reflexive human actors who in the same process are shaping their own selves, with the aid of discourses and practices (like those of financial self-help) that shape ethical orientations. In short, economic performativity offers little in the way of insights about humans as subjects.[6] Recent theoretical and empirical work on accounting and governmentality, however, has shown that calculative tools shape more than our economic conduct. Calculating is constitutive of one's self; calculation makes up who we are. According to Peter Miller (2001:392), "the calculative practices of accountancy are intrinsic to and constitutive of social relations, rather than secondary and derivative. . . . Accounting practices create a particular way of understanding, representing and acting upon events and processes" (Miller 2001:392–393). Financial self-help users change their notion of what makes a liability and what makes an asset, or start dividing income between "passive" and "active," and they do this in a very practical way, resorting to board games, sheets, and lists. This change is enormously consequential for how they calculate, but also because they simultaneously transform how they see themselves and who they want to be. Calculation makes identity and personhood (see Miller 2008:57–58). Conversely, embarking on a particular project of the self makes particular calculative tools meaningful for financial self-help users. Acquiring these calculative tools becomes part of that project; if calculative tools are like "prostheses," as Michel Callon called them, subjects actively strive to make those prostheses "fit" them correctly. Therefore, the technical transformation into a person who acquires financial intelligence is entangled with the ethical transformation into a person who strives for financial freedom. With one set of technologies and practices, financial self-help shapes readers both into market actors in financial capitalism and into neoliberal subjects that strive for freedom and autonomy. All the activities that financial self-help practitioners perform to enhance their financial skills and knowledge and to make money are at the same time *practices of the self*. Learning to calculate as an investor is also a way of cultivating an entrepreneurial spirit, liberating oneself, and showing that one is not afraid of taking risks and is not dependent on institutions or others to take charge of one's own financial life.[7]

How This Book Came About

This book is the result of two years of research in two countries: attending meetings of financial self-help clubs, interviewing their members, reading their online forums, and consuming the same media (books, games, DVDs) as the club members. Financial self-help resources and their global use allow us to understand the impact of neoliberalism in everyday life and the configuration of economic subjects as a process of self-transformation. This book is about how the macro transformations of the economy in the last three or four decades have been accompanied by powerful, pragmatic, simple, everyday forms of expertise. In a world that has increasingly deprived citizens of the safety nets that characterized the welfare era (job stability, solid retirement plans, and strong welfare programs), individuals turn to popular books for guidance in order to make sense of their circumstances and try to adjust to new conditions. These books and the groups they foster provide the techniques necessary to turn the self into the subject imagined by neoliberal governmentality.

In spring 2006, I serendipitously came across an article in an Argentine newspaper about fans of the best-selling book *Rich Dad, Poor Dad*, written by American financial guru Robert Kiyosaki. The article mentioned that there was an online club with four hundred members (the club in which Guillermo participates, and which today has over sixty thousand registered members) that organized meetings to play a board game called Cashflow as a means of enhancing their financial skills and mindsets. I had seen Kiyosaki's book in bookstores a few years before, but, like Guillermo, for a long time I never paid much attention to it. It seemed to be just one more of the dozens of "how to become a millionaire" books that I assumed existed in the world. After reading the newspaper article, I started seeing the book everywhere—at bookstores, newsstands, and airport shops. A few months later, I came across a long TV advertisement on PBS, part of the U.S. public television channel fundraising campaign, for a DVD featuring Kiyosaki. This was the first time I had heard him speak, and I saw much more than the motivation and hope I imagined popular best-sellers contained. His speech provided a theory (in popular form, but with some substantive sociological content) of the transition from industrial capitalism to financial capitalism (he called them industrial age and information age), and urged people to change inside (their selves) and outside (in their planning and strategizing) in order to succeed in the new economy. Eventually, I decided to buy the Spanish translation of *Rich Dad, Poor Dad* for five dollars on the streets of Mexico City (the majority of Mexican street book vendors gave a privileged space on their tables to Kiyosaki's books—a testimony not only to their popularity but also to their global reach). I also started skimming the online forum mentioned in the newspaper and exploring online material about Kiyosaki and other financial gurus.

What makes Robert Kiyosaki and the Rich Dad groups stand out? First, Rich Dad has been the most successful brand of financial self-help in the last decade. Kiyosaki, a fourth-generation Japanese-American born in Hawaii in 1947, published his first books in the late 1990s. His publishing endeavors now include more than thirty books translated into dozens of languages, targeted at children, teens, men, and women.[8] He also offers various seminars, TV broadcasts, videos, and coaching services. The sales volume of Kiyosaki materials cannot be compared to those of other authors in the genre. Estimates vary from ten to twenty-eight million books sold worldwide, and his books have been consistently top ranked in the United States, Argentina, and many other countries since they came out.[9] The *Rich Dad* books are not only the most popular; Kiyosaki's ideas are most often the point of entrance for people into the world of financial self-help, and *Rich Dad* is an appealing book that is easy to read, which many readers recommend (and even give as presents) to friends, family, and acquaintances. Kiyosaki's pervasiveness is truly impressive.

Second, the Rich Dad series provides a specific tool, the Cashflow game, which brings people together and sparks networks of practitioners. Attending a Cashflow game provides an opportunity to play and enhance one's financial skills, but it is also a chance to meet "like-minded" people, such as those Guillermo and his wife sought to find, and build community. Cashflow has contributed to creating new social worlds of fans of financial self-help. While participants in Cashflow clubs use and discuss other materials, Kiyosaki's ideas give these groups their *raison d'etre*. Even activities not explicitly inspired by Kiyosaki's work are still largely influenced by it.

Third, Kiyosaki's world offers a defined set of ideas about the self, the economy, the structure of social classes, the nature of investing, and more. His ideas are reasonably consistent throughout his books and other products as well as the various spin-offs by other authors and gurus. The common complaint (even by committed fans) that most books largely repeat the same few ideas over and over at the same time could be said to reveal their consistency.

Finally, Kiyosaki's products are an explicit response to late modern capitalism, which is what makes them different from classic nineteenth- and twentieth-century varieties of financial advice. On top of more general motivational and financial advice that has been common since the nineteenth century, Kiyosaki developed a popular social theory of the transition between the industrial or corporate period in capitalism and the late, financial or neoliberal stage (under the labels of industrial age and information age). The core recommendation for the current era, unlike with most corporate self-help books, is that people should make a plan so that they can eventually quit their jobs and receive "passive income" from investments.

One of the first things that struck me when I started learning about Kiyosaki, long before beginning the research for this book, was his international reach. As I mentioned earlier, my first encounter was when I read about Cash-flow clubs and online communities in a newspaper from Argentina (the country where I am from and where I have conducted much of my scholarly research). The article mentioned that clubs had been created in places as disparate as California, Bulgaria, and Indonesia. I learned a little more about the ideas of *Rich Dad* watching American public television and, as I mentioned, it was in Mexico where I bought my first book. It seemed to me that there was something profoundly American about Kiyosaki's ideas, actual examples, and financial advice, yet they somehow managed to travel successfully to countries that had little to do with the U.S. economy and culture. It is of course not unusual or new that cultural products from the United States make their way into other countries and quite successfully. As in most households with a TV set around the world, growing up in Argentina I only had to turn on the TV to watch dozens of dubbed American shows and movies in which one has to imagine, for example, what on earth a fraternity is or why the prom is so important. In other words, consumers of American cultural products worldwide have to understand them outside their original context of production. Yet American financial self-help resources are not movies or TV shows, which one usually consumes for entertainment, but technologies of the self; the relation between users and product is a practical one, aimed at self-transformation. Therefore, their consumption in a different context from where they were produced cannot be taken for granted: how do fans in those other countries make sense of advice and techniques that were not created with their economic contexts in mind? To find out, I decided to conduct fieldwork in financial self-help groups in the United States (where most financial self-help resources are produced) and in one other country. On the one hand, looking at practices that were similar across the two cases ensured that my analysis was not driven by the particularities of one country or the other, but by the characteristics of financial self-help as a global phenomenon. It also ensured that I was not referring to some peculiarly American occurrence. On the other hand, studying financial self-help in a country other than the United States allowed me to observe the process of adjusting and adapting imported American resources, which is the subject of Chapter 5.

While I could have chosen several other countries, I selected Argentina because it offered a particularly illuminating case to study the global diffusion and use of American financial self-help (in addition to the obvious advantage that it is a country I know well). More than other countries, its cyclical economic crises and perennial financial instability make Argentina a place in which using the same financial self-help advice and tools as those used in the United States would seem particularly difficult. To give but one example, during the financial crisis of 2001, the government froze bank deposits and customers simply could not get a hold of their own money deposited in savings accounts. A walk in the financial district of Buenos Aires in 2002 was a surreal experience, with angry depositors hammering the sturdy metal gates that banks were forced to add to their entrances. This was just one in a long history of financial and currency crises Argentina has undergone, a history that makes Argentines feel that they are always walking on shaky economic ground.[10] Despite such recurrent financial crises and pervasive distrust of the banking system, Argentines use American financial self-help books and develop similar clubs and activities. Argentine users, however, actively "translate" American products to make them fit their context, and some local authors try to fill the "applicability gap" with their own books. By studying how American financial self-help is collectively adopted in and adapted to another economic context, I want to contribute to a view of globalization as a social practice rather than as an abstract force.[11]

Throughout this book, I show that financial self-help has substantial effects on users, on how they see the world, themselves, and their social positions, and how they reconfigure some of their economic and non-economic practices. However, my research does not try to determine whether or not financial self-help *works* in terms of leading users to wealth or financial freedom. It would not be possible to determine with this kind of research whether users end up becoming rich or not, or if there are traits that would make someone more likely to succeed than others. The irony is that in conversations with fans of financial self-help throughout my fieldwork, *they* saw that question as the most worthy of investigation. A long-term, quantitative, longitudinal assessment would likely be necessary to answer such a question. Most important, the question of effectiveness would merely end up in either a celebration of financial self-help (if the answer is positive) or an exposé of the lies of the genre (if negative).[12] Instead, this book takes a step back and questions the *question of financial success itself*. My goal is to offer a careful analysis of the ideas and practices of financial self-help and to understand what participants of fan groups are doing, their categories of meaning, and the context in which their ideas and practices emerge. Whether they become "rich" or not depends on many more factors than a person's will, unlike what the main teaching of financial self-help assures. Whether financial self-help succeeds or fails in terms of leading users to riches, it still *does* something.

One afternoon in 2007, I timidly attended a Cashflow session organized by a group based in a predominantly black and Latino neighborhood in New York City.[13] Until that day, I had only read about Cashflow; I had no idea how to play the game. That was the beginning of my two-year ethnographic journey through the Rich Dad clubs of New York and Buenos Aires. Within a few weeks, I was regularly attending games organized by Sonny, a white man in his late forties who worked in a community mortgage firm in Manhattan. At my first Cashflow game, I also met Steve, an African American man who was the soul of the group. In many ways, Steve's story was a perfect rags-to-riches American tale of redemption. He grew up in a poor family in the South, supported only by his mother's disability income. When he was young, Steve decided that he would attend college and, after overcoming various obstacles, he earned a university degree. Since his childhood, Steve had felt that he did not want to spend his life working for a salary, and that there had to be more to life than school, four decades of labor, and then retirement. He found a more articulate formulation of his feelings when he read *Rich Dad, Poor Dad* as an adult. "After the Bible, it was the best book I've ever read," Steve told me and every new member of his group. He had tried to talk to his friends about the book, and even gave it as a present to some of them, but they didn't show much interest. For two years, he dug into financial self-help, reading books and attending workshops, but not taking much action. Eventually, he decided to start a local group that would motivate him, where he could also share his acquired wisdom about real estate investing. By the time I attended my first group's meetings in the spring of 2007, Steve was already an expert in the business (he owned several rental properties) and was educating and motivating others to follow in his steps.

The group gathered once a month on Saturdays, and between thirty and sixty people attended each time. It was a diverse group, with a majority of African Americans, but also Latinos and whites, which was more or less representative of the neighborhood's population. At each meeting, Steve combined heavily technical information about becoming an investor (particularly in real estate) with motivational tools to work on the self in order to become a successful person on the way to financial freedom. Yet Steve defied the popular image of a financial guru. He did not wear expensive suits or aggressively preach like late-night infomercial hosts. He always dressed in jeans and t-shirts, and he lived in the neighborhood. The meetings were organized in whatever place could be found in the community, usually at local schools or a meeting room in a member's workplace. Most of the New York portion of my fieldwork occurred at these Saturday meetings and in the Cashflow games organized by Sonny in the city between 2007 and 2009.[14]

I spent eight months in 2007 and 2008 in Buenos Aires, where I searched for equivalent local groups and found two large financial self-help communities, both inspired by Kiyosaki's books. One was the online forum that Guillermo joined. Born as an e-mail fan group in 2005, the forum grew from five thousand to eight thousand users throughout my time in Argentina and today boasts more than sixty thousand members. The forum has many sub-sections, not only on financial self-help books but also on general advice about investing and entrepreneurship. Members call it a "community," and it has certain rules of etiquette, such as the courtesy of introducing oneself when entering for the first time, and the commitment to be polite and congenial. Users are supposed to contribute as much as they can to collective wisdom, and moderators regulate business proposals in order to prevent fraud or misconduct. People post questions and business opportunities and also receive feedback and encouragement about their investment ideas and entrepreneurial projects. The forum is headed and maintained by Luis, a computer technician in his mid-thirties who, like Steve and others, became hooked on financial self-help after reading Kiyosaki. Luis sees himself as someone that connects entrepreneurs, investors, and businesspeople in order to make successful investments happen. The forum officially sponsors a few business opportunities, and there have been several cases of collective projects with a plurality of investors who met in the forum.

The second group that I found in Argentina was led by Matías, a salesman and marketing consultant who created his own website devoted to *Rich Dad* in Argentina in 2006. After a friend recommended it to him, Matías read *Rich Dad* in one weekend, and within a couple of months he had finished reading all of Kiyosaki's books. He then asked a friend who was traveling to the United States to bring back the Cashflow game, which was not yet available in Argentina. Matías started playing with family members and officemates in early 2006, and a few months later, as he was attracting more people to the games, he started a website. When a major national newspaper published an article about Kiyosaki, featuring a link to Matías's website, the web server exploded with interested people. By the end of that year, he had organized public Cashflow sessions with over fifty people at coffee shops in Buenos Aires. He later assembled a team and started offering full-day workshops featuring talks on specific financial topics in the morning and Cashflow sessions in the afternoon. His group (Financial Freedom Argentina) organizes workshops throughout the country and has teams in several provinces.

Besides attending and participating in the activities of these clubs, I conducted fifty in-depth interviews with people I met at games and workshops or through online forums. I interviewed and had informal conversations with a wide variety of fans representing the diversity of the financial self-help world: from a school teacher to a professor of economics, from real estate agents to artists, from factory workers to insurance agents, from bank employees to engineers, as well as several enthusiasts who simply defined themselves as "entrepreneurs." Like the people whom Guillermo met at his first Cashflow game, they had heard about the game in different ways. Some had found a financial self-help book in a bookstore or had a friend who insisted that they read one. Others had been dragged to a game by a friend or family member. Regardless of their paths, they had all found in the financial self-help world the narratives to explain why they were there and why it was necessary for them to change. They may not have thought that there was anything wrong with them before, but they discovered their financial deficiencies as they started their journeys.

An Overview of the Book

In Chapter 1, I define contemporary financial self-help and distinguish it from two of its closest relatives: general self-help and "get rich quick" schemes. I then turn to the diagnosis provided by Kiyosaki regarding the end of corporate capitalism and the end of job security. According to him, the number one task for those who do not want to be crushed by the "information age" is understanding that prosperity in this day and age has little to do with schools and jobs. Financial education, which is acquired through more informal channels, is the only indispensable education individuals should acquire, he argues. Kiyosaki also provides a theory of the class structure of capitalist societies (called the *Cashflow Quadrant*) that associates certain objective positions (employee, self-employed, business owner, and investor) with distinct forms of subjectivity. He suggests that individuals should understand what their social position is and plan to leave "quadrants" in which they work for their money and move to those in which they receive money from the work of others.

Predictably, moving between quadrants is not easy. Financial self-help authors suggest that one truly has to become a new person. Chapter 2 describes what kind of person users are urged to become. The answer is simple: financially free. Financial self-help puts freedom even above wealth itself. In a discourse with roots in American libertarianism, Kiyosaki tells readers that they have to combat their conformist self engendered in the welfare era and resist the temptation of security in favor of a quest for freedom and autonomy. Readers are exhorted to fight external dependence on institutions, but also their internal dependence on conformity and fear, and to essentially control their selves, in a discourse that echoes that used in the addiction recovery movement. In this chapter, I provide four examples that illustrate this project of financial freedom: the rejection of family education, the rejection of the school system, the rejection of frugality as a means of social mobility, and financial self-help's discourse on gender.

In Chapter 3, I move from ideas to practices, by looking at the Cashflow game and its players. First, through the practice of Cashflow, players acquire definitions of what being rich means in the context of financial capitalism and establish financial freedom as a specific goal. Second, they develop calculative tools adjusted to the idea of financial freedom and incoming rent (called "passive income"). For example, they learn to distinguish between various forms of income, expenses, assets, and liabilities, and learn to place each of them in the correct columns of a balance sheet. Third, players work on the self by playing the game. They see themselves "in action" and identify what must be modified in their selves in order to produce the right subjectivity that will lead them to financial success. Finally, I analyze the work of translation that participants perform in practice in order to fit what happens in the game with what they call "real life."

Chapter 4 engages with the collective dynamics of the world of financial self-help. Although the ethics of financial self-help appear to be about pure self-interest, there is space for generosity and disinterest in economic gains. While pure economic self-interest is not acceptable, pure generosity is deemed suspicious. People recognize that there are and should be economic gains for someone, and do not see helping others and making money out of it as contradictory. This conflation of interest and disinterest rests on the notion that pure disinterest is a sign of a yet unchanged "poor" self that lives in a "world of scarcity." The rich, in contrast, live in a world of abundance in which there is enough for everyone, and therefore, the dual aims of interest and generosity are not contradictory. I examine two instances that illustrate this noncontradictory character of interest and disinterest. First, I analyze what users say about the fact that financial gurus live off their fans. Second, I examine an economic activity closely related to financial self-help: multilevel marketing (MLM) companies. These organizations sell products or services through independent affiliated members and are very popular (although controversial) in financial self-help circles.

Chapter 5 addresses the transnational circulation of financial self-help. Financial self-help is a global phenomenon with its epicenter in the United States: most resources are produced there and exported to other countries. But a great deal of local work is needed to make idiosyncratic American products work in the starkly different contexts of developing countries. Local networks of fans are crucial in "globalizing" financial self-help products. In this chapter, I draw on my fieldwork in Argentina to scrutinize the local interpretations and adaptations of American financial self-help. Users in Argentina are well aware of the American character of the genre and products, and they actively try to adapt the theories and advice to their more vulnerable (and less wealthy) economy and financial system.

In the Conclusion, I return to some of the theoretical and political issues discussed throughout the book and suggest some connections between financial self-help and the growing attention to financial literacy and entrepreneurship in policies by governments, NGOs, financial institutions, and international agencies. Finally, the methodological appendix presents details about the research process that led to this book as well as a reflection of my experience as an ethnographer in a world that is significantly different from my own. I reflect on the utility of ethnography as a participatory method that allowed me to learn a great deal about the world of financial self-help through my own participation, reactions, and observations, as well as those of my research participants such as Guillermo, Sonny, and Steve.

Contemporary Financial Self-Help
and the Rise of Neoliberalism

1

LIKE ANY BROAD CONCEPT that attempts to include a number of heterogeneous components, the term *financial self-help* is not perfect. Simply put, while it references what is traditionally considered the self-help genre (resources, including books videos, group meetings, audio recordings, and so on aimed at improving some area of one's life), it encompasses only those that apply mainly to the financial realm. Some types of self-help obviously are excluded from this definition. A book about improving one's love life or working on one's body image is self-help, but is certainly not *financial* self-help. A textbook about micro-economics belongs to the universe of financial expertise, but no one would call it self-help. But other cases are harder to classify. There are some self-help resources that touch upon prosperity and economic advancement, but do not make economic issues the main focus. There are also training workshops and websites about stock market trading which might not be self-help per se, but are important resources that are very popular among users of financial self-help.

Defining too strict a set of boundaries would not be productive. I use *financial self-help* to identify a very fluid set of cultural resources, practices, techniques, and expertise that is more a hybrid of related knowledge, practices, and techniques than a clearly bounded world.[1] I prefer to define the field of financial self-help not by its boundaries but rather by the presence, with various degrees of salience, of three features:

1. A technical economic component: technical expertise loosely related to professional investment and accounting

2. An emotional or motivational component: techniques of the self used to produce changes in dispositions, attitudes, and behavior, aimed at dealing with fears and emotions in economic behavior and planning, particularly in terms of risk-taking, managing, and thinking about money

3. A sociological component: social theories about how the world works (the economy, the social class structure, and so on), and what people's goals should be under those circumstances.

Using this definition, financial self-help resources can be classified not by being inside or outside a delimited universe but rather by being closer or farther to or from a center. In that epicenter is the work of Robert Kiyosaki and the groups inspired by it. Kiyosaki's products most clearly combine these three dimensions. He provides resources to increase users' "financial intelligence," such as real estate training and accounting tools; he encourages readers to examine their upbringing and subjectivity and to identify those parts of the self that are impeding their financial improvement; and he offers an account of the shift of capitalist societies from the "industrial age" to the "information age." Other gurus combine the three components in different forms and with different intensities. Author Suze Orman (1997, 2007a), for example, provides investment and personal finance advice coupled with motivational material and self-help, but she does not focus as much as Kiyosaki on offering an account of the structure of social classes in the current world.

Financial self-help borrows much of its discourse and knowledge from several forms of related expertise, some of which enjoy a more legitimate status than others, including economics and finance, coaching, corporate success literature, personal finance, professional investing, neurolinguistic programming, leadership, and psychology. All of these fields are largely autonomous, and financial self-help authors frequently legitimate claims on their basis. Although they are all related to financial self-help, they should be differentiated. Corporate success literature, for example, is closely tied to financial self-help in its advocacy of individual strategy and positive thinking. But although financial self-help takes that flavor from corporate success literature, it explicitly disregards the corporate world as an adequate setting for the pursuit of financial success.[2] In other words, financial self-help would not see much use for resources that help people succeed inside the firm. Financial freedom, the goal of financial self-help, is precisely the liberation from the constraints of that world, not the mastery of a corporate ladder.

The field of personal finance or household finance is very close to financial self-help. They both advocate a balanced family budget and careful expense recording practices. But financial self-help is not just personal finance. It promotes self-regulation of spending practices as only one part of a quest for wealth, success, and, ultimately, "financial freedom." Achieving a balanced household budget and healthy personal finances is seen in financial self-help as a very limited goal, perhaps one step on the way to financial freedom and a sign of improved financial intelligence. But for authors like Kiyosaki, only "losers" would conform to that goal alone.

Those unfamiliar with the genre often think that financial self-help books are nothing but glorified "get rich quick" schemes. But authors, group leaders, and practitioners in general emphasize how financial self-help is *not* such a scheme. There is a paradox here. Get-rich-quick schemes are a presence in the world of users and fans of financial self-help. Late-night infomercials abound, promising that without any financial expertise, and by just clicking a few buttons, one may become wealthy in a short time, as do pyramid network schemes that promise to multiply one's income almost overnight. While those schemes often use similar discourses, they have little to do with the core discourse of financial self-help that I examine in this book. Both approaches argue that anyone can be rich if they really want to be, but the paths to riches each of them promotes are quite different. Most financial self-help resources stress that becoming rich is difficult and make quite clear that get-rich-quick schemes are illusory. Financial self-help users are told that they need to understand financial goals correctly, acquire technical tools, and work on the self. Devotees of this discourse are taught to forget much or all of what they have learned thus far, and to combat all the dispositions that prevent them from achieving financial freedom. For example, in *Rich Dad, Poor Dad*, Kiyosaki writes,

> I wish I could say acquiring wealth was easy for me, but it wasn't. . . . I believe that each of us has a financial genius within us. The problem is, our financial genius lies asleep, waiting to be called upon. It lies asleep because our culture has educated us into believing that the love of money is the root of all evil. It has encouraged us to learn a profession so we can work for money, but failed to teach us how to have money work for us. It taught us not to worry about our financial future, our company or the government would take care of us when our working days are over. . . .

Unfortunately, 90 percent of the Western world subscribes to the above dogma, simply because it's easier to find a job and work for money. If you are not one of the masses, I offer you the following ten steps to awaken your financial genius. . . .

If you ask most people if they would like to be rich or financially free, they would say "yes." But then reality sets in. The road seems too long with too many hills to climb. It's easier to just work for money and hand the excess over to your broker. (Kiyosaki and Lechter 1998:213–14)

Financial self-help tells readers that becoming rich is not as impossible as their family upbringing suggested, but it's not going to be easy, and it's not going to be quick. Those attracted to get-rich-quick schemes, in contrast, attempt to circumvent the crucial work of acquiring financial education and working on the self. Get-rich-quick schemes and financial self-help look alike not because they are alike, but because they compete to attract the same clientele.

The more general self-help genre, like get-rich-quick schemes, is related to but also distinct from financial self-help. Most people I interviewed had read a self-help book at some point before reading Robert Kiyosaki. But there were significant variations in how much contact they have had with nonfinancial self-help, and in how they saw the financial integrated into other spheres of life improvement. Nicolás, whom I met early in my fieldwork in Argentina, offers perhaps the clearest example of a complete integration of financial self-help into a whole program of self-improvement. Nicolás was introduced to financial self-help books by a friend from his church in Buenos Aires. An extremely eager nineteen-year-old and a committed fan of Kiyosaki (whom he referred to as "Robert" when I interviewed him), he saw financial self-help as one component of his overall project of self-improvement and success. His church, where he started going after his mother passed away, was led by a local pastor who authored several spiritual self-help books and often appeared on radio and television. He narrated the details of purchasing and reading *Rich Dad, Poor Dad* for the first time as a moment of epiphany:

My friend from church—we were going to take the bus and we saw a bookstore, and we went in, and went to the business books and leadership section, which is perhaps my favorite now. And he said, "Look at this book, I recommend it. It's spectacular, it would be great if you could buy it." And I had the money in my pocket, picked up the book, took it to the cashier, paid, went home and started reading it, and loved it. That night I read it for about three hours, and I was halfway into it and realized it was like 2:00 a.m. So I went to bed but with an amazing desire to continue reading it the next morning. So, from then on, I started devouring Kiyosaki's books.

Nicolás then proceeded to name the titles of each of the eight books by Kiyosaki he had read. He said that he also bought the Cashflow game and played with friends, to whom he would offer *Rich Dad, Poor Dad* as a gift "so that they could read Kiyosaki and share my experience on this new path." For Nicolás, being introduced to Kiyosaki was the consequence of his participation in this particular church. He sees religion, health, spirituality, and finance as one unified project:

> I believed I could [make it] because of the church, because of all the growth in that explosive moment I had in the spiritual realm . . . mostly. I felt connected because it was all new to me. So I was thrilled, enthusiastic . . . so it was easy for me to read Kiyosaki, to soak in his books. And I love going to the church. I go every week, I love it. I love it . . . persisting in this path, even if the initial motivation wanes a bit. And, well, all this [influence] became visible in my personality, in how I move, how I communicate with others, in the words I started using, because with our words and thoughts one creates one's world and creates the world. A world that when Kiyosaki appeared [in my life], it expanded from the spiritual sphere to a lot more areas, and that was the idea: to cover many areas—really important areas that we all need—basic ones, and try to grow in each one of them evenly.

Nicolás was an avid reader of self-help, and even his words echoed the linguistic style of self-help manuals. He told me his readings covered "the physical, the spiritual, the mental, and the emotional" and finances were part of the mental sphere, "the most rational part, the cold part that links more to strategy." I asked Nicolás how important finances were in his activities with the church, and he told me,

> Yes, we take into account freedom in all senses: physical, emotional, spiritual, financial. Yes, we talk a lot about that. That's why they recommend *Rich Dad, Poor Dad*. We constantly talk about assets, business, being a leader for others. Lots of freedom, a field of the human being free of conditionings we inherit, perhaps from taboos, money, sex, a lot of things, and try to break with it so that the human being can be free and unfold its potential.

Financial self-help is for Nicolás one component of a regimented set of practices for self-improvement involving physical well-being and spiritual growth. He integrates what he learns in church with other popular self-help books:

> I contemplate the results in all those areas, and I see progress and growth. For example, every morning I make the same breakfast: one liter of water in a bottle with two lemons and two oranges. I mix it with two spoons of aloe vera, with two spoons of all the minerals, and two spoons of fructose corn syrup. I mix everything and I drink 250 milliliters of that juice and then I do yoga. . . . I learned that in John Gray's book, *Men Are from Mars, Women Are from Venus.* I read that one, and one called *The Mars and Venus Diet and Exercise Solution.* And, well, it explains how the body is designed to heal itself, and to give the best, all the time, making your body a "supermachine." So while you do the yoga exercise, the power of lemon, minerals, and aloe vera purifies everything inside you, it cleans everything. . . . After fifteen minutes of exercise, I drink another cup of that juice, and two garlic cloves, I put them in the food processor and mix them with water. It destroys all virus and bacteria, everything bad in your body. And after that, he [John Gray] says, you drink the morning smoothie.

Nicolás's words show a serious commitment to everyday techniques for improving health and well-being, which for him are part of an overall program of self-improvement in which Kiyosaki also fits. Nicolás's story is not the most typical in terms of the extent of his commitment. For example, his level of devotion to church participation as well as regimented physical and spiritual improvement was not remotely as strong in most other participants I met. Yet it illustrates not only the enthusiasm most fans develop after first reading Kiyosaki, but also the way financial self-help integrates into a larger project of self-help that is not centered solely on finances. However, other fans stumble upon financial self-help books without having read so many other self-help genres like Nicolás had, and even without a high regard for self-help in general.

Iván, for example, a professional economist who taught at a prestigious university in Buenos Aires, said that for a while he refused to read Kiyosaki, just because it was self-help, and he simply did not like self-help. When I met Iván, he had just published an article on Robert Kiyosaki for a local financial magazine, and he had started teaching courses on personal finance organized by the same magazine. I was surprised to see Kiyosaki's ideas treated seriously by an academic expert and in a magazine targeted to more experienced investors. While his background was in corporate finance and capital markets, Iván told me that he grew attracted to personal finance and the latest developments in behavioral economics. Even with a strong academic background in economics and finance, and with suspicion of self-help, he soon became a fan of Robert Kiyosaki.

> I don't like self-help. . . . But, well, a friend started telling me some things about the books and I realized they were interesting. Perhaps I found resonance with things I had been thinking before. And that was the big break. Besides reading him, phrases by Kiyosaki have stuck in my head . . . like, for example, he talks a lot about emotions, which is very interesting—emotions in investment and decision making. And he says that when you look for a safe job, the emotion that drives you is fear.

I attended a few sessions of Iván's courses for aspiring investors, and in his lectures he frequently used concepts from Kiyosaki's books. Iván later published his own book on personal finance and became a columnist on personal finance for a major newspaper. Kiyosaki also had an impact on his personal life. Not long after he was introduced to Kiyosaki's work, Iván quit his job at a major oil company—a dream career for an economist with his specialization—to become an entrepreneur, writer, and personal finance educator.

Although they are extremes—Nicolás is probably the most committed fan I met, while Iván is atypical in that he was an academic and a specialist in finance—Nicolás and Iván's stories demonstrate how wide the variety of users of financial self-help can be, ranging from fans who are regular consumers of self-help in general to those for whom financial self-help is tied to business and money and don't highly regard the self-help genre itself. This amplitude contributes to the success of financial self-help and the breadth of its audience, because people with different goals and different attitudes toward self-help can feel comfortable with it.

The distinctions and connections between financial self-help and general self-help may have little value for users themselves, given that they simply use resources as they run into them and find them appealing or useful. But it is important to clarify what, in my view, makes financial self-help unique: the fact that motivation, optimism, and positive thinking are only part of the components that define it. One recent successful (nonfinancial) self-help resource illustrates the singularity of financial self-help. In 2006, the book and DVD *The Secret* were published globally and became an immediate sensation, partly because of their exposure on American celebrity Oprah Winfrey's television show. Echoing a long tradition of self-help focusing on "positive thinking," the central tenet of *The Secret* is that people attract outcomes with the power of their minds. Whatever people want in life, they have to truly wish for. Positive thoughts attract positive outcomes. The visualization of wishes is what brings about their realization in the future (Byrne 2006; *The Secret* 2006). *The Secret* and resources like it do not have a specific domain of application. The "law of attraction" that it promotes can be equally applied to health issues, financial issues, or one's love life. In essence, *The Secret* discards any external constraints and makes individuals the only party responsible for what they achieve, regardless of whether it is riches, happiness, or good health. Several authors have criticized self-help for being oppressive, and for blaming individuals for circumstances outside their control. Essayist Barbara Ehrenreich (2009:42), for example, states in her critique of positive thinking, "Without question there is a problem when positive thinking 'fails' and the cancer spreads or eludes treatment. Then the patient can only blame herself: she is not being positive enough; possibly it was her negative attitude that brought on the disease in the first place." The scattered scholarship on self-help of various sorts has stressed its extreme individualism and voluntarism.[3] This literature is useful to understand this particular feature of self-help, which financial self-help shares, but not other characteristics that make contemporary financial self-help unique.

Products like *The Secret* tell people to think positively if they want to attract good financial outcomes. They also tell readers and viewers that they have only themselves to blame for their failures. But *The Secret* does not tell users that they have to proactively learn about the financial world. It does not recommend or provide any kind of technical tool or form of calculation. In addition, it does not diagnose the current state of the economic world. The addition of the technical and the sociological components makes financial self-help a new species, one that contains the DNA of other varieties of self-help but is indeed different. As noted earlier, what distinguishes financial self-help is the weaving together of three components: the emotional or motivational, the technical, and the sociological.

Financial self-help is not just based on belief, although belief is a crucial component. Although practitioners believe that they are the almost-exclusive creators of their destinies, that does not mean that they simply reflect on the desire for more money and expect the law of attraction to do the work for them. Financial self-help enthusiasts use the motivational component of self-help to set themselves in motion toward actual accounting and investing practices. For example, Raquel, a high school teacher who discovered financial self-help while she was going through a divorce, describes how financial self-help allowed her to initiate investments:

> Raquel: Many people don't decide to change their situation because they are scared. It happened to me, too. In many situations in my life I said no as a result of fear, for not knowing [any different].
>
> Daniel: What sorts of things?
>
> Raquel: Like investing. In my life I would have never thought that I would put money into a call center [an investment she started]. I would have never thought about that. Even if I had said, "Cool, investing!," I would have had it on paper, not in action. I had to lose that fear, and I did. . . It changed my thinking a lot. If I have money, I don't want to leave it stuck in the bank, because it is not helping. It changed my thinking a lot. [Before engaging with financial self-help] maybe I could think about it, but I wouldn't have put it into practice.
>
> Daniel: Are your expenses different?
>
> Raquel: Yes, my control of spending is very different now. I have a record of what I spend; I'm much more systematic now, much more orderly. I have an Excel file with all the income and all expenses.

For Raquel, financial self-help was instrumental in shedding her fear, but she sees this loss of fear in connection to concrete new accounting practices and renewed ways of thinking about and managing money. Financial self-help is a complex set of narratives and practices that puts together partly somewhat mystical beliefs—according to which inner thoughts and desires outweigh external conditionings on financial outcomes—with techniques for rational economic calculation to maximize incoming cash flow. In one of Kiyosaki's manuals, called *You Can Choose to Be Rich*, he writes,

> Financial literacy requires proficiency in several areas: economic history, accounting, taxes, investing, and building businesses. These are difficult subjects to master, particularly accounting and investing. But don't let the level of difficulty scare you off. Anyone can master these subjects, including you. It's a matter of choosing to do so. (Kiyosaki 2005b:1-30)

The manual provides recommendations about how to eliminate negative thoughts and internal obstacles (for example, Kiyosaki implores readers to "remove the mines blocking your path"), but also suggests that there still is a complex external world that has to be understood and mastered in addition to the technical expertise required to attain financial freedom:

> So far, you have been focusing on internal things that you have the power to change. What happens when your internal self meets the external world over which you have so little control? In truth, you have more control over that world than you think. It has been said that luck is what happens when opportunity meets preparedness. . . . When it comes to financial matters, it's important to keep your eyes and ears open—and to know where you are. Only then will you spot opportunity when it crosses your path. In a broader sense, it's important to know where you are in history and in the world at large. (Kiyosaki 2005b:I-8–I-9)

Adding to the long tradition of self-help resources, financial self-help calls readers to acquire technical financial tools (often called financial intelligence or financial literacy) and an explicit diagnosis of the current stage of capitalism and how it affects individuals. Financial self-help combines these three components to produce a subject whose main responsibility is to successfully navigate the mysterious web of contemporary financial capitalism.

Financial Self-Help and the Rise of Neoliberalism: A Brief History

Financial self-help is a product of the neoliberal transformation of the last four decades, a change that, among other effects, has shifted social risks to individuals and has increased the role of finances in everyday life. Of course, books offering advice on how to become rich are far from a new phenomenon. What distinguishes contemporary financial self-help from its antecessors is its explicit disregard of any form of work as a viable means for financial success (the mantra is "make your money work for you, don't work for your money"). The recommendation to quit one's job in favor of investing is only possible under economic conditions that emerged in the last quarter of the twentieth century. Contemporary financial self-help arose as part and parcel of the enormous transformations of capitalism that started in the 1970s and 1980s and brought about a new, unprecedented stage in capitalist development, alternatively called "neoliberalism," "globalization," "financial capitalism," or "the new world order" (Ranney 2003). This transformation has taken place in different forms and with varied intensity, but it has been a global transformation. Neoliberalism has not just prompted a transformation of the economy—it has shifted our contemporary understanding of how societies are organized and governed and what individuals are asked to do in that context (Foucault 2008:130–31).

In several areas of social and economic life, we have witnessed a shift over the past several decades from models of socialized risk that guaranteed certain safety nets and protections of work (such as social security, labor regulation, welfare, and so on) to models of privatized risk in which individuals are left largely to their own devices (Foucault 2008:144; Hacker 2006; O'Malley 1996). Both in developed countries like the United States as well as in countries that were in a process of late industrialization like Argentina, production started shifting around the 1970s from manufacturing to financial and other services (Basualdo 2001; Davis 2009; Krippner 2011; Lin and Tomaskovic-Devey 2013; Villarreal 1985; Whitford 2005). Employment has become much more flexible, with increasing temporary work, subcontracting, precarious or non-unionized positions, and employee turnover, while wage-earners have lost their sense of job security and stability (Boltanski and Chiapello 2005; Fraile 2009; Frenkel and Ros 2004; Kalleberg 2011; Novick, Lengyel, and Sarabia 2009). Capital has become much more mobile, partly due to technological transformations (Castells 1996).

These changes have given individuals access to parts of the world of finance that were previously restricted to experts. Today, investing in the stock market or having an Internet business (like an e-shop) does not sound like an impossible venture for the common citizen. Alongside this opening of the world of finance to everyday people, the deregulation of financial systems has increased the levels of consumer credit and home loans, enabling individuals to invest in products, stock, property, and business endeavors that were previously unattainable for many and expanding financial reasoning to an increasing number of areas of life (Ailon 2015; Chiapello 2015; Fligstein and Goldstein 2015; Langley 2008; Leyshon and French 2009; Martin 2002). As a consequence, finance today is much more than a growing sector of the economy; it is "a model of how things are done" (Davis 2009:xi). It is in this context of a post-industrial, finance-oriented society that the financial self-help notion that money should work and not people emerges victoriously in popular culture.[4]

Although financial self-help is a relatively new species, explicitly tied to the changes brought about by neoliberalism, it is also a descendant of the American tradition of the *success manual*, which goes back to the eighteenth century (Baida 1990).[5] American founding figure Benjamin Franklin, famously characterized by Max Weber as the ideal type of the spirit of capitalism, may be one of the first ancestors of financial self-help. For psychologist Steven Starker, who traced the history of self-help, Franklin represents the secularization of popular literature on mobility and financial success out of its religious origins (2002:14–15). Franklin's iconic publications *Poor Richard's Almanac* (1732–1758) and *The Way to Wealth* (1758) contained several exhortations popular in today's financial self-help culture, such as the notion that a dollar spent instead of invested could very well jeopardize one's chances of becoming wealthy.

Following in Franklin's footsteps a century later were popular moral tales of mobility like those penned by American hero Horatio Alger. Alger was a prolific nineteenth-century author famous for his stories about impoverished boys who escaped their humble backgrounds and rose to financial security through their own hard work and determination. Alger's books were formative in American culture during the country's Gilded Age, an era of rapid economic growth. But Alger was nothing like today's financial gurus. According to historian John Cawelti (1965), Alger's "rags to riches" stories should have been called "rags to respectability." Most of his stories were tales about how the development of moral character ensured mobility to the middle class, but money, or even financial independence, was not central to his message. In fact, he believed the biblical motto that money is the root of all evil, an idea that fans of Kiyosaki not only despise but regard as one of the mistaken truths acquired from one's family that has to be combated through intense work on the self.

During the twentieth century, most success manuals shifted from the goals of superior moral character or middle-class respectability to either a vague sense of "internal peace of mind" or the pursuit of material wealth as an end in itself (Biggart 1983:308; Cawelti 1965:209–18). They also included advice on improving people's chances in the labor market, particularly in large businesses. Many of the books published in the decades after the Great Depression were attuned to the emergence and consolidation of the large corporation in the U.S. economic landscape. According to Starker, the famous Dale Carnegie's *How to Win Friends and Influence People*, published in 1936, responded to the new managerial class's need to survive in the new corporate environment:

> By 1930, the 200 largest corporations controlled nearly half of all nonbanking corporate wealth in America. A large managerial class had been created, but it had also been badly burned by the Great Depression. Finding and keeping a job, being liked by one's supervisors and coworkers, being selected for promotions— these were matters of extreme concern, and Carnegie offered to help (2002:66).

Carnegie's book sold more than six million copies in the United States between the 1940s and the 1970s, and remains one of the most famous success manuals to date.

Sociologist Nicole Woolsey Biggart (1983) analyzed thirty best-selling success manuals published in the United States between 1950 and 1980. Like previous researchers of the 1960s and 1970s, Biggart examined postwar industrial societies characterized by the importance of organizations and the stability of employment. Consistent with Starker and others, Biggart found that books tailored for workers in corporations were the most important and widespread type of success manual in this period.[6] With the erosion of job security and the increasing flexibility of work since the 1970s, the tone of success manuals started to change. Sociologist Micki McGee, who examined the self-help genre in the 1990s, observed a subtle but visible shift. New self-improvement books, more than providing advice on how to succeed in the corporation, urged readers to remake themselves on a constant basis in order to remain competitive in the job market, and provided "exactly the kind of motivation required of a new labor force of women and men faced with temporary positions, downsizing, and non-elective self-employment." New books adapted "to a lifestyle of economic insecurity" (McGee 2005:41). "In the place of a social safety net," McGee argues, "Americans have been offered row upon row of self-help books to boost their spirits and keep them afloat in uncharted economic and social waters" (McGee 2005:12). McGee uses the concept of a "belabored self," which works on two levels. A belabored self is the result of individuals having to work on themselves in order to remain merely employable in a neoliberal economy. The existence of a belabored self also means that people are now asked to discover and craft an authentic and stable self that "might function—even thrive—unaffected by the vagaries of the job market" (McGee 2005:16).

Contemporary financial self-help is a response to the same economic conditions that led to the growth of the books McGee evaluated, which offer advice on how to be flexible enough to survive in a declining and unstable job market. Like the literature McGee analyzed, Kiyosaki also exhorts readers to find a way to be unaffected by the rollercoaster of labor markets in the neoliberal era. However, the novelty of current financial self-help is that, on the basis of its analysis of current economic conditions, it completely discards employability as a worthy goal. McGee compares books published in the 1990–1997 period with those published from 1998 to 2003. She found similar titles in the two periods, with the "important exception of an increasingly financial approach to daily life" (McGee 2005:196). While many popular books from the past are still widely sold today, since Nicole Biggart's study of the 1950–1980 period and McGee's study of the 1990s there has been extraordinary growth in the sophistication and sales of success manuals supporting entrepreneurial strategies outside the world of labor, particularly those that take advantage of the financial system and real estate markets (Olen 2013). These books were not particularly significant before the last decade of the twentieth century, but with the advent of neoliberalism and the expansion of the financial system, the very definition of success changed. While success manuals before that time were predominantly about achieving prosperity through formal organizations like the corporation, contemporary financial self-help is explicitly about escaping the corporate environment—or any other work environment for that matter—and making a living through "passive income." The very definition of success in Robert Kiyosaki's books is *financial freedom*, which is the total abandonment of work: "If you go with me, you'll let go of the idea of working for money and instead learn to have money work for you" (Kiyosaki and Lechter 1998:44).

Social Theories People Live By

Contemporary financial self-help shares much with nineteenth- and twentieth-century success literature. However, contemporary financial self-help does not simply provide generic or timeless financial advice; it is rather explicitly tied to the particular historical conditions in which we live. Kiyosaki tells readers that his advice is tailored to the current era. As such, the ideas of *Rich Dad* are not just a technique or theory of the self; I argue that they make up a social theory (albeit more accessible and less rigorous than those to which social scientists are accustomed). He inherits the extreme voluntarism common to all self-help, but also has quite a sophisticated reading of social and economic reality.

Current financial self-help is not simply about motivation and positive thinking. The goal of these ideas and practices is not just to acquire peace of mind, feel good about oneself, attract good things, or strike a balanced self. It is not just about being a more positive or happier person. Neither is the goal of current financial self-help just making money, which theoretically could be achieved by climbing the corporate ladder. The stated goal is *freedom*. Freedom, as I will explain in more detail in the next chapter, means liberating the self from its own limitations but also from the constraints imposed by the real economic world. As I discussed earlier, attaining financial freedom demands working on the self, controlling emotions and fears, and disciplining the self, but also going out and learning about real estate investing, tax law, stocks, and so on (as I heard time and again in my fieldwork, "educating yourself financially"). Current financial self-help tells you that you have to think in certain ways and become a certain kind of person to achieve financial freedom, but also that you need to make the effort and take the time to technically understand and acquire the tools for the global economy of the twenty-first century.

Authors of financial self-help books, particularly Robert Kiyosaki, do not ignore or disregard the changes in the economy and labor market brought about by the neoliberal era—quite the contrary. Kiyosaki offers his consumers a description of the historical conditions that made his own ideas possible—one that, as I will show, is not farfetched. He presents his work to readers and practitioners as a merciless illumination of the conditions of the world in which we live, not the ones we imagine. Paraphrasing George Lakoff and Mark Johnson's book title *Metaphors We Live By* (1980), Kiyosaki offers what I call *social theories people live by*. He presents a popular theory about the transition from the corporate and welfare society to the more recent investor society and of what forms of action and subjectivity fit well in the new order.

Kiyosaki links his ideas to the transition between what he calls the industrial age and the information age. Although he does not use the term, I find that the concept underlying his theory is *inertia*. According to Kiyosaki, people have become accustomed to the order of the industrial age, although we no longer live in this period. They still use the concepts, categories, and ideas that made sense for that age. They still behave according to classifications, values, and cultural ideas associated with social and economic forms that do not exist anymore. I distinguish three levels at which people are asked to correct this maladjustment (although Kiyosaki does not separate these levels explicitly). First, at the level of concepts and goals, what people should try to achieve today is different from what their parents tried to achieve. Second, at the level of calculative tools and other cognitive resources, whoever wants to succeed in the current economy will need to perform calculations that their parents did not even know existed. Finally, at the level of the self, for Kiyosaki there is no point in our post-industrial world in waiting for institutions (the state, the corporation) to take care of you; you should care for yourself and be prepared to take risks. He says all this while citing great economists (Kiyosaki did not like school, but, he adds, he always liked economics). In one of his presentations on an instructional set of CDs, Kiyosaki argues that although Marx and Keynes

were the economists of the industrial age, Joseph Schumpeter and Intel CEO
Andy Grove are the economists of the information age:

> What Schumpeter and Grove believed is that this new unleashed capitalism will
> greatly brutalize and batter anyone who is still thinking old industrial age ideas.
> So, much of this program is really about having you examine your current ideas,
> your current beliefs and hopefully and maybe, if they are not already changing,
> change your ideas or thoughts into what I consider information age ways of
> thinking about money, employment, business, and investing. (Kiyosaki 2000a)

Kiyosaki forcefully tries to persuade his readers that they ought to understand and accept that the world has changed and correct the self in order to
abandon their welfare society ways (see Binkley 2009). Much of his description
of the transformations of the last three decades is largely a simplified version
of the way social scientists have depicted the transition from industrial to post-
industrial societies and its profound effects on labor, finances, and communications.[7] The first step for success in this age is to combat those inertial ideas
that no longer belong in financial capitalism. His first and foremost target is
the illusion of job security inherited from corporate capitalism. For Kiyosaki,
job security is completely obsolete and most people have not yet realized it.
The notion that a good job in a large corporation would provide good benefits
and a safe pension at the end of the road was the great "agreement" of the industrial age. The most important moment of social mobility was the moment
of entry into a setting that assured workers that they would have continuity, a
salary, and the safety that comes with knowing their company would take care
of them. Once there, the path was clear—the positions to strive for were well-
defined, and staying on the same rung of the corporate ladder was not grounds
for being fired. Workers could count on having the same job until retirement,
or eventually moving to a similar or better one. The choice of corporation made
all the difference because a good set of benefits meant lifetime security. For
those born before 1935, Kiyosaki says, this may have been a reasonable course
of action, but clearly not for others.[8]

Kiyosaki's bashing of the industrial era that ended in the 1970s rides a wave
of critique of the rigidity and bureaucratization of managerial society that
started in the 1960s. In *The New Spirit of Capitalism*, sociologists Luc Boltanski
and Eve Chiapello (2005) argue that while the first spirit of capitalism (the one
Weber traced back to the protestant ethic) was constructed around the image
of the bourgeois entrepreneur, the second spirit was molded by the large in-

dustrial firms that emerged in the twentieth century, and based on the heroic figure of the salaried managers of those firms. This second spirit of capitalism valued economic efficiency and growth but also security: it promised stable careers, a protective work environment, and fairly predictable economic paths for wage-earners, in addition to a secure pension down the road. Individual self-realization was deeply tied with that promise. A well-defined place in the rational bureaucratic structure of the firm and the possibility of progress were seen as conditions for self-fulfillment and freedom of action. However, by the 1960s these work arrangements came to be seen in a negative light in several industrialized countries. Students, countercultural movements, and even many employees forcefully critiqued the impersonal rationality of industrial society, which did not leave much room for individual creativity and autonomy. Boltanski and Chiapello argue that capitalism is capable of embracing and incorporating critique, and that is what happened in the 1970s in response to the countercultural mobilization of the 1960s. This wave of critique gave birth to the current spirit of capitalism, which values flexibility, self-expression, and adaptability. The complaint that employees at all levels were cogs in the bureaucratic business machine of Fordism and the demands for individual autonomy and spaces of creativity were taken seriously by firms and governments and led to important changes in workplace organization. Boltanski and Chiapello compare the workplace management literature of the 1960s and the 1990s, and find an increasing attention to these demands. For example, a management manual from the 1990s stated that the firm "must be a site for creating meaning, for shared goals, where everyone can simultaneously develop their personal autonomy and contribute to the collective project" (Boltanski and Chiapello 2005:63). The rigid hierarchies and occupational categories of the industrial age were replaced by firms that function as networks, with flexible positions, teams, and projects, under a leader's vision instead of a manager's orders. All of these changes were meant to make the workplace a place where feelings, meaning, and creativity would flourish, instead of the rigid bureaucracy of the past, although the cost was to give up job security and protections from risk. In his analysis of the transition to post-industrial societies, Kiyosaki does not seem to buy into these new forms of workplace organization. While the themes of flexibility, adaptability, and autonomy that emerged in the critique of industrial capitalism of the 1960s are indeed at the center of financial self-help, the workplace is still not seen as the place where people will find freedom. Work today provides neither security nor autonomy and self-fulfillment. For Kiyosaki, not only are most people still caught up with what Boltanski and Chiapello call the second spirit of capitalism, expecting a job security that is long gone, they have also failed to see that finance is now at the center of capitalism, and passive income is the only viable outlet for their desires for freedom.

Kiyosaki's diagnosis of current economic conditions and how they affect the world of work is disseminated not only in his books, CDs, DVDs, and interviews, but also in multiple seminars and Cashflow game sessions organized by fans. In the fall of 2007, I traveled with the leaders of Financial Freedom Argentina to Mar del Plata, a coastal city five hours from Buenos Aires, for a three-day annual event on entrepreneurship. As part of the event, the founder, Matías, was given a one-hour slot to promote the Cashflow game among attendees from all over the country, and asked me to help participants with their first steps of the game. One hundred and twenty people who had never played Cashflow and many of whom had never heard of Kiyosaki sat around tables ready to play. Before play, Matías gave participants a short lecture appealing to their own experiences in a labor market full of flexibility and tied them to Kiyosaki's core ideas:

> The advice to "study a lot, get a good job, and with that you will be able to get far" belongs to a mindset of the industrial age when there were large corporations that took care of their employees. This happened in the time of my parents, my grandparents, when they took a job in a company, and they surely retired in that same company. Today, we know that this doesn't happen. I don't have to give any examples. If all of you have worked, you know you worked a year in one place, two years in another one, and so on. And due to the market, the state of the company, or how things change, you have to adapt yourself. You have to improve, know more, and update yourself. So, the current mindset of the information age, and not the industrial age, is a mindset of openness to understand how the wave is moving and how to adapt to it.[9]

Given the unstable and unsettling conditions of work in the neoliberal era that Matías describes, success is redefined by financial self-help in a very specific way: it is the possibility of liberating yourself from the tyranny of the labor market. The world of work does not offer the possibility of security that it used to, and by no means provides financial freedom. Success within today's labor market is not really success; according to Kiyosaki, financial freedom can only be achieved through incoming cash flow based on financial investment and not on labor. As Iván, the professional economist who became a personal finance writer, explained to me:

> This is one of the most important things Kiyosaki talks about. Passive income is an income for which you do not have to work, so ideally you have a passive income column that generates an incoming [cash] flow every month. When that income is more than your regular expenses, you reach financial freedom, which doesn't mean that you are a millionaire, but that the income you don't have to work for covers all your needs.

In other words, financial freedom is mathematically defined as the possibility of covering one's expenses without having to work. According to Kiyosaki's social theory, in the bygone industrial age, job security was directly tied to one's formal education. One needed to attend school to obtain the certification and credentials necessary for suitable entry into the formal labor market, but this is much less important today. In books, workshops, and informal conversations, I repeatedly heard the argument that the age-old advice to "get good grades, in order to get a good job with good benefits and a good retirement plan" is now obsolete, yet people mistakenly cling to it. Kiyosaki essentially sees school as training for a stable labor market—a stability that has now disappeared. If all one had to do was get a job, then a good education was all one needed. In the contemporary information age, however, formal education is not as important as "street smarts," partly because educational credentials do not help outside the formal labor market. Several financial gurus adopt this tactic of presenting themselves as academic failures. Kiyosaki never misses an opportunity to remind his audiences how poorly he did in school and college, how much he hated it, and that the intelligence that helped him become rich has little to do with formal schooling.

Kiyosaki sees the skills learned in school as useless in the pursuit of financial freedom. This is due to the distinction between the "real" financial world and that of the security of formal organizations. Kiyosaki repeatedly says that in order to be given a loan, people are not asked to show their school report card but rather their financial statement. Report cards, he argues, are to school what financial statements are to real financial life: they demonstrate to someone how well you are doing. Since laypeople have not been taught how to read financial statements, they do not know how well they are doing financially. Individuals do not learn how to read or write financial statements in school, or any practical, real-life financial skills.[10] While Kiyosaki's father taught him that reading

books was important, his financial mentor taught him that it was more important to know how to read financial statements than books (Kiyosaki 2000a).

Kiyosaki's first book was unambiguously titled *If You Want to Be Rich &*
Happy Don't Go to School (1993). This topic is perhaps the most disputed among
his devotees. Although fans share the general idea that school is not a great help
for financial freedom because none of the necessary skills are learned there,
many middle-class fans do not feel so comfortable with this maxim. Those who
have already missed the train of higher education (that is, they did not attend
college when they were young) find a comforting narrative that tells them that
it was unnecessary anyway. But those who have gone to college or further, and
those younger fans whose middle-class background is associated with a high
regard for higher education, are still likely to consider formal education important, if not helpful financially. Sergio, a twenty-four-year-old engineering
student who works in computer networking, and whom I met in a Cashflow
game, told me in an interview,

> Suddenly, you read that and the first thought is, "I'll drop everything [univer-
> sity] and start investing, what the hell." Obviously, it crosses your mind, but then
> you say, "I can't leave everything because I read a book!" But the first thought is,
> "I'm a jerk, look how I'm studying and they [the rich] are laughing their asses
> off." But well, you can't give up everything you are for financial freedom. I think
> you can slowly fuse them together. I'm not going to drop years of studying com-
> puter science and delve into the stock market. All right, I would make money,
> but what about what I like doing: computer science?

Like Sergio, Raquel was attracted to Kiyosaki because of her initial aston-
ishment at his positions on formal education. Being a math teacher, she was
at first very angry about the author's discouragement of formal education, but
then she partially accepted the idea:

> How can anyone say that school is not useful?! No! Terrible! I said, "He's crazy,
> how can he say that!" But when I read it . . . I was angry, nitpicking, but then I
> started to understand what he said, about why school was not convenient for
> our financial life. And I started thinking about our system, and how one teaches,
> and I said, "He's right, because you are not really teaching children to get ahead.
> You are really teaching them so that they become employees. You say, 'You need
> a degree.' What for? In order to look for a better job." And we say that systemati-
> cally. Nowadays, for some things you need a degree, but for others . . . you don't!
> It's not necessary. But the system makes you repeat those conditionings. So, in

some ways, he's right, but not in everything. I believe that a base of knowledge is necessary to face life. Even though the more intuitive part of a person helps in what decisions you are going to make in life, a methodical and systematic form of thought is also necessary. So, at least the school system works for that, to teach you how to be systematic.

Degrees are not a significant source of prestige in the financial self-help world, but fans do not readily accept that not studying might be better than studying. On Argentine online forums, younger members often ask for advice on what to do about their higher education plans, and most people respond that they should study, but knowing that if they want financial freedom, they will have to educate themselves financially outside of the university.[11] A real estate attorney in New York told me during a Cashflow game that if she had known all that she knows now after reading financial self-help, she would not have attended law school. Or perhaps, she said, she would have made money and gained financial freedom before attending school. Although some people may think along these lines, it is by no means a common belief. Cashflow organizer Matías told me,

> I don't think people who studied regret doing so. I don't see that. They regret what they were not given in school, what they didn't learn. But they don't regret studying. I have two degrees, and I don't regret it. Were they useful for my financial freedom? No. But perhaps with the extra ingredient I'm adding now, it'll probably be better than if I hadn't studied. I have an MBA. Was it helpful for my financial freedom before I read Kiyosaki? No. But perhaps Kiyosaki was the missing ingredient.

Of course, in his books Kiyosaki recognizes that there are some useful things that people learn in the educational system. But for him, those with adequate financial training—a kind of training that you do *not* get in school—can always hire those with other skills that will also be needed to conduct a business or an investment venture. Outside of the school system, you do not have to perform well in all subjects. People hire others to complete tasks at which they are not skilled. For example, if one has the means, one can (and will have to) hire the best lawyers and accountants.[12] Thus, the skill of choosing the right people to cooperate in the quest for financial freedom is essential and cannot be learned in school. The idea of "building your team" and relying on the expertise of others is an important value in current financial self-help, which makes both education in general and certain expert skills in particular non-essential on the way to riches. Kiyosaki suggests that being school smart is not necessary: the C student can always hire the A student.

There are two skills, however, that are nontransferable and that any person who wants to achieve financial freedom has to acquire. One, as I have just mentioned, is the ability to select the right people with whom to work collaboratively. The second is financial intelligence. Readers are encouraged to delegate in any other sphere, but the use of financial planners or financial advisors is despised. There is an important dictum: while you can pay others or collaborate with them in entrepreneurial activities, no one cares more about your money than you. Financial planners are usually salespeople that benefit from customers' investments independently of the outcomes of those investments. The use of mentors (wealthy people who have made it themselves) is encouraged, but to let someone else handle your finances is a sin. Financial literacy and financial planning are the only nontransferable, essential skills. In this sense, although there is nothing wrong with obtaining several useful skills, financial education is the only essential education. No one can read a financial statement or design a business plan for you, Kiyosaki reminds his followers.

According to Steven Starker (2002), self-help generally competes with established forms of expertise. Popular psychology books, for example, compete with professional psychologists. Diet books compete with nutritionists and doctors. I suggest that the case of financial self-help, however, is different. Financial planners might be seen as the experts challenged by financial self-help, but financial self-help goes further than seeking to replace what financial planners do. It responds to the rise of a whole new set of concerns that were previously nonexistent. Independently of the financial self-help boom, financial knowledge has become increasingly necessary just for survival in current capitalist societies. Financial gurus like Kiyosaki have been complaining for years of the deficiency of the school system due to its lack of financial education. But this issue is not one that only the financial self-help world cares about. In the last few years, educators and policymakers in the United States and other countries have been discussing the challenges of establishing and improving financial education in schools.

While education for household finances was a relatively simple field until recently, the increasing complexity of finances and the entanglement of financial institutions at all levels of society have made financial training for laypeople a growing concern for educators (see Bernheim, Garrett, and Maki 2001; Lyons, Palmer, Jayaratne, and Scherpf 2006; Lyons, Chang, and Scherpf 2006; Mandell

2008). The establishment of retirement systems based on individual manage-able accounts such as IRAs or 401(k)s, which demand from citizens much more knowledge than before, is one of the reasons why financial education is increas-ingly a need and not a choice.[13] This is a dramatic change that current financial self-help acknowledges as confirmation of the need for a new financial mind-set. Sociologist Brooke Harrington regards changes in retirement laws in the United States (although it has happened in other countries too) as the explana-tion for the growth of investment clubs in the 1990s:

> Until the 1970s, most American workers could expect to receive traditional pen-sions—known as "defined benefits" plans—upon retirement. Under this regime, employers took full responsibility for setting aside and managing employees' retirement funds. But after the laws governing private pension plans changed in the mid-1970s, employers began shifting the risk and responsibility of retire-ment savings to employees. Out of this change emerged the so-called "defined contribution" plan—the most common of which is the 401(k)—in which em-ployees must decide for themselves how much money to deduct from their sala-ries and how it should be invested. . . . This has created a new imperative for individuals to become informed about investing and financial planning. (Har-rington 2008:19–20)

The shift of financial risk and calculation from organizations such as the state and companies to individual workers is a trademark of neoliberal govern-mentality (O'Malley 1996) and a source of terrible anxiety. It is hard to overstate the concerns workers have today about their retirements. Individuals are now on their own in regard to retirement planning, which demands much more from them. The levels of financial knowledge and skill required for adequate financial planning a few decades ago pale compared to those needed now. The issue of financial education is not just a problem for those who want to be rich. The mastery of complex financial calculations has become a minimum requirement for survival. The problematization of financial education is com-mon to self-help and consumer economics, and it is likely to grow in the future (Lusardi and Mitchell 2007a, 2007b).

Financial self-help authors cash in on the anxieties that the transforma-tion of finances has created. On top of trying to convince readers to accept the new retirement situation and do something about it, Kiyosaki tells them that they should not delude themselves into thinking that having a 401(k) ac-count makes them investors. He argues that these retirement accounts are just savings plans and not really investment plans (and he repeatedly states that "savers are losers"). Kiyosaki fuels readers' fears about retirement and tells fans that they cannot expect too much from Social Security and their 401(k) accounts. For Kiyosaki, demographic variables, such as the massive retirement of baby boomers, will wipe out most of the retirement savings of employees in just a few years. If they want to find comfort in retirement, he implores, it is not enough to save money through conventional retirement accounts. They need to become real investors—a task that, of course, adds even more anxiety.

Class Structure and the Logic of Social Mobility

Follow along with me, for a moment, to imagine a possible diagnosis of modern capitalism: capitalist societies are divided into two fundamental classes—the workers and the capitalists—more specifically, those who work for their money and those who benefit from the work of other people. Societies are not divided into classes according to the amount of money people make, but rather by the source of their income. Those lucky enough to find employment with a higher salary than the mean are not saved from remaining on the poor side of society. They might have more money at their disposal, but they do not own the means of production that make it possible, by employing others or investing in businesses that employ others, to profit without working. Their only property is their labor power, and if the company in which they work fires them, they have nothing left but their capacity to continue working if another employer wants them. Those who belong to this group (I'll call them the poor) always have just barely enough or perhaps a little more than what is needed to survive in a consumption-oriented society. They end up working all their lives without being rewarded for their efforts, never enjoying the benefits of a free and full life unburdened by alienated work. Meanwhile, capitalist societies have a formidable mechanism to reproduce this dichotomous and unequal structure: the school system. In the educational system, people learn to become good workers. Teachers encourage conformity, reward character traits that fit well with being a worker, and discourage independence. Those who perform better in school will most likely end up in higher-paid positions, but they will never learn in a classroom that there are two social classes and that, as far as they may go in their jobs, they will still belong to the workers' group. This system guarantees an adequate supply of workers at all levels of skill that the capitalist system needs. These workers believe that their actual position is the best they can achieve and rarely question why they are where they are. Meanwhile, although the state is supposed to represent everyone equally, it clearly favors the rich. The taxation system is obscenely structured in a way that gives enormous benefits to those who own the means of production while taxing more heavily those whose only property is their labor power. Thus, the state is in collusion with the rich so that they can easily reproduce their advantages. As a result, the rich tend to get richer.

The preceding diagnosis could very well have come from a Marxist critique of capitalism. It has all the elements of such an analysis: the notion of class structure based on ownership of the means of production instead of level of income; a hint at Marx's idea of alienated labor; the idea of social reproduction based on education, which resembles Marxist philosopher Louis Althusser's analysis of the school system; and the certainty that the state contributes to the reproduction of the conditions for capitalism and the advantages of the capitalist class. This diagnosis, however, is a summary (using different jargon) of some of Robert Kiyosaki's ideas, and those of related popular financial self-help authors, who confess no major issues with capitalism itself. Rather, these authors advise readers about what kind of person they should become if they want to be on the advantageous side of a capitalist system. I present this parallel to highlight how Kiyosaki's theory is not just a theory of the self, but a theory of how the class structure of capitalist society works. However, financial self-help and Marxism or structural social analysis could not be further apart. Perhaps where financial self-help departs from Marxism is in the idea that capitalism is not necessarily unfair, and that there are ways to move from one class to the other that fully depend on changing oneself: "Unless you change your ideas, nothing outside of you will change. The good news is that if you want to be rich and wealthy, it's as simple as changing your ideas, your thought. The bad news is that for some people those are the hardest things to change" (Kiyosaki 2000a).[14]

While he frequently refers to the rich, the middle class, and the poor, and suggests that the rich think differently from everybody else, Kiyosaki's "class structure theory," to give it a name, has four categories, described in his book *The Cashflow Quadrant* (Kiyosaki 1999). The concept of the quadrant is widely used by Kiyosaki's fans, and it is, unsurprisingly, repeated throughout Rich Dad materials and their related activities. This book is seen by many fans as more "serious" than *Rich Dad, Poor Dad*, and it is usually read after the latter. The image of the Cashflow Quadrant is one of the most important symbols of the

Kiyosaki brand (it is actually trademarked). The leaders of the group Financial Freedom Argentina have a small image of the quadrant printed on their distinctive shirts, while their website registration form asks people in which quadrant they are located—the logic being that this should be an obvious answer. In the Argentine *Rich Dad* online forum, members also display their quadrant affiliation in their online profiles. Kiyosaki's first recommendation is that people understand where in the quadrant they would fit, or in other words, their objective position in society. That position is determined by a person's source of income, not by the level of income or the type of activity ("The important words are 'generate income from.' It is not so much what we do, but more how we generate income," says Kiyosaki).

A representation of the quadrant can be seen in Figures 1.1 and 1.2. In the figures, E is employee, S is self-employed, B is business owner, and I is investor. Those at the top of the quadrant work in formal organizations while those at the

Figure 1.1. The Cashflow Quadrant
SOURCE: Kiyosaki, 1999. Reprinted with permission of CASHFLOW Technologies, Inc.

Employees (have a job) **E**	**B** Business owners (people work for them)
Self employed (own a job) **S**	**I** Investors (money works for them)

Figure 1.2. The Cashflow Quadrant
SOURCE: Kiyosaki, 1999. Reprinted with permission of CASHFLOW Technologies, Inc.

bottom work in a more autonomous fashion. The vertical division is the most significant: those on the left of the quadrant work for their money, while those on the right have other people (if they are B = business owner) or money (if they are I = investor) work for them. Those on the left seek security while those on the right seek freedom. On the left side, those above (E = employee quadrant) receive a salary and have a boss while those below do not have a boss but still work for their money. Being in the E quadrant is associated with a quest for security, while the S quadrant denotes an appreciation for independence. Yet, those who are self-employed, regardless of prestige and income—from doctors and lawyers to shopkeepers, real estate agents, plumbers, and cleaners—are very different from the business owners of the top right quadrant. As a rule of thumb, people can determine if they are in the S or the B quadrant by performing a thought experiment. If they could possibly leave their business for a whole year and yet find it successful after this sabbatical, they are business owners. If going on vacation means that income disappears, then they are in the S quadrant: "Saying it simply, an 'S' owns a job. A 'B' owns a system and then hires competent people to operate the system. Or put it another way: In many cases, the 'S' *is* the system. That is why they cannot leave" (Kiyosaki 1999:27). The levels of income have nothing to do in principle with the position in the quadrant: "employees can be presidents of companies or janitors of companies. It is not so much what they do, but the contractual agreement they have with the person or organization that hires them" (Kiyosaki 1999:21). In essence, Kiyosaki's idea about what puts a person in one class or another is closer to the basic Marxist sketch than one would think a financial self-help book would be at first sight.

Most participants in financial self-help are initially in one of the two quadrants of the left side, and they hope to move to the right side. Among those registered on the Financial Freedom Argentina website until late 2009, 50 percent defined themselves as members of the E quadrant; 18.5 percent were in the S quadrant; 16.7 percent were in the B quadrant (although this may be overestimated due to the frequent confusion between S and B: they own a business, but not one from which they can take a year off); 5.6 percent categorized themselves as I; and finally 9 percent chose "none," which probably reflects people who are unemployed or not in the labor market (full-time students, for example).[15] However, people do not have to belong to one quadrant exclusively; they may have portions of their income coming from different quadrants.

One of Kiyosaki's basic messages is that people should have their money work for them instead of them working for their money. The abbreviations

OPM and OPT are widely known in the world of financial self-help. They refer to *other people's money* and *other people's time*. The rich, who populate the right side of the quadrant, get rich by using the time and money of others. Those others are the people on the left side. Kiyosaki is quite explicit in stating that a minority of people appropriate resources (time and money) from the rest, and he suggests that it is only natural to try everything one can to join that minority.

Kiyosaki describes several patterns of mobility between quadrants. Each of them is associated with a specific goal. Those who look for job security might occasionally change jobs or ranks, but they invariably revolve around the employee quadrant. Some people, tired of having a boss, might decide that enough is enough and start their own business, which does not change much in terms of their position in regard to financial freedom. Members of the middle class may have a good job or be self-employed and also invest some of their income in order to secure retirement. Kiyosaki calls this pattern "financial security," which is still far away from the notion of financial freedom—not having to work *before the time of retirement*. They are still in the left side of the quadrant, where people who work for their money stay. His recommendation is to follow a path from the left side to the B quadrant (becoming business owners), and then move down to the I quadrant, where financial freedom lies. This transition through business ownership provides people with the necessary skills, mindset, and capital for a successful venture into the I quadrant, where they can finally live off of their investments.

Another major difference between the left and right sides of the quadrant, and a major theme of Kiyosaki's advice, is tax benefits. Kiyosaki repeatedly states that people that work hard make the least money and pay more taxes. Even people with higher levels of education and income, as long as they remain on the left side of the quadrant, pay immensely more taxes than business owners and investors. Most people, he says, do not realize that tax laws are designed to favor the rich. The harder people work, the more they are taxed. For most people, taxes are their highest expense. Because the rich make their money through real estate or business revenue, they do not have to share such a large portion of their income with the government. In contrast, when those who belong to the employee quadrant get a raise, the government gets one, too. A book sponsored by the Rich Dad series that provides advice on taxes is unambiguously called *Loopholes of the Rich: How the Rich Legally Make More Money & Pay Less Tax* (Kennedy 2001). Neither in Kiyosaki's material nor throughout my fieldwork have I found any moral questioning of the fact that the tax structure favors the rich, or a suggestion that the tax structure should be reinvented more equitably. Financial self-help rhetoric seems to imply instead that if the rules are designed or bent to favor the rich, then this provides more reason to try to join their ranks. In fact, it confirms how financially smart the rich are. For Kiyosaki, the tax code is designed in a way that incentivizes business, and people should try to benefit from that opportunity. Taxes are a good example of how conditions external to the individual are regarded simply as unquestionable facts and not as objects of political or moral objection. The idea is that, to be rich, one has to master the external rules, not complain about them.

.   .   .

Kiyosaki tells readers that those who want to be successful in today's economy have to understand that the world has changed and assess where they are located in the Cashflow Quadrant. Those positions are based on people's sources of income. If they work for their money, they are on the left side; if they benefit from the work of others, they are on the right side. Eventually, they should plan to reach the Eden of the investor quadrant. For Kiyosaki, the first step is to understand the quadrant structure.

Acquiring financial skills is another crucial step. Like get-rich-quick schemes, Kiyosaki promises that riches are within reach. But, unlike those schemes, he tells readers that not everyone can be rich. Becoming rich is difficult, but not because of the structure of economic opportunities or factors like financial crises or the shrinking and volatility of the job market. It is difficult because it demands an internal change of the self to face the challenge:

> Anyone can change. But changing quadrants is not like changing jobs or changing professions. Changing quadrants is often a change at the core of who you are, how you think, and how you look at the world. The change is easier for some people than for others simply because some people welcome change and others fight it. And changing quadrants is most often a life-changing experience. (Kiyosaki 1999:18)

Like Marx, Kiyosaki sorts people into classes according to their source of income. But in Kiyosaki's model, those individuals who do not move upward have only themselves to blame—quite the opposite of Marxism. Mobility between quadrants is largely an internal process of the subject, and financial self-help provides the rationale and the tools to forge a neoliberal self that should make that shift possible. Moving depends on each person's ability to develop the skills and self that will succeed in a given quadrant. That transition has to be carefully planned and demands a great deal of effort and work on the self:

> When people come up with those objections [when they say they cannot change quadrants], there's some validity to it. The number one reason I say it's valid is because most people have been trained to be employees or to be self-employed. They've never been taught how to be business owners or have financial skills. The second reason people are not able to make this shift from quadrant to quadrant is very simple: the most important control they must have is control over themselves, or control over their emotions. If a person cannot control that, or control themselves, making the transition from one quadrant to the other is very difficult. (Kiyosaki 2000a)

Ultimately, adequate control of oneself is seen as the key to mobility. The efforts of understanding post-industrial society and of acquiring financial knowledge will not pay off unless they also engage in the hard work of changing themselves. In this sense, financial self-help is an ethical program for the transformation of the self. How do financial self-help fans have to change? What kind of people should they become? The answer lies in the basic key phrase of financial self-help: *financial freedom*, a phrase that appears simple at first sight, but that requires further examination.

It's Not About Money, It's About Freedom

2

AS DESCRIBED IN CHAPTER 1, one of the most important things people learn from contemporary financial self-help is that they should not just be trying to make money, they should instead achieve *financial freedom*. Kiyosaki tells people who are looking for get-rich-quick formulas that success is not so much about money as it is about freedom. They will only be rich when they have liberated themselves. In his books, Kiyosaki says that when he was young and his financial mentor offered him work for zero pay, he complained:

> He said to me at that moment that one of the biggest mistakes people make is that they work for money. They become addicted to a paycheck. Many people actually sell their soul and their good sense and work for that money. He says: if you work for me for free, you will learn more about how to be free from money. (Kiyosaki 2000a)

In this passage, the main target of self-transformation appears to be not merely the ability to make money, but rather one's dependent relationship with it, which leads people to "sell their soul" and remain an employee forever. Financial freedom is partly seen as a liberation of the soul from the vagaries of money.

At the level of accounting, the definition of financial freedom is quite simple: once one's passive income (that is, from investments) surpasses one's expenses, one is financially free. Note that there is no concrete dollar amount given in this definition. Financial freedom, Kiyosaki argues, does not come when someone reaches X million dollars in assets or earns Y thousands of dollars a year. Two people with substantially different levels of income and expenses can both be financially free, following this logic, as long as they have "their money working for them," regardless of how much money. This may be interpreted as an optimistic trick designed by an industry that runs on hope, and which convinces people with no money that they can also reach financial salvation. While that is one effect, there is much more to the concept. Kiyosaki does indeed tell readers with low incomes that they too can dream of becoming financially free, but he also tells the wealthy CEO that as long as she has to work for money, she is no different from her low-income brethren. As long as the high-income worker can be fired, and depends on an employer for his or her income, he or she is not free. In financial self-help, freedom has a higher value than riches. Thus, money does not appear as an end in itself, but rather as a means to attain freedom. In financial self-help, *the rich* are role models not just because they have money, but also because they are *free*. Readers of financial self-help are taught to understand how post-industrial capitalism works and to acquire adequate financial skills not just because this knowledge and skill set will help them attain wealth (or purity, wisdom, or power), but because such skills will set them free.

While financial freedom is a measurable and observable, even mathematical, condition, it is also framed as a mindset, or a condition of the self. The concept of freedom can be in opposition to different qualities or states of being, such as oppression from an authoritarian regime or restriction of movement. In financial self-help, freedom is opposed to *dependence*, both external and internal. People might be dependent on external institutions, such as an employer, the state, social security, or so on. They can also be dependent on something less visible, inside the self. Financial guru Suze Orman, for example, says that "financial freedom is when you have power over your fears and anxieties instead of the other way around" (Orman 1997:2). In other words, one can be betrayed by one's own subjectivity, which consciously or unconsciously does not want to or does not know how to be free.

These two interrelated concerns (*external freedom* from collective institutions and *internal freedom* from one's fears and weaknesses) are brought together in contemporary financial self-help, while echoing a variety of discourses on freedom that have grown and expanded in scope throughout the twentieth century and the beginning of the twenty-first. As sociologist Nikolas Rose points out, freedom has become a priority both in how individuals are governed and in how individuals govern themselves:

> As the twenty-first century begins, the ethics of freedom have come to underpin our conceptions of how we should be ruled, how our practices of everyday life should be organized, how we should understand ourselves and our predicament. . . . There is agreement over the belief that human beings are, in their nature, actually, potentially, ideally, subjects of freedom, and hence that they must be governed and must govern themselves as such. (1999:61–62)

This exaltation of autonomy and questioning of dependence is not exclusive to financial self-help, and it is a crucial part of both political and self-improvement discourses in neoliberalism. As the literature on governmentality has illustrated, the idea of free and autonomous individuals is at the center of neoliberal discourses and rationalities of government. The reframing of the seemingly abject goal of "making money" into a quest for freedom does much more than give the project of financial self-help a patina of respectability. The centrality of freedom in financial self-help aligns this discourse with the neoliberal dictum that the free, autonomous, and risk-taking individual is the political subject from which all social organization should begin, and for which any form of government or social organization is worth having. Neoliberalism's distinctive character as a rationality of government is that it does not assume the freedom and autonomy of individuals, but rather seeks to create spaces and configure subjects so that autonomy becomes possible (Barry, Osborne, and Rose 1996:10). Financial self-help is a neoliberal project not just because, as I showed in the previous chapter, it explicitly regards itself as a product of the neoliberal transformation of the global economy, but mostly because it supplies practitioners with discourses and practices that seek to turn them into autonomous subjects responsible for their financial well-being and who value individual freedom above all else. But the similarity between financial self-help and neoliberal rationalities of government does not mean that the state is necessarily involved, directly or indirectly, in the enterprise of creating that subject. Government, as Foucault has shown, should be treated as the "conduct of conduct" more than as a particular sphere of social life (Foucault 1982:790; Dean 1999:17). The notion of *governmentality* treats government not as a specific activity limited to states, but rather as scattered and varied forms of thinking about the government of conduct. For Nikolas Rose, government

> refers to all endeavors to shape, guide, direct the conduct of others, whether these be the crew of a ship, the members of a household, the employees of a boss, the children of a family or the inhabitants of a territory. And it also embraces the ways in which one might be urged and educated to bridle one's own passions, to control one's own instincts, to govern oneself. (Rose 1999:3)

With its attention to internal and external dependence, financial self-help problematizes the dynamics between the government of others and the government of oneself. It hits exactly on the link between how one is governed by others (the state, institutions, the labor market, the family) and how one ought to govern oneself to achieve true freedom and independence (Binkley 2009; see Foucault 1988:19). Financial self-help denounces at once subjection to collective organizations and subjection to oneself. This dynamic between internal and external dependence shows, perhaps more than any other cultural product, the connections between *technologies of the self*—the ways in which we attempt to shape, improve, and govern ourselves—and neoliberal technologies of government. Much of the ethical message of financial self-help lies at the crossroads between internal and external dependence. Financial self-help suggests that internal slavery to fear and anxiety leads to external dependence on institutions by prompting the individual to lean toward the security of a paycheck instead of the risks of freedom. In turn, the commitment to the security of institutions provides a false sense of comfort that leads to a weak subject who will grow too afraid of exploring the possibility of attaining financial freedom.

External and Internal Dependence: Libertarianism and the Recovery Movement

The concern for dependence espoused in financial self-help has its intellectual roots in two largely independent worlds of ideas and practices: libertarianism and the recovery movement. Some of the basic tenets of classic liberalism outlined in the philosophies of European thinkers such as Adam Smith and John Stuart Mill in the eighteenth and nineteenth centuries already anticipated the libertarian individualism of the twentieth century.[1] But the writings and proselytizing of thinkers such as Ayn Rand, Milton Friedman, Murray Rothbard, and Fredrich Von Hayek—an explicit reaction to New Deal and welfare policies since the 1930s—contributed to a rebirth and popularization of the idea of individualism, particularly in the United States. The concern with individual autonomy from the state and collective institutions that is central to financial self-help discourse is also a core theme of libertarian ideology.

Libertarianism starts from the assumption that individuals are endowed with the potential to do great things, and that in order for that potential to be realized in the world, they have to be freed from constraints and guaranteed autonomy. Given that human achievement comes only from individuals, autonomy and personal choice are the most important values in libertarianism. Collective organizations, particularly the state, are seen as mechanisms that stifle individual potential, so this tradition rejects the influence of social organizations whenever they do not fulfill the task of merely securing individual autonomy and the correct operation of market forces. Unions and social security are seen as harmful because they deprive people of their ability to realize their potential. Libertarianism frames individuals in terms of their entrepreneurial capacities—the state, the corporation, and welfare institutions, instead of helping individuals, are merely strangling and discouraging those capacities. When provided with enough security, citizens become dependent on institutions and lose their entrepreneurial spirit. These basic liberal tenets are at the core of the moral message of financial self-help, particularly its encouragement to avoid succumbing to the lure of a secure paycheck. As I will show later, these same principles also influence Kiyosaki's rejection of formal schooling for being an institution that strangles entrepreneurial capacities.

Writer and philosopher Ayn Rand is perhaps the clearest exponent of libertarian individualism and is widely considered the most popular advocate of individualism in the United States (Doherty 2007:11–12). Financial self-help is partly an inheritor of the resurgence and popularization of libertarian ideas since the 1960s, much of which is owed to the circulation of Rand's novels and treatises in business circles (Burns 2009:4).[2] In contrast to the work of other neoliberal thinkers like Hayek or Friedman, who were economists concerned about public policy and the government of the economy, Ayn Rand's writings are mostly about entrepreneurial heroes who clash with "parasitic" non-entrepreneurs and the state. These themes are closer to the pragmatism of the financial self-help world, in that practitioners only marginally care about state policy, while they mostly care about the question "What should I do?"[3] Rand, like other libertarians but with the dramatization added by her novels, saw individual will and creativity as the only true engine of the world, and considered collective arrangements (government in particular) as the obstacle that clogged the engine and snuffed out individual spirits. Rand was one of the first outspoken advocates of egoism as a virtue and argued that individuals should not be ashamed of it. For Rand, one of the most important virtues humans should pursue is independence, both material and intellectual. As Rand scholar Tara Smith explains, making money is seen in Rand's Objectivist philosophy not as an end but as a means to guarantee one's autonomy and choice:

> Wealth represents time liberated from the task of tending one's most basic, day-to-day subsistence needs through physical labor. The greater a person's reserves of wealth, the less labor he must exert in the future to achieve the same standard of living that that wealth can buy. The more money a person has, the more easily he can meet those needs and the more time he can devote to more desirable activities. Consequently, money is valuable not only for providing a person with more material goods. It gives a person more options; it allows a greater range of choices in his activities. Money enables a person to enhance his life in whatever ways, material or spiritual, are most conducive to his overall well-being, giving him more time to cultivate friendships, for instance, or to enjoy his love of opera. (Smith 2007:219–20)

Material independence, according to Rand and echoed by financial self-help gurus, is crucial in the mission to achieve true freedom. From both perspectives, one of the beliefs that we need to eliminate through working on the self is the Christian-inspired dictum that "money is the root of all evil." A famous speech in Rand's novel *Atlas Shrugged*, like Kiyosaki's books, combats this idea by praising money as the product of virtue and merit and as the enabler of freedom (Rand 2007:380–85; see also Smith 2003). For Rand, pursuing money is virtuous not for religious reasons but because it represents values traded within market arrangements. Libertarianism sees the market as a fair and transparent mechanism to recognize people's worth and independent qualities, and rejects any intrusion in that mechanism (Fourcade and Healy 2007:289–91).

Libertarianism is at the core of the conception of freedom as autonomy from external institutions that pervades financial self-help. But there is also a long tradition of discourses and movements about the care of oneself, particularly what came to be known as the *recovery movement*, which is echoed in current financial self-help. Historian Trysh Travis (2009) defines the recovery movement as the matrix of ideas, practices, and institutions that since the 1930s has framed multiple individual problems as addictions and their solutions as recovery from addictions. For Travis, the logic of addiction and recovery has become naturalized in American popular culture. Central to the recovery movement is the appeal to gain autonomy from one's own demons—what sociologist and legal scholar Mariana Valverde (1998) calls "slavery from within." This rhetoric differs from the libertarian call to denounce the "slavery" that results from attributing too much power to collective forces to the detriment of the individual. The recovery movement, in contrast, is much less explicitly political and is preoccupied with the internal slavery to oneself. This preoccupation with internal slavery gave birth to a myriad of techniques of the self to deal with a variety of social problems.

According to Travis (2009), the very notion of "recovery" has its origin in the twelve steps developed by Alcoholics Anonymous (AA) in the 1930s, which were later replicated in various recovery groups. For Valverde (1998), alcoholism has largely eluded the jurisdiction of both physicians and psychologists. Remarkably, the AA 12-Step Program has been the most widespread treatment for alcoholism for eight decades, and it is based on the notion that alcoholism is neither a problem of the body nor of the mind, but rather a disease of the *will*. Valverde points out that some tests meant to determine whether someone is an alcoholic do not ask any questions about the amounts of alcohol consumed, but rather about how alcohol is consumed. These alcoholism tests are "not an inquiry into drinking as much as a test of the soul's relation to itself. Do you feel free and happy? Or do you feel constrained, depressed, and guilty about the behavior that you engage in to relieve depression and guilt?" (Valverde 1998:25). Just as alcoholism is not measured only by the amounts of alcohol consumed but by the level of control of that consumption, financial freedom has little to do with a concrete sum of money and more to do with an internal mindset disposed to freedom. Thus, financial freedom changes from a measurable external condition (when passive income is equal to or higher than expenses) into a certain frame of mind, in which self-control and the will to be free become defining features of the self.

Suze Orman's definition of financial freedom—the control of one's fears and anxieties—ties financial self-help to the problematization of the will, which is at the root of the therapeutic movements to recover from addictions such as alcoholism. Since the 1970s, discourse about the weakness of the will and the self-help recovery techniques associated with it has expanded from the specific problem of alcoholism to cover several other behaviors also considered to be addictive (drug consumption, overeating, love) and even to behaviors that were once considered healthy, such as taking care of one's family or spouse. Like alcoholics, readers of financial self-help are urged to recognize that there is something wrong inside of them and that they should work, like people "in recovery," to control their impulses and their will.

Since financial self-help's main agenda is to combat one's dependence and achieve individual autonomy, all the activities recommended to become financially free—educating oneself financially, understanding post-industrial capitalism, investing in the stock market, playing the Cashflow board game, attending seminars, reading, or buying real estate, and so on—are two-sided. On the one hand, by participating in these activities, users may approach that observable condition called financial freedom, in which one doesn't have to work to receive income. On the other hand, these practices are also *practices of the self*. As Valverde observes, "In the self-help technologies of edifying videos, self-esteem workbooks, and codependence support groups, freedom is both the end of the recovery and the means. It is the supreme value for the sake of which we work on the self and it is simultaneously the technology through which we act on the not-yet-free-self" (1998:32). Learning accounting techniques, playing Cashflow, jumping on an investment opportunity, or buying trading software are then not merely mundane techniques to accumulate money. They are, above all, ways of working on the self in order to rid it of conformity and attempt to develop an entrepreneurial self that stops drifting to the alluring security of collective organization.

Financial self-help is a modern technology of the self, a sort of therapy to turn individuals from subjects determined by dependency (both internal and external) into entrepreneurial subjects who can call themselves free and autonomous. Financial self-help exhorts users to examine the parts of themselves that involve dependency and to work on correcting them. By engaging in this self-reflection, one is already considered freer than before, and by leaving the safe haven of dependency and being unafraid to "take action" in the world of investing, one is already producing a new, free subject. Financial self-help gurus imply that money will be almost a natural side effect of turning oneself into a subject that strives for freedom.

Financial self-help urges individuals to become free, self-reliant, and entrepreneurial by working on their internal and external dependencies. In the following pages, I will review more specifically how those ideas appear in financial self-help discourse and practice. First, family education is seen as one of the main culprits in people's conformist attitudes that strive for security instead of autonomy. Second, the school system is regarded not only as useless because it does not provide financial training, but also as harmful because it produces the opposite of entrepreneurial subjects: people who are too afraid of taking risks. Third, the long-standing method of being frugal as a way of accumulating wealth is rejected as meaningless for financial freedom. This rejection illustrates why financial self-help discourse is more about freedom than about money. Finally, discourses on gender, particularly Suze Orman's work, tie financial self-help to a long tradition of technologies of the self that combat women's dependency on men, particularly the discourse of codependence and the recovery movement.

Family Life and the Failed Financial Self

"Pull out a hair," David told the audience. "I know this part is not nice . . . if you are on the edge [losing hair], pull it from your arm or something," he joked. "But please, pull a hair!" In the midst of jokes about the strangeness of his request, audience members complied. "Now hold the hair in front of your eyes," David went on.

This scene took place during a one-day financial freedom workshop in Buenos Aires, organized by the incipient group Financial Freedom Argentina. When David took the floor, the seventy attendants had already heard a presentation on leadership and were finishing the first coffee break. They still had a long day ahead, including lunch, coffee, presentations, and a four-hour-long session playing the Cashflow game. The workshop had started at 8:30 a.m. with all the attendees introducing themselves. A few managed to get some laughs from their fellow attendees and helped to break the ice. Liliana, who was studying tourism and hotel management and who, like a few others in the workshop, had traveled a long distance to attend (about three hours in her case), said that the main reason she came was "to accompany my husband and understand him a little better." People smiled, understanding that her husband had probably been talking a lot about financial freedom, rich dads, and poor dads, and she just wanted to know what all the fuss was about. Leonardo, an electronics engineer in his thirties, also made participants laugh when he told them that he had just put all of his savings in the stock market and said, "I would like to learn more, I'm a newbie and I'm scared shitless of losing all my money."

Attendees came from all walks of life, from teachers to MBAs, engineers to a professional singer, housewives to real estate agents, lawyers to factory workers, accountants to administrative employees, and even an evangelical priest. A few were working part-time in network marketing companies. In their introductions, most people mentioned that they were there to learn and meet people, that they were open to new ideas, and that reading Kiyosaki had awakened in them the will to achieve financial freedom. People talked about opening their minds, overcoming their fears of investing, and finding out what investments were within their reach. Forty-two-year-old Fabio introduced himself as an employee and said that, after reading *Rich Dad, Poor Dad*, he decided that he would retire by the age of fifty. Mabel, an accountant also in her forties, corrected herself when she said that she wanted to become financially free. She said, "Sorry, it's not *I want*, it's *I will*, because that's the goal I set for myself." She was attending her second workshop and was happy to see a few familiar faces. Pablo, who worked in a large telecommunications company, said that he was present because just a few months earlier, all he dreamed of was reaching the top of the corporation where he worked. After reading Kiyosaki, he changed his goals accordingly and sought to achieve financial freedom.

Many participants had university degrees. Miguel, who had an MBA and was studying to become an accountant, complained that all his university education had done was prepare him to be an employee. After reading "the book," his thinking changed, and he was now seeking financial freedom. Lorena, a twenty-five-year-old student and administrative employee, mentioned the important issue of her family expectations in her introduction: "I have a very structured family for whom working means sticking to a work schedule and receiving a paycheck at the end of the month, and I want to prove that that is not true, and make money work for me." A few participants spoke of Kiyosaki as a new father or mentor. For example, Marcos blamed his own "poor dad" for his setbacks in the real estate business. He was now back on track thanks to finding a new rich father in Kiyosaki.

The introductions helped to break the ice, but what created a truly friendly and enthusiastic atmosphere was David's presentation. He was a warm and funny man in his early forties from the province of Córdoba (a province known in Argentina for the cheerful, comic spirit of its inhabitants). He said that he did not come from the world of business. He was a pastor and did social work with young students. When I later asked him about his religious activities and how they fit with his speeches on financial improvement, he touched my shoulder with the tip of his finger. "Do you feel that?" he said. I nodded. He explained to me that spiritual well-being is not everything, and that material issues—ones you can see and feel—are as important as spiritual matters. David began his presentation recognizing the efforts of the organizers and asking for a round of applause. He then joked that he would try to be brief because he was worried about Carmen, who in the introductions had said that she was probably the oldest person at the workshop (she was sixty), so she had to learn fast because she did not have that much time. Partly thanks to his warm personality and jokes, David created a relaxed and participatory environment. He later explained to me one-on-one that while attendees start the day a bit shy and timid, by the afternoon they act as if they have known each other forever.

Around sixty workshop participants responded to his odd request of plucking out a hair and holding it before their eyes. "How many of you can see the DNA of poverty in your hair? How many of you can see the DNA of richness?" David asked. "You were not born to be poor or to be rich. This is what Kiyosaki teaches in his books. Our environment, our context has been creating the operating system inside of us that has placed us in the situation we are in. What is your financial position today? Well, you have not been born for that financial position. It was determined by a whole lot of 'sowing the seeds' [siembra] around us."

David then asked the audience to remember phrases about finances and money that they had heard at home while growing up. Audience members called out: "That rich people do not make their money honestly!" "Life is sacrifice!" "To make money, you have to have money first!" David repeated the phrases as people uttered them and added, jokingly, "The only people who make money are those who work at a mint! All those concepts have marked you and me and have placed us where we are. We have grown up with a sense of conformity: 'Well, that's what I am. I was born for this. My parents had this financial position, my grandparents had this financial position so, hey, I'm not doing that badly!' But Kiyosaki's concept is that our financial position has to do mostly with our education."[4] When he said "education," David was not implying that the more one studies the better off one will be. He was referring to the financial education we receive at home: "How many of you, before you were twelve or so, had your parents telling you, 'Now I'm going to teach you how to manage your money, because throughout your life, that's what you're going to do.'" No one raised a hand.

This reference to family upbringing and its connection with conformity is not random. One's upbringing is thought to be a crucial time to revisit to focus on changing oneself into a successful subject—one capable of achieving financial freedom. In fact, Kiyosaki's most popular book actually takes the form of a family tale. Much of David's presentation was taken from *Rich Dad, Poor Dad*, a book that tells the story of the author's two "dads," which allows him to represent two attitudes toward money, autonomy, and social mobility using two clear-cut characters. Kiyosaki's real father, the "poor dad," represents a social path of conformity to welfare society, someone who values security over freedom. He was a highly educated man and the head of education of Hawaii. He was also an employee who received a salary all his life and repeatedly advised his son to take the same path he took: study hard, get good grades so that you can find a good job with a good salary and good benefits. In contrast, his "rich dad," who was the father of his childhood friend, was a businessman who became his financial mentor. This adopted father represented the spirit of entrepreneurship and individualism. While fans still debate if the story of the two dads is real or fictional,[5] it certainly offers a simple scheme that dramatizes the opposition between the quest for security and conformity and the quest for freedom and self-sufficiency (Binkley 2009):

> One dad believed in a company or the government taking care of you and your needs. He was always concerned about pay raises, retirement plans, medical benefits, sick leave, vacation days and other perks. He was impressed with two of his uncles who joined the military and earned a retirement and entitlement package for life after twenty years of active service. He loved the idea of medical benefits and PX privileges the military provided its retirees. He also loved the tenure system available through the university. The idea of job protection for life and job benefits seemed more important, at times, than the job. He would often say, "I've worked hard for the government, and I'm entitled to these benefits." The other believed in total financial self-reliance. He spoke out against the "entitlement" mentality and how it was creating weak and financially needy people. He was emphatic about being financially competent. (Kiyosaki and Lechter 1998:16)

The tale of the two dads puts family upbringing at a central location where one can begin to question one's instincts about security and freedom. This narrative provides a blueprint on which people can project their own biographies. Readers can examine their own lives and reinterpret them in accordance with the patterns of the two dads. They revisit their family histories to find similar milestones of financial poverty. As several workshop participants mentioned in their introductions, many believed that they needed some kind of mentor, like the "rich dad." I heard many times, in multiple forms, stories about how parents could only think of education and a good job for their children, but never offered a real financial education. For example, in the case of Sergio (age twenty-four), even though his family had a business, he saw his parents as too timid about their entrepreneurial spirit. He came to recognize their failures after reading Kiyosaki:

> Look, my mom is a hard worker, very good in what she does. She has a business, with her current husband, they have a dollar store. But they don't have the mindset to go out and open branches, as Kiyosaki says. . . . "Not being a slave to your business, but having your business work for you." . . . So, my parents worked from Sunday to Sunday. They would come home for a little while, on Sunday at lunchtime, but they didn't have enough brains to search for a way of generating more income and having their money work for them. As I said, they are dedicated, but they never had the culture of saying, "Look, try to find the way to. . . . " They are great examples of the second quadrant [the S quadrant], you have your own business and you work for it, you are self-employed. So, I started realizing that when I started reading Kiyosaki.

Although Sergio admired his parents' work ethic, he did not admire their seven-day-a week jobs, and sought financial freedom in a manner very different than the one modeled for him growing up. Similarly, Joaquín, who is one of the moderators at the Rich Dad online forum in Argentina, echoes this narrative shared by several fans I interviewed about wanting to diverge from their families' slave-like adherence to traditional routes to financial security:

> So, the book [*Rich Dad, Poor Dad*], I'm not lying, I read it in two days at most. What particularly caught my attention was that it presented things in a different way. To me, since I also was of the typical family, what they always said was "work, study, get a good job," the typical message. I see the history of my grandparents, my parents, my family, and so on, and it's all the same, working, studying, and that's it.

This archetypal divergence from the family that runs throughout *Rich Dad, Poor Dad* seems to resonate with many readers. Another Argentine fan, Gabriel, says that his family never encouraged him beyond a vague sense of "moving ahead," and only realized that after reading *Rich Dad, Poor Dad*. He also identifies his own uncle as the representation of the "poor dad":

> Daniel: And what did your parents transmit to you?
> Gabriel: "Work, work." I mean, "Try to move ahead all you can, but don't go crazy. . . . Don't do what I did, OK?" But they wouldn't encourage me to give my best. So I read *Rich Dad, Poor Dad* and it blew my mind because

deep down I had been ruminating on the idea that . . . "I don't want to study to be an employee, I want to study to be an owner and you can't study that anywhere." But I never had it organized in my mind as clearly as it was there in the book. It became clear to me: employee never again.

Daniel: Did you have conversations about this with your family?

Gabriel: Yes, with my mother, my wife. . . .

Daniel: And how was it?

Gabriel: With my mother it was. . . . "Hey, look how nice. . . . Yes, it would be beautiful," but she's still sitting with the sewing machine working ten hours a day. She never really got it. My uncle is sixty-two years old and has almost thirty-five years of public employment. To me, he's like my poor dad; I could define him like that after reading the book. I mean, beyond all my affinity with him, for everything he meant and represented for me, I discovered the exact example. He is the guy that wouldn't risk a dime—no fucking way. He prioritizes the security of the paycheck at the end of the month. And he comes from the time when a manual laborer's son could become a doctor, a time in which people would actually say "The Doctor!," and the respect he would get [as the father]! He has that era marked on him. The industrial age, the laborer and the son/doctor who's the pride of the family. So for me, he's the poor dad of Kiyosaki.

Gabriel has thought deeply about how his family's story parallels the one told in *Rich Dad, Poor Dad.* Although he clearly cares for his parents, he pities them and their strict adherence to jobs that don't pay off. He defines his desire for financial freedom not only on the basis of Kiyosaki's categories but also in opposition to the values and behaviors of his own family, which he identifies with the industrial age. In the beginning of the financial self-help journey, practitioners question the education and influence they received from their parents. The question of what one's parents taught one about money, or the fact that they did not teach one anything positive about it, is the beginning of the knowledge of the self.

Parenthood is vital in the narrative of financial freedom because the family is seen as the area of life in which people most easily succumb to the lure of security over freedom.[6] In their well-intentioned concern for their children, parents consciously or unconsciously teach children to conform and not to strive for freedom, transmitting their fears and their own "poor" mentality. In interviews and activities I attended, most participants with children said that they plan to teach their own children differently from what they were taught, giving their kids financial education and encouraging them to pursue financial freedom, start their own businesses, and so on. David said that people with poor mindsets blame the obligations brought by children for not having made money while the rich have a commitment to freedom partly as a duty to their children. The sense of responsibility that parents have about their children is transformed into another reason to achieve freedom and abandon security.

Using Kiyosaki's ideas, David lectured the audience on the differences between the advice the rich give to their children and the advice the poor give theirs: "The poor work for their money, while the rich make their money work for them. The poor are motivated by fear and anxiety. And the rich? They are motivated by dreams. This is very important." As a pastor who has worked with poor communities, David clarified that he didn't intend to denigrate the poor. He said that although we have to be merciful with people who go through difficult times, we have to bluntly recognize that some people work for their money while others don't. The opposition between the motivation of dreams and the motivation of fear and anxiety highlighted a main point of financial self-help: the rich are free and can pursue their dreams while the poor are limited by their own fearful selves.

David continued to present differences between rich and poor dads: "When it comes to money [the poor dad said], 'Do what is the most secure. Don't take risks.' And the rich dad said, 'When it comes to money, learn to manage risk.'" He interrupted himself, "Are you realizing what operating system you have?" David then stopped and said, "Hey, don't get distressed! We're trying to change the operating system. I see some faces that seem to say, 'I was programmed really badly!' Me too! I was terribly programmed! The important thing is that when I realize that there is an operating system and I see that the results are not good, I can work on the operating system." It is rather common for people to feel bad about themselves when they are exposed to Kiyosaki's arguments. Only an hour before, the previous speaker had asked participants if they had felt bad the first time they read *Rich Dad, Poor Dad*, and most of them nodded in agreement. "I was very comfortable, working in a company. . . . Thank God I dared to break with that job security. I felt bad realizing how comfortable I was. . . . It sounds strange, but I felt really horrible," the first speaker of the day shared. The sense of security and comfort that wasn't a problem before became, after reading Kiyosaki, a source of shame.[7]

David moved on in his presentation to explain that consumption practices vary according to class. His message was that consumption practices are perfect expressions of the "operating system." Just by looking at consumption practices, he said, you could figure out if a person was poor, middle class, or rich. "The poor buy filling, the middle class buy commitments, and the rich buy assets," the PowerPoint screen showed. David explained, "The poor receive an income and spend it on *filling*. What's that? Filling is unnecessary items that were a great bargain! Say you have all the pennants of all the countries in your living room. When someone asks you why you have them, you say, 'All of these . . . fifteen pesos!'" In a humorous and unpretentious way, David explained that the poor concentrate so much on finding bargains, they spend much of their salary on worthless items that have one single benefit: they are cheap or on sale. Middle-class people, in contrast, want to see themselves as rational spenders, different from the poor, but end up spending most of their income on "commitments." Although they believe that they are investing, they are just acquiring a "commitment cloud." In fact, David argued, middle-class finances are usually even more strained than those of the poor. A new car, a bigger house, a better neighborhood—all these expenses bring an illusion of improvement, when in fact they drown people in more severe financial commitments that put them further from financial freedom. In other words, spending money can further conformity and fear instead of making one more autonomous, both internally and externally. The consumption pattern of the middle class pushes them to cling to the security of their paychecks. "The rich," David continued while jokingly pointing to the speaker that presented before him, "receive income that may be huge or not, but they invest that income in assets. Those assets generate income, which generate more income, which generate more income . . . and that's the seed that Kiyosaki sows in his books." Workshop participants had a chance to experience what an asset is, as I will show in the next chapter, when they played the Cashflow game later that day.

David went on to say that people's thoughts determine their feelings, which are in turn translated into results. The problem, he said, is that we only evaluate the results. We are angry about our current financial position, which is nothing more than the result of a process that started with our thoughts. Those thoughts are influenced by everyone we interact with, particularly family and close friends. He then asked participants to think of how much money their six closest acquaintances made. "The average of those six people determines how much you make," David asserted. The idea that you have to reconfigure your social relations and start surrounding yourself with the kind of people that you want to be is also very important in financial self-help. Many collective activities like the workshop David conducted are held with this goal in mind. While in their everyday lives people usually find that their friends and family are wary of these new ideas, at these events fans find "positive" people who will encourage them in their financial pursuits. Much of the collective life of financial self-help has the rationale of expanding one's social world to make one's conformist background less influential.

School, Failure, and the Entrepreneurial Self

Besides deficient family education, there is one institution that is seen in financial self-help as responsible for producing dependent and conformist subjects who do not want financial freedom: formal schooling. In the previous chapter, I explored some of Kiyosaki's complaints about education regarding its lack of instruction in financial skills, which means that people have to look for those skills elsewhere. If this was the only problem, school would just be a waste of time, or a place where people learn abilities necessary for other pursuits but not financial freedom. But for Kiyosaki, school also has some evil effects that linger in people's subjectivity and which will eventually require intense work on the self to correct.

Kiyosaki continues a long popular American tradition of anti-intellectualism that opposes school-smarts to street-smarts, but he also incorporates more recent libertarian arguments against the educational system. Not unlike many social scientists, he sees the educational system as an apparatus designed to reproduce the social order by creating people with skills to work and a sense of obedience. According to Kiyosaki, schools produce conformist workers who will not develop a sense of entrepreneurialism:

> We go to school to get a good job. We are taught to work for the rich, shop at the stores of the rich, borrow money from the banks of the rich, invest in the businesses of the rich via mutual funds in our retirement plans—but not *how to become rich*. (Kiyosaki 2009:36)

Once again, it is not just money that one gives away by attending school, but also one's freedom. Kiyosaki argues, quite boldly, that the educational system intentionally deprives students of financial education so that they become dependent on the government and their salaried jobs:

> If people do not learn about money, they end up exchanging their freedom for a paycheck—for a steady job and enough money to pay their bills. Some people

spend their lives in constant fear of being fired. The lack of financial education in our schools has resulted in millions of free people who are willing to let the government take more control over their lives. Because we do not have enough financial intelligence to solve our own financial problems, we expect the government to do it for us. In the process, we surrender our freedom and give the government more and more control over our lives and our money. (Kiyosaki 2009:38)

Kiyosaki took inspiration from John Taylor Gatto, a former New York City teacher who in the early 1990s wrote a manifesto against the educational system in the United States (Kiyosaki 2009:37). In *Dumbing Us Down*, Gatto asserts that mandatory schooling is nothing but a system designed to "*prevent* children from learning how to think and act, to coax them into addiction and dependent behavior" (1992:xii). With a libertarian individualist approach, Gatto rejects the educational system indoctrinating students in the name of providing skills and knowledge. He suggests that education should be limited to bringing out individual creativity by securing a space of autonomy: "teaching is nothing like the art of painting, where, by the *addition* of material to a surface, an image is synthetically produced, but more like the art of sculpture, where, by the *subtraction* of material, an image already locked in the stone is enabled to emerge" (Gatto 1992:xii). For Gatto, the only reason why education is wrongly seen today as an addition and not a subtraction is because the state wants to create citizens who are "addicted to dependency" (99). Teachers, he argues, are simply part of the bureaucratic army of experts that the welfare state provides in order to discipline citizens, strangling their creativity and entrepreneurial spirit, killing their self-esteem, and launching them into a life of emotional and intellectual dependence.

Kiyosaki's rejection of school report cards is partly inspired by Gatto's ideas. As observed earlier, Kiyosaki says that once you finish school, you will not be asked for your grades but for your financial statement. This criticism is embedded in a neoliberal rejection of expertise in the form it takes under the technologies of government that characterize welfare society.[8] The expert sanction of teachers is seen as part of a bureaucratic and controlling machine that annihilates the individual's self-reliance. Gatto (1992:11) states that "the lesson of report cards, grades and tests is that children should not trust themselves or their parents but should instead rely on the evaluation of certified officials. People need to be told what they are worth." The judgment of certified bureaucrats, expressed in arbitrary report cards that are only valid in enclosed institutions, contrasts with the dynamism of the market, which is seen as an impersonal evaluator for which only one's financial statement is the measure of one's worth.

For Kiyosaki, school discourages risk-taking by punishing mistakes, which in turn creates the fearful and conformist subject of the welfare era. In the "real world" of financial, entrepreneurial capitalism, the road to financial success is paved with a great number of mistakes. Mistakes are required in order to learn and improve. As in learning to ride a bicycle, Kiyosaki sees magic in mistakes because one learns from them. The narrative goes that in the real world (outside of school and the workplace), those who make more mistakes end up making the most money. When people "play it safe" (or place security over freedom), not risking their money, they are reproducing the pattern learned in school, an institution that punishes those who deviate in any way from the norm. Trying to avoid making mistakes means denying oneself the possibility of becoming rich. In contrast, taking small risks since childhood and incurring mistakes makes people smarter. Since people learn more vividly from their errors, those who commit them end up being more intelligent than those who don't. When introducing people to the Cashflow board game, Argentine organizer Rolo likens failure and mistakes to "payment for a course." Whatever is lost financially from failures is considered an expense in self-education. The problem with straight-A students, Kiyosaki says, is that they make mistakes only when they are old, and they cannot recover. They get stuck with their first mistake.

The theme of failure and the importance of mistakes is one that extends beyond the issue of formal education. Kiyosaki shares with most financial gurus a narrative of initial failure from which he rose up and became wealthy. Donald Trump, for example, with whom Kiyosaki has coauthored two books, published in 2006 and 2011, is seen as an icon for how many times his businesses went bankrupt but he kept resurrecting himself. What many people would probably see as irresponsible cowboyism is regarded in financial self-help as the necessary bravery to take action. Kiyosaki himself flaunts his being practically homeless in the 1980s, living with his wife in a basement before he became financially successful again. In fact, he argues that this temporary crisis was the price he had to pay to pursue freedom; if he had wanted security, he could have had it, but he never would have been financially free. Having failed and been deep in debt and broke is seen as a positive lesson from which people benefit in the long run. According to Kiyosaki, avoiding risk due to fear is seen as worse than failing but having tried.

In 2006, a twenty-four-year-old investor from California became famous for getting into the real estate flipping business, having aggressively followed the advice of financial gurus such as Russ Whitney and Kiyosaki. Without using any of his own money, Casey Serin purchased eight properties in a year by rolling over cash made in each closing. He was planning to "flip" the properties (sell them shortly after purchasing, thus making an immediate profit), but things went badly, and he was left with several mortgages he could not afford and a huge credit card debt. He started a blog to report his failures and appeared in the media, becoming a minor celebrity in some circles (Knox 2006). Kiyosaki, who at the time had a TV show on an Arizona network, invited Serin and presented him as a hero. With $140,000 in credit card debt and five properties in foreclosure, Serin seemed more like the poster boy of failed financial advice than a hero, but the theme of the show was about mistakes. Mistakes, Kiyosaki wrote on a whiteboard while on air, are sins only when people don't admit them. Unlike most people, Serin had taken action and made mistakes. If he learned from them, he would be successful. Those who make no mistakes have not done anything and are guaranteed to stay poor. After going through the lurid details of his failed experience in the world of real estate flipping and generous credit, Serin asked Kiyosaki how he would respond to critics who said that the young man had been intoxicated with financial success books and workshops. Kiyosaki responded that he would not judge them because giving and receiving criticism was part of the human condition, but he did not like people who pretended to be saints but never took action. It takes "getting pounded," he said, to learn good lessons. "The world is pounding you, and we at Rich Dad salute you for what you are doing because five years from now you'll be further ahead than those critics out there." Kiyosaki recalled his personal experience: "If I hadn't taken those risks, I wouldn't be what I am today. . . . I'd still be a salesman for Xerox. A loser," he said while making an "L" with his fingers in front of his forehead. "With my 401(k), hoping that someday I would be promoted to executive VP of Xerox. Geez, give me a break!" he continued in a mocking tone. The broke Casey Serin did not stand out for the wisdom of his financial decisions. Yet he represented the entrepreneurial spirit of risk and adventure that defines neoliberalism, which in Kiyosaki's eyes made him morally better than salaried workers.[9]

The praise of failure and the embrace of mistakes as a stepping stone to future success are key in financial self-help because they leave it impervious to criticism. If success is success, and failure is ultimately success, then when investments go wrong, it can always be read as a temporary stage in the path toward final success. While mistakes are not sins, pessimism is. Thus, financial self-help practitioners can always be "on the way to success," regardless of their current position. However, this praise is more than a tool for selling more books and making financial self-help infallible. The ode to failure shows how financial self-help is a technology of the self to produce a subject more than it is a method to make money. Taking risks, jumping on opportunities, making investments, or starting businesses are all techniques to work on the self. The very fact that a person has taken the risk instead of valuing security means that they are already freeing themselves. In financial self-help, it does not matter so much if those investments succeed or fail. The important achievement is to have overcome internal slavery.

Rich and Cheap? Frugality and Freedom

The morality tales of Horatio Alger and the success gurus of the eighteenth and nineteenth centuries taught their followers that riches would result from the development and practice of certain human virtues. Even Benjamin Franklin prescribed living a moral life to succeed in business. Industry and frugality were moral values that put those who practiced them on the way to wealth, success, and respectability. Franklin famously advocated frugality, not just because a penny saved could become a penny invested, but also because industriousness and frugality would show creditors that one was a trustworthy person. But the virtues advocated in nineteenth-century books are different from the ones advocated in the twenty-first century. The main moral value of current financial self-help is freedom. Frugality, a central moral value for Franklin, is seen as yet another example of a dependent mindset, even if it is conducive to wealth.

In the Cashflow game—which I will explore in detail in the next chapter—"doodad" cards show players vividly how money misspent on consumer items can instead be used for investments. By being forced to spend their game money on golf clubs or a cup of coffee, players see that consumption is an obstacle to financial freedom. In this regard, it seems to be similar to Franklin's advice. For Franklin, every penny spent superfluously today was not just a penny, but all the pennies that would have followed if that one had been carefully invested. The protestant ethic highlighted by Max Weber that connects so well with Franklin's capitalist spirit drove Calvinists in the sixteenth century to live frugally for moral and religious reasons, and to then reinvest their earnings. In addition, since financial freedom as an equation between expenses and passive income means that it would be easier to achieve it by lowering one's expenses, it seems to follow logically that being frugal should be an important dictum of financial self-help. However, the idea of frugality that is at the origin of the capitalist spirit is associated in current financial self-help with the working-class mindset that Kiyosaki rejects. Franklin's idea that money should be seen as potentially more money is obviously not rejected, but the moral dictum of living frugally is. Kiyosaki sees frugality as an attempt to get rich by being cheap:

> A very popular theme today is the attempt to get rich by being cheap. We know some of those books out there that stress frugality. But my rich dad said that the problem with getting rich by being cheap is that you're still cheap. In other words, why in the world would you want to have a lot of money and be cheap? It doesn't make any sense to me. Yet for a vast number of people, especially today, they're talking about cutting back, living a simpler life and all that. And you can get rich possibly that way. Yet my rich dad said: "It's people who are rich and cheap who give the rich a bad name." . . . And today, there's many people espousing that idea of getting very rich living below your means, drive a pickup truck, and all that other stuff . . . live in a cheap neighborhood. In my opinion, that's selling your soul to money. It's no different than marrying somebody for money. (Kiyosaki 2000a)

Frugality, while seen as a virtue in itself in old financial advice, is seen by Kiyosaki as a vice, comparable to marrying for money instead of love. Frugality might be a reasonable method if the goal was just money, but it is a poor method if the goal is freedom. Living frugally is no different than being a slave to a paycheck. To Kiyosaki, frugality is a form of internal slavery comparable to selling one's soul. Kiyosaki criticizes this strand of financial advice that is very popular and which attracts the attention of many of his own fans. Perhaps the best example is that of Oprah Winfrey's columnist David Bach and his book *The Automatic Millionaire*. This strand is closer to Franklin's advice of frugality. The main idea is that, to become rich, you do not need much financial intelligence and knowledge of the market and the economy. You do not even need to make as much effort as authors like Kiyosaki suggest. You just need a little self-control. In fact, Bach (2004) advocates that by simply taking a small consumer expense like daily coffee and placing it instead in an interest-bearing bank account—essentially automating the process—you can almost eliminate the need for conscious self-control and become a millionaire in a few years. He presents calculations proving how five dollars a day, by the magic of compounded interest, can become a fortune by the age of retirement, and concludes that daily lattes can cost you about two million dollars in the long run. This is obviously very similar to Franklin's reasoning, in which one has to focus on the potential investment value of every expense.

On a 2009 television show in which celebrities are interviewed on the front steps of a New York City building, the famous financial advisor Suze Orman scolded a man who was walking by with a cup of coffee from Starbucks. She stopped him, asked him how much he paid for it, and calculated how much that daily pleasure was truly costing him over the years. This kind of advice is very popular, particularly with people who see themselves as uncontrolled spenders. For some time in the Rich Dad group that met monthly in New York City, members used to set themselves the task of working on one expense item from one month to the next. These were committed fans of Kiyosaki, yet they believed that freeing some money from superfluous consumption for investment was a smart decision and had no moral qualms about it (no one objected that this was cheap). People tried to make their own daily coffee or avoid banking fees by walking a few more blocks to a machine that would not charge them. Even Steve, the leader of the group, who had plenty of investments, followed this collective practice. No one, however, suggested that this alone would make them rich.

But David Bach has a different idea than Kiyosaki and his followers: "In order to become an Automatic Millionaire, you've got to accept the idea that regardless of the size of your paycheck, you already make enough money to become rich" (2004:36). In this strand of financial self-help, people are not prompted to quit their jobs, change quadrants, or reconfigure their selves, just to have a bit of discipline to save some money every day by eliminating superfluous consumer expenses. In fact, the idea of *The Automatic Millionaire* is that disciplining yourself is such a hard task that the most effective way to do it is to eliminate the need for it. His idea is *pay yourself first*, automatically setting aside a small amount from one's paycheck each week.

While Kiyosaki would probably not overly mind if his readers used these techniques, and the "latte" or "cappuccino factor" is popular among financial self-help groups, he despises the moral implications of it (as shown above) and would identify it as just one more piece of advice coming from poor mindsets. He repeatedly reminds fans that "savers are losers." During an interview with a television network, a viewer sent a message in response to Kiyosaki's repeated slogan, saying that if he wanted to go on vacation, saving was the only way he could think of to make it happen. Kiyosaki responded that the viewer was thinking like a consumer, not like a rich man. He said that he had a lot of money and could go on vacation any time he wanted because he did not work for his money. The viewer, Kiyosaki said, had a working-class mentality that conditioned him to work and save (Al Jazeera English 2009). Kiyosaki did not explain to the viewer how to go on vacation without saving. His tacit point was that the viewer's mindset led him to figure out how best to spend what he earned working instead of how to use it to generate the passive income that would lead to financial freedom—a permanent vacation of sorts. Passive income is seen to have a higher moral status than money saved from work. While it may be a step ahead from a pattern of living off debt, which is widespread in the United States, saving is still seen within the bounds of a poor mentality because it means internal dependence. Saving and living frugally are associated with a poor mentality that sees the world as a world of scarcity. The rich, in contrast, see the world as one of abundance. Those who have not reached the visible and measurable condition known as financial freedom can start working toward it by trying hard to see the world like the rich see it. Richness is, more than an economic condition, a condition of the self, a way of seeing the world. According to Kiyosaki, if they are not yet in a position to quit the slavery of the paycheck, people can start by avoiding their internal slavery to their own selves. Unlike getting out there, investing, and taking risks, frugality will make people more dependent.

Women, Dependence, and Financial Freedom

Financial self-help resources targeting women offer yet another example of the significance of individual autonomy and the fight against internal and external dependencies for the making of the neoliberal self. The issue of gender ties financial self-help to a long tradition of "recovery" resources aimed at women audiences. In fact, for several scholars, feminism is ironically at the root of the recovery movement (Rapping 1996; Travis 2009; Valverde 1998). Ideas about women's independence and the dangers of codependence are at the core of financial self-help tailored for women.

Not surprisingly, in a world in which people think that the determinants of social outcomes are within the self and the class-based family education which initially configures that self, there are few regular explicit references to gender or race. Kiyosaki was asked in an interview about the impact of culture in financial success, and he minimized any variable besides class:

> [Interviewer:] Do you find variations in people's culture, in the way they approach [financial matters]?
>
> [Kiyosaki:] Yes, I would definitely say so, but more than just culture, I would say from economic class. If you come from a poor family, what I'm saying is pure heresy, and if you come from an academic family like my family,

with all PhDs, it's academic heresy. And for the rich they go: What's so hard about this?! So, it's not so much about ethnicity or anything like this, because every country has its rich and its poor and middle class. It's really what economic class you come from. (Al Jazeera English 2009)

Most financial self-help resources, and the *Rich Dad* series in particular, are not marketed to particular segments of the population in terms of gender, race, or ethnicity.[10] I have found women as captivated by *Rich Dad* as any man, even though the book is a story about two dads, in which mothers do not even appear. And, while *Rich Woman*, written by Robert Kiyosaki's wife and business partner, Kim, came out in 2006 (almost a decade after *Rich Dad, Poor Dad*), there is not a book called *Rich Mom, Poor Mom*.[11]

In most activities that I attended both in New York and in Argentina, there were a few more men than women, but men were never an overwhelming majority. This includes events organized by Financial Freedom Argentina. However, data from their newsletter subscribers in 2009 show that 79 percent were men ($N = 5,148$). In the case of the Argentine online forum, while I did not have access to quantitative data, the forum organizer told me that only 20 to 30 percent of members were women. While I have no quantitative evidence for these differences, my ethnographic observation shows that many couples attend events together, which may explain some of that gap. So while men participate more than women in forums, they engage more equally in offline activities.

Financial self-help material exclusively targeted to women has been growing, perhaps encouraged by this gap, but also by the recognition that women face different challenges in the realm of personal finance (Bernard 2010; Hira and Loibl 2008; Lusardi and Mitchell 2008). The themes—empowerment and independence—are not so different from gender-neutral books. Authors and gurus urge women to see themselves as powerful beings who do not depend on men in their quest for financial freedom. Most titles somehow reflect this idea: *Rich Woman: Because I Hate Being Told What to Do!* (Kiyosaki 2006); *Women & Money: Owning the Power to Control Your Destiny* (Orman 2007a); and *Make Money, Not Excuses: Wake Up, Take Charge, and Overcome Your Financial Fears Forever* (Chatzky 2006), for example. It would not be impossible to imagine similar titles for general books, not particularly targeted to women. For Kim Kiyosaki, depending on a man is no different than depending on the government or a corporation (Kiyosaki 2006:11). The assumption is that, in the quest for financial freedom, women have to do more than men to achieve autonomy and empowerment because they may have an additional layer of dependence.

The challenge for women is framed within the same conceptual structure as that of men: they have to abandon their conformist, dependent, and weak welfare society mindset in favor of the independent entrepreneurial self of neoliberal governmentality. Thus, women have to do the same as men do, but they also have to free themselves from the additional chains of economic dependence on husbands.

Consistent with the general spirit of voluntarism and individualism, financial self-help targeted at women does not advocate any general social change, activism, or new legislation. Instead, authors of such books write about the obstacles that women's selves place between their present situations and their financial prosperity. Jean Chatzky writes,

> The *reason* most women aren't richer—and the *reason* you aren't as rich as you'd like to be—is that you can't get out of your own way. That's right, *you* are a big part of the problem. You set up roadblocks that stop you on the way to wealth. You have a million excuses that prevent you from earning as much as you'd like, saving as much as you'd like, keeping as much as you'd like for the future (Chatzky 2006:2).

Most writers feel the need to justify publishing a book for women alone, and authors like Chatzky accomplish this by putting the blame for women's lack of wealth on their own shoulders—they are their own greatest obstacle to success and must therefore be taught how to transform themselves to be financially free. For Kim Kiyosaki, women are indeed different from men when dealing with financial matters, and although that is a shame, the market itself is a gender-blind mechanism of distribution of wealth according to merit:

> Whether stocks, bonds, or real estate, investments do not care if it is a man or a woman who is doing the buying, selling, holding, remodeling or renting. So why is there a need for a book on investing, just for women? The answer is because *when it comes to money*, men and women are different—historically, psychologically, mentally, and emotionally. . . . Am I saying that women are stupid? Absolutely not. Nothing could be further from the truth. I am saying that we do some incredibly foolish things. And most of these things are directly related to money. (Kiyosaki 2006:7, 9)[12]

Kim Kiyosaki suggests that if women can overcome their internal issues with money, they can take advantage of the market just like men do. These ideas lie entirely within her husband's conceptual framework; that is, she advocates financial freedom and moving to the right side of the *quadrant*, becoming an investor or a business owner. The corporate world, in addition to being the realm of work and not of financial freedom, imposes the famous "glass ceiling," which truncates women's upward mobility (a mobility that the Kiyosakis see as meaningless anyway). In contrast, Kim Kiyosaki argues that the world of investing is one of equality, in which markets break any social conditionings:

> In the world of investing the markets don't care if you're female or male, black or white, a college grad or a high school dropout. The markets only care about how smart you are with your money. The key is education and experience. The smarter you are with your investment choices the greater your success as an investor. There are no limits, no ceilings, glass or otherwise, for women in the world of investing. (Kiyosaki 2006:62)

Similar to Kim Kiyosaki's rationale for writing *Rich Woman*, Suze Orman (2007b) explains in her *Women & Money* DVD special that, after a long career as a financial advisor, television celebrity, and best-selling author, she never expected to prepare a lecture for women only. She had always been convinced that gender had nothing to do with finances, but after hearing many stories, she recognized that women had a harder time than men in feeling and using their power. While highlighting all the weaknesses that women in particular have in regard to money, she clearly states that they are women's fault: "This has nothing to do with men. Men are not the reason we are in this situation. It's our fault, for not taking our own power." Just like Kim Kiyosaki, Orman maintains that the issue to correct is between women and their money and nobody else. Consistent with the general spirit of financial self-help, structural factors constricting women's access to and knowledge about investing are not a consideration.

Most financial self-help material for women defines the female character in the context of relationships with others—a characterization that aligns closely with traditional stereotypes of women as more community-oriented than men, who are thought to be oriented toward independence. The case of Suze Orman is the most illuminating because she most clearly echoes the long tradition of self-help addressing women's "codependence," outlined in the famous book *Women Who Love Too Much* (Norwood 1997; see also Rapping 1996; Travis 2009; Valverde 1998:29–35). Orman addresses women as people who care about others before themselves, who are extremely powerful in taking care of multiple tasks and people simultaneously, except when it comes to money: "We take the money that we are making and we use it for everybody else's benefit before our own. Our nature is to nurture. When it comes to money it means that whatever we get we have to give. We have to use it to protect everybody." She addresses women as those who ensure that the care of everyone is guaranteed (spouses, parents, children, best friends). So she encourages women to start caring more about themselves, but not necessarily caring less about others. Basically, Orman tries to shatter the contradiction between caring for the self and caring for others. Since she frames women as *caring subjects*, she pushes them to think about their financial well-being as a matter of caring for both the self and others. She urges women to be as generous with themselves as they are with others: "When you change your behavior with your money, it enhances those that you love, it doesn't take away from them. You can just see that by giving more to yourself (financially speaking) you can give more to everybody else. Then you start to become a powerful woman, who could truly own the power to control her destiny."

Orman makes a point of being inclusive to different family structures, referring to single women as well as women with life partners, thereby including same-sex or unmarried couples, and women living alone. Yet she addresses women almost exclusively in the context of personal relationships. Echoing a vast self-help literature for women with a similar tone, "relationships" is the frame through which women are supposed to understand, among other things, money. Women have a dysfunctional relationship with money, gurus like Orman claim, and all they have to do is work on this relationship, in the same way that they work on their relationships every day: "I want you to get involved with your money. I want you to treat it like a friend, like a family member, like an entity that will support you and take care of you throughout your entire life." Money becomes one more entity for women to nurture.

While financial self-help resources for women circulate much more in the United States, at the time I did fieldwork in Argentina most of these books had not yet been published there. The field of women's financial advice has been slowly growing, and most women I interviewed there had not thought much about finances from the point of view of gender. Only one of the women I interviewed had read Kim Kiyosaki's *Rich Woman* (only published very recently). While she was very involved in financial self-help collective activities, and worked side by side with her husband, Alejandro, importing and selling Cashflow games and organizing events with Financial Freedom Argentina, Valeria was appalled by some of Kim Kiyosaki's ideas. Like other resources for women,

Kim Kiyosaki urges women to be financially independent from their husbands. In doing so, she recommends that they consider the fact that divorce is a possibility. She laments the reality that many women stay in unhappy marriages only because they do not have the financial independence to leave, and regrets that many women find themselves in a financial disaster after divorce for not having made the right decisions early on: "Unfortunately many marriages do not pass the test of time. The divorce rate is up; one out of two marriages ends in divorce. I'm not saying plan on a divorce. I am saying be realistic and set yourself up financially no matter what happens" (Kiyosaki 2006:14). Valeria told me that while she understood the argument and recognized that there was a point to it, she just could not include in her financial calculations the possibility of divorce. She did not ignore that it was a possibility; after all, she was in her second marriage. But she saw this level of calculation and strategy as a distinctly American cultural feature. While, as the "baby" square in the Cashflow game demonstrates, financial self-help pushes people to consider their life events as financially calculable ones, some users refuse to infringe on the imaginary boundaries between money and intimacy (Zelizer 2005).

In sum, books targeted to women illustrate the main argument of this chapter: that financial self-help is more about fighting dependence than about making money. For women, money becomes another vehicle for working on oneself, adding to a long historical list of suggested targets (including relationships and codependence). These books also show the connection between financial self-help and one of its intellectual predecessors, the recovery movement, of which codependence became a central concept. Ultimately, the consistent suggestion in financial self-help (both general and gender-specific) is that individuals have to look inside and work on the self if they ever want to achieve "freedom."

.   .   .

The Rich Dad fan group with which I spent the longest time in New York dedicates substantial time in its long monthly meetings to various complex technical issues that I had a difficult time understanding. In the meetings I attended over two years, most time was spent talking about real estate investing techniques such as how to find rental property, perform proper due diligence, and calculate potential cash flow; how to repair damaged credit scores in order to finance real estate ventures; how to open a business line of credit; or what to consider when starting a business. Steve, the founder and soul of the group, would generously answer specific questions from members who were taking their first steps in business and investing. Some days, instead of coaching members, he would tell the group what business he was investing in or the story of a property he was trying to buy, and he would give detailed and valuable technical information about the accounting and legal intricacies of his deals. Steve also helped members understand the state of the economy. When Lehman Brothers drowned in September 2008, for example, Steve offered a long and careful explanation of what he thought would be the causes and consequences of the crisis. All of this technical expertise, however, was never separated from preparing the self for the challenge of financial freedom. At the end of the day, technical expertise had its limits. One of the maxims that Steve repeated in every meeting was that "all you need to know is that you never know all that you need to know." Steve, who genuinely cared about the members of his group, was interested in their learning, but he constantly reminded them that there was a component deep inside the self on which they had to work if they were ever going to achieve financial freedom. At some point, they would need to jump and take risks, and that was a matter of fostering a desire for financial freedom greater than the fear of risk. Most important, money had to move to the background: "What I observe from successful people," Steve told the group, "is that money is just a by-product of something else." He said that he became more successful when he stopped caring about money, when he gave up the fear of ending up with no money. He encouraged people to start with small deals and leave their comfort zones. The point was not making money, but rather cultivating the internal freedom that would eventually lead to money. "The fact that you tried makes you successful. The only failure is not trying." As in the case of Casey Serin, the failed California real estate investor, the worst sin is letting the conformist self of welfare society beat the neoliberal self who calculates, takes risk, and launches itself into the adventure of creating money from nothing. Every step in the world of investing is also a step in a project of changing oneself.

Paradoxically, Kiyosaki is not oblivious to the costs and risks involved in suddenly jumping into business and investments, big or small, in order to start working on the self. He therefore developed the Cashflow board game, a learning tool that allows readers to experience what it means to invest, generate "passive income," and achieve financial freedom. Cashflow is a widely popular game in financial self-help circles that allows readers to incorporate the teachings of Kiyosaki, pretend to be investors, and see themselves in action.

From Rats to Riches

3

IT WAS AROUND 7:30 P.M. on a Thursday, and everyone was focused on the Cashflow boards and their financial statements. There were five players on one table and four on another. Game organizer Sonny walked around the tables, coaching players and offering explanations. Except for Joe and me, who had played several times, the rest (Mark, Victor, and Elise) were playing for the first time. Sonny interrupted the game: "Ok, guys, now listen, you've been playing shy of an hour and a half. What have you learned so far, if anything?" Mark was the first to respond to Sonny's question; after a short pause, he sighed, "I have a lot to learn." Victor nodded, "Yes, I understand the game so far. . . . I'm just trying to suck it in, basically." "Ok, but what did you learn? Did you guys learn anything? If not, I'm wasting my time. Either you play this like Monopoly and you go home, or you play this in real life and hopefully you make positive financial steps," Sonny replied. Elise intervened, "Kind of what is a good deal and what's a bad deal." Mark added, "Yeah, I'm having a difficult time determining what's . . . like, you guys look at the cards and immediately you're like, 'Oh, it's moving slow, tah-dah!' I'm not seeing that at all." Joe comforted Mark, "It's just practice. You'll notice a good deal and a bad deal when you get there. And if you're leveraging too much or if it's worth it to do it, if you take a loan. . . . " Victor added, "I learned that I could take more risk in the game, you know . . . take more risk and just see what happens." Mark reiterated the difficulties he was facing: "My inability to understand the card, it's probably making me lose out on a good deal. In one of the opportunities I had before, I wasn't sure . . . it might be a

good deal, but I put it back in the deck, 'cause . . ." Sonny offered to help by saying, "Next time, pull me over, and I'll go over it with you, OK? In real life, I now
have people helping me analyze deals. But I've made my mistakes." Joe threw
the dice, and we continued playing for another hour.

This scene took place in a public space inside a corporate building's plaza in
midtown Manhattan, where people gathered to play Cashflow, a board game created and marketed by financial guru Robert Kiyosaki. During games, passersby
usually looked curiously from afar, and sometimes stopped and got closer to the
tables to see what these adults were doing huddled around boards full of little
plastic rats for game pieces. The reactions of Joe, Mark, Victor, and Elise are a
good illustration of the kinds of learning that happened around Cashflow boards.
At first a bit confused about the game dynamics, through repeated play participants learned to recognize deals, gauge their risk aversion, and contrast the game
with real life. And all of this happened under the gaze of Sonny, who tried to
coach players into understanding what it was that they were supposed to learn.

Cashflow at first sight resembles the famous game Monopoly. It represents
a fictitious market in which players buy and sell assets with the ultimate goal of
obtaining profit and improving their virtual economic positions. Unlike Monopoly, however, Cashflow is explicitly designed and interpreted by players as a
tool for preparing oneself for real-life financial mobility. Players and organizers
repeatedly stress the fact that it is more than a game. "It is not really a game;
it is a tool to condition our minds for finances, accounting, and business," said
Matías, the creator of Financial Freedom Argentina, when introducing the
game to new players. Playing Cashflow is for the most part a fun experience
(and depending on the players, it can be a lot of fun). However, it is also serious
business. A full game demands several hours and significant effort, occasionally
including traveling long distances when games are not held in players' home-
towns, as was the case of a few players I met in Argentina. At the beginning of
a weekend game session, Matías distinguished playing Cashflow quite clearly
from playing any other game: "I believe you are not here for a weekend distrac-
tion. You are interested in financial freedom. There's a great place around here
if you just want to kill time, where you can play bridge or bocce. But that's not
what we are here for." Cashflow is not a game that people play only once. A
statement printed on the board says, "The more you play, the richer you become." Robert Kiyosaki and group organizers recommend playing the game
periodically, weekly or monthly. Even experts and group leaders continue to
play from time to time. In this regard, playing the Cashflow board game is not

that different from sports training, in which exercises are repeated countless times, and in which learning is necessarily practical (Wacquant 2003:58–60). It requires discipline and routine practice to become proficient.

Cashflow is a practice that embodies the three components that define financial self-help (the sociological, the technical, and the emotional or motivational). First, Cashflow provides definitions of what the goals of people living in an era of financial capitalism should be and what these goals mean. Following Kiyosaki's diagnosis of current capitalism, users reframe their goals and principles of economic action and financial planning. Whether they have read financial self-help or not before playing—although most players have, there are always players who have been invited by friends or relatives and who do not know much about Kiyosaki—the game reinforces the notion of financial freedom in a practical way. The crucial difference between having a fortune and being financially free is dramatically conveyed by the board game. In Cashflow, players do not change their status in the game until they convert money into incoming cash flow from investments. Second, by using specific technical devices, particularly the financial statement form that the game provides, players can acquire and cultivate what Michel Callon (1998) has called "calculative tools" in line with the neoliberal project of "financial freedom." Players learn some of the technical nuances of bookkeeping; investing; calculating returns; and distinguishing various sorts of income and expenses, assets, and liabilities. Those distinctions, purely technical in appearance, push players to change their everyday calculative practices into ones that should set them on a course to financial freedom. Third, players not only learn what financial success entails and the technical skills that such a mission requires, they also look inside their selves to determine what may be fostering or limiting their chances of success. Throughout the game, players have opportunities to reflect on and redefine their financial selves in order to effect changes in their attitudes toward financial success by working on the emotional manifestations of a certain kind of self (fear, anxiety, risk, hope, and so on). Players can start cultivating an autonomous, brave, and entrepreneurial self as a first (or simultaneous) step into the real financial world. They are encouraged to draw lessons from every step of the game and to apply these to "real life." Cashflow serves all of these purposes, besides being an excuse for consumers of financial self-help to get together, creating networks that not only bring social support but may also eventually lead to joint business opportunities. Much of the collective life of financial self-help revolves around Cashflow encounters.

The Game and the Clubs

Ironically, Robert Kiyosaki's *Rich Dad, Poor Dad*, his most successful book, was at the time of its publication just a means to an end: promoting his newly created board game, Cashflow. Consistent with his apparent strategy of using each of his products to promote the others, his books and DVDs recommend playing Cashflow as a means of becoming financially literate and starting on the path to "financial freedom" (Kiyosaki 1999, 2000b; Kiyosaki and Lechter 1998). Playing a game is considered a unique practice because, unlike other financial self-help resources, players can see themselves "in action," both getting to know themselves and starting to develop the necessary tools and mindset to achieve financial freedom. Many players recognize that Cashflow is a more effective way to learn than any other resource, just by virtue of it being a game. In any given game session, there are players for whom Cashflow is one of their first encounters with financial self-help technologies as well as players who arrive to Cashflow after having started their journey into financial self-help via other media (books, the Internet, and so on). Of course, no one expects to "change their mindset" by only playing the game; the game is meant to be combined with other practices and training that make up the holistic enterprise of "financial intelligence." As I suggested before, financial freedom is not an easy accomplishment; it demands a serious commitment from the individual. Playing Cashflow is partly a testimony to that commitment.

Fans can order Cashflow online (or, as they do in Argentina, buy it from a local distributor) and play at home with family or friends, which is what some fans initially do. There is also an electronic version available on CD to play individually. However, getting together with others provides opportunities to network and interact with people who have the same interests and similar attitudes toward financial freedom. Networking is one of the mandates of the Rich Dad literature and other financial self-help books. Readers are told that interacting with people with similar concerns will help them work more actively for their financial success. They also use networking to find financial opportunities or business partners. Also, given that the game is expensive (around $200), for many players it makes more sense to try playing with someone else's board first, and perhaps buy a game set later. Playing Cashflow is one way of fighting the initial sense of being overwhelmed that many readers experience when they read financial self-help for the first time and discover that, according to the books, they may have been managing their finances poorly for quite some time.

Players often express a feeling of relative isolation, of not having anyone close who shares their new interest in financial freedom. Omar, a thirty-six-year-old fan from Argentina, felt that the mere desire to and conviction that he would succeed financially pushed him away from his friends:

> I didn't buy the game because I didn't have anyone to play with. In my circle of friends, no one shared my ideas about *Rich Dad*, about Kiyosaki. They didn't even know who he was, and they were not interested in knowing. Among my friends, I am the crazy one who thinks that he will become rich. I don't think I'm crazy; I'm just pursuing a goal.

Many players feel that their close friends may not be interested in playing with them, so attending a game organized by a club may be their only chance to play. Alejandro, one of the organizers of Financial Freedom Argentina, who also imports and sells games, told me that he knew of people who purchased the original game but could not find anyone to play with. Several players fear that they will not be taken seriously by their friends if they suggest playing Cashflow. After all, Cashflow is a game, and games are thought to be for children only. As thirty-five-year-old Santiago put it,

> [The game is] more than a hundred bucks!. . . . I thought, "Even if I buy it, who's going to play with me?" My friends are all grown-ups, married. "Look, I have the little rat game, you have the black rat, I have the red, he has the orange, [with] the little cheese. . . . " They would think I'm insane.

While playing what might look like a silly game "makes sense" for someone who is already exposed to the world of financial self-help and who can therefore appreciate its importance, others may be tougher to convince.

The global Rich Dad website has a "community" section where one can register a Cashflow club and find the contact information of club organizers anywhere in the world. Registering a club is so easy that many groups who are largely inactive are still published on the website. When Matías, the leader of Financial Freedom Argentina, signed up with one of those groups, the reply was that the group would perhaps organize a game many months ahead. So he organized his own group, and a few weeks later, Matías created his own independent website. Like Matías's group, some clubs have become more permanent and semi-institutionalized, developing their own websites and online forums.

A Cashflow game requires at least three players (two players is possible, but somewhat boring; five or six players is ideal), a game set (including copies of the financial statement, which can only be used once), a few pencils and erasers, and calculators. Between 2007 and 2009, I played or observed thirty-five games in New York and Argentina (mostly in and around Buenos Aires, but also in the cities of La Plata and Mar del Plata). Because a game session can last from two to six hours depending on the rules used, I observed (and most times engaged in) more than one hundred hours of play. Cashflow is played in two main types of settings: (1) sessions with one to three boards and five to fifteen attendants, which are held in a public space like a coffee shop or in an office or private home (these are informally organized through online forums or webpages and are free or very cheap); and (2) sessions that are part of one-day workshops organized by Financial Freedom Argentina. These are typically more expensive.

In New York, several permanent clubs organize small games (among other activities) and two clubs tend to dominate the Cashflow scene. Most of these clubs' games are facilitated by the same person, Sonny, a fifty-year-old mortgage consultant who brings the games, paper, pencils, and other materials needed to play. Sonny is the most active game organizer in the city.[1] He is a well-known character in New York's financial self-help world and participates in several groups and activities. Sonny is in many ways New York's proverbial King of Cashflow. At various events held by different New York groups, Sonny gives short presentations on how important it is to play the game in order to achieve financial freedom. Sonny tells me that he enjoys facilitating games and coaching players. He often insists that "the quicker you can move the balance sheets, the quicker your brain moves." He offers encouragement to players with statements such as, "You see, you could be playing cards now, but instead you're learning about the global economy." His enthusiasm for and dedication to Kiyosaki's teachings are palpable. Sonny had the largest collection of financial self-help and personal improvement media I had ever seen. In his home, he had bookshelves and drawers full of books, CDs, DVDs, folders, and other materials. "What do you think, that you become rich and *then* buy the books?" he asked me. Thanks to his job as a mortgage consultant, he had a stable income and commissions. But since a few years earlier, when he read Kiyosaki and started networking and facilitating games, he had purchased two rental properties in a large eastern city, close to a university campus. Forced to deal with difficult tenants, his investment properties were giving him many headaches instead of the passive income they were supposed to provide. Sonny told me that if he could go back in time, he would seek other sources of passive income; real estate was feasible only after acquiring more capital and experience. But even if things were not going well for him, Sonny was a firm believer in and disseminator of the tenets of Kiyosaki and other financial authors.

Sometimes Sonny charges a small fee of five dollars per player, but in general he holds the games free of charge.[2] Game announcements are published on the clubs' websites and broadcast by e-mail to previous attendants; usually between five and fifteen people attend. Since the game can be played by up to six people, there are most often two simultaneous games at separate tables. The games are held once or twice a month, sometimes more, depending entirely on Sonny's availability and will, and each session takes about three hours. Occasionally, some players exchange phone numbers and organize their own games independently.

In Buenos Aires, I attended sessions organized by members of a popular online forum organized by Kiyosaki fans. These small games (five to ten people) were generally held in someone's apartment or office, and people would chip in to buy refreshments and food. Sometimes, members organized meetings in a coffee shop that was closed to the public for the occasion, charging the price of a fixed menu. These events were attended by around twenty players. The second setting, the large one-day "financial freedom workshop," is very popular in Argentina. These workshops are organized by Financial Freedom Argentina. In Buenos Aires, they are usually held once a month, sometimes more frequently, in a rented conference space, and attendees are charged a moderately expensive fee (the equivalent of $70 to $150US), which includes lunch and coffee. Games are held in other big cities around Argentina with similar frequency. Attendance is usually fifty to seventy people, who occupy ten to twelve game tables, and the duration of games is at least five hours. In a display of institutionalization that other groups lack, team members of Financial Freedom Argentina wear distinctive t-shirts and answer questions around the tables throughout the game.

Regardless of the setting or country, the dynamics of game playing are rather informal. During weekend games, it is rare to see people in business attire, although there were usually a few attendees dressed formally at the events organized by Financial Freedom Argentina. Wearing a tie or suit on a weekend signals to others that one is treating the meeting as a business event more than a day of fun. However, wearing casual clothing does not signify to others that the player is less serious. In fact, most of the organizers dress casually. When a game is organized on a weekday, most people attend after work, so it is more frequent to see participants in their office attire. But in general, Cashflow participants follow no particular dress code.

The structure of the Cashflow game leaves significant time for conversation between players. Before, during, and after games, players talk and interact with each other and the organizer constantly. They ask for help or offer it to others; talk about the rationale for their decisions; and comment on their own activities, books they have read, seminars they have attended, investments they are considering, and so on. Although organizers and players often comment on the seriousness of the game and the importance of applying Cashflow principles to real life, having fun is both accepted and encouraged. To participants, Cashflow is as much about socializing and networking as it is about playing. At large events, one can hear people laughing loudly, celebrating, and complaining about their bad luck. In my experience, Argentine games are usually louder than games in the United States, but this is likely unrelated to Cashflow itself—Argentines are famous for being noisy and theatrical. Depending on the personalities of those playing at a given table, I found that playing a game of Cashflow can be a very fun experience. In one game organized through the online forum and held in a private home in Buenos Aires, two players seemed devoted to making everyone else laugh, taking every opportunity to make a joke. To this day, I remember that afternoon for how much I laughed. At other times game sessions are less eventful.

A Cashflow table is often messy (Figure 3.1). The board itself usually takes up most of the table space, but each player also has two pieces of paper (a financial statement and a tracking sheet) and one or more pencils. In addition, several calculators (sometimes people use their cell phones), erasers, and pencil sharpeners are usually scattered around the table. The rest of the table is usually filled with the dust generated by the erasers, game cards, and sometimes individual business cards that players give to each other when chatting about who they are and what they do for a living. In addition, depending on the setting, players often have water, sodas, coffee, or snacks (they may have chipped in for supplies or purchased a flat-rate menu prearranged with the coffee shop). I never saw alcoholic drinks at games, and I never saw anyone suggesting or banning alcohol.[3]

Cashflow is a complicated game, and it takes some time playing it to fully understand how it works.[4] The board contains two tracks, the "rat race" and the "fast track," and four piles of cards: "big deals," "small deals," "the market," and "doodads" (Figure 3.2). Each player has his or her own financial statement that displays their income, expenses, assets, and liabilities. Players initially copy the numbers from a profession card they randomly select from twelve options

Figure 3.1. Playing Cashflow
SOURCE: Photo taken in a meetup group.

(mechanic, lawyer, teacher, secretary, and so on) before the start of the game, and then make changes to their financial statement throughout the game. The goal in the first track (the rat race) is to invest in assets (stocks, properties, businesses) that generate enough incoming cash flow to surpass one's monthly expenses. When that occurs, a player is allowed to move from the rat race to the fast track. Once in the fast track, a winner is crowned when (1) she lands on her dream (which is chosen by each player before the game starts) and has enough money to buy it,[5] or (2) she accumulates $50,000 in monthly cash flow from investments in the fast track.

Participants take turns throwing the die and moving among the twenty-four squares that form the wheel of the rat race. They land on one of seven different alternatives: "paycheck," "opportunity," "the market," "doodad," "baby," "downsized," or "charity." Landing or passing over a "paycheck" square provides a player with his monthly cash flow, a number that is different for each player and is determined by each individual's financial statement. The monthly cash flow is the difference between the player's monthly total income and monthly expenses as determined by his or her financial statement. Each paycheck rep-

Figure 3.2. A Cashflow Board
SOURCE: Photo taken by the author.

resents a month of the player's life, in which he or she normally saves some money. While this adds some money to players' pockets, the "opportunity" and "market" squares are what get the game moving.

When landing on "opportunity," the player picks a card from either the "big deal" or the "small deal" pile, depending on how much cash she has available to invest (Figure 3.3). All cards are seen by all participants, regardless of whose

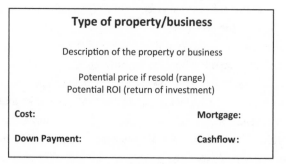

Figure 3.3. Opportunity Card (Big Deal or Small Deal)

turn it is, and are read out loud. Opportunity cards offer real estate properties, stock, or businesses. Each real estate card provides information on (1) the amount of the down payment, (2) the total amount of the mortgage, (3) the total cost of the property, (4) the potential range of the value of the property if it is resold in the future and the return of investment, and (5) the incoming monthly cash flow provided by the property.

The incoming cash flow generated by the property is often confusing the first time one plays. It is assumed that the property is automatically rented out and, after covering monthly mortgage payments and other expenses (which do not appear on the card), it provides a positive monthly cash flow. Stock market opportunity cards offer stock shares at a certain price and provide information on the predicted price range of the given stock, so that the player can evaluate buying (if the price offered is close to the lower bound) or, if he owns the stock and the price is high, selling his shares. In the case of stock, the player who picked up the card may buy stock from the market, but anyone is permitted to sell (players do not trade stocks—or anything except for cards—between themselves). Similar to real estate cards, each business card offers an opportunity to purchase a business with a cost and a fixed incoming monthly cash flow (unlike property cards, however, most business cards do not mention the potential value if the business is sold in the future).

Landing on a "market" square allows a player to pick up a market card, which presents cash offers for real estate or businesses. All players who own the type of property that the market demands can sell it back to the market, normally at higher prices than the original purchase value. The downside of selling is that players then have to give up the incoming cash flow generated by the rental of the property. Throughout the game, players may buy and sell assets several times in order to increase their wealth, reinvest, and eventually seek to have their income from investments surpass their expenses.

Landing on a "doodad" square is bad news, since it forces a player to pick a doodad card and spend the money indicated on the card on some consumer good (ranging from a $10 cup of coffee to contributing $2,000 to a player's daughter's wedding). When landing on a "baby" square, the player has to add a new item to the monthly expenses column representing the regular expenses incurred in raising a child, which varies according to each profession.[6] Landing on a "downsized" square represents a player losing her job, which means that she loses two turns and has to pay her total monthly expenses once. If a player lands on a "charity" square, she has the option of donating 10 percent of her monthly income once in order to throw an additional die during each of her next three turns. The advantage of throwing two dice is moving faster along the board, and therefore receiving more paychecks since it symbolizes a faster passing of time.

In most cases, new players sit with participants with more game experience. When games are held as part of a one-day workshop, players receive a brief lecture on the rules and goals of the game. Most times, however, participants just sit down and follow the informal instructions of the leader or other players. For beginners, the rules, goals, and accounting of the game may be hard to understand. The first time I played, in New York, I told the rest of the group that I didn't want to play and I would just watch, because I had never played before. They smiled and said that everybody had to play. But they didn't sound as if they were forcing me—more as if they knew that I would learn fast. I insisted, saying that I didn't want to make the game slower, and Robert, the experienced player on that board, said that it wasn't a problem since other people were also playing for the first time. Even if they received an explanation before playing, participants (including myself) may not know exactly what they are doing during their first few experiences with Cashflow. They become familiar with the objects of the game as they use them and as other players help them interpret their actions. Even if beginners are lucky enough to win during their first game, understanding and incorporating all of the game's concepts often takes several sessions.

Acquiring Definitions

Each rule and each step of the Cashflow game conveys a specific definition of economic success. The basic structure of the board, with its two distinct tracks, sets up a binary that is central to Robert Kiyosaki's books: that there is a substantial difference, both in cognition and content of character, between the rich and everybody else. The "rat race" track is drawn in a circle, representing a rat's running wheel. The game pieces are small plastic rats meant to represent players in their financial travails. For Kiyosaki, most poor and middle-class people behave financially much like rats on their running wheels: they run and run but always stay in the same place. The "rat race" represents the idea that, no matter how hard people work and how much they may feel they are moving ahead, they do not change their financial positions. This image is used to characterize, for example, middle-class financial burdens, in which more income means higher expenses, more debt, and greater needs—essentially the act of being trapped in a perennial cycle of hard work and financial difficulty. As David explained in the workshop discussed in Chapter 2, while the working class buy "filling" (trivial or unnecessary belongings) and the middle class buy a "commitment cloud" (more expensive items that require pricey upkeep or continual investment), only the rich, who buy assets, are liberated from the rat's running wheel.

The rat has a powerful symbolic meaning. Many workshop participants explicitly reference their goals to "stop being a rat" or to "get out of the rat race in [X] years." For example, during the introductions at a workshop in Buenos Aires, one of the participants said, "I'm here because I read Kiyosaki and immediately felt that I was one of the small rats running on a wheel." The pieces that represent players on the board are little rats of different colors, standing on their hind legs, dressed in human clothes. The board also features various images of male and female rats wearing costumes that identify different professions (cop, secretary, pilot, doctor, and so on). In the center of the wheel is an image of a male rat wearing a millionaire's robe, with a bundle of dollars in his paws. The rat race is a simple but effective metaphor. Everyone in the world of Cashflow clubs knows what "getting out of the rat race" means—having all one's expenses covered by an income that does not require work. That is "financial freedom."

By practicing Cashflow, players acquire specific definitions of what being rich entails. Throughout the game, they visualize one of the central tenets of financial self-help: that having a huge amount of money is not the same as financial freedom, and that they should strive for the latter instead of the former. Financial freedom is, in its most basic form, the possibility of having one's spending needs covered by investment revenue (or "passive income"). In Kiyosaki's language, financial freedom, or an escape from the rat race, is attained once one's passive income equals one's expenses. Financial freedom means that a person does not need to work any longer to maintain his or her current lifestyle. In the game, if a player has a lot of money, but has not acquired passive income, nothing really happens—he does not leave the rat race and is no closer to winning than before. The only event that gets a player out of the rat race and onto the "fast track" is when he has enough passive income to cover his expenses.

At the beginning of the game, new players are informed by the leader or by other players that they are only allowed to leave the rat race track when they achieve this goal. However, in the midst of learning the rules and making calculations on their financial statements, new players often lose sight of this goal (although it is printed prominently at the top of their financial statements). On several occasions, I saw new players identify the passive income box on their financial statements and understand its meaning only well into the game. As I suggested in previous chapters, the project of financial success does not start by learning "how" to be financially free, but rather by learning for "what" one should strive.

For people who thought that being a millionaire simply involves having lots of money, this shift means reconfiguring their goals. As a group leader said in a post-game discussion, "It is not enough to turn $1,300 into $90,000, like you did in the game. The point of the game is that you understand that you are not free until you make money work for you and generate incoming monthly cash flow." Experienced players know that profession cards that represent lower-paying jobs have also fewer expenses. Since financial freedom (or the chance to leave the rat race) is achieved when passive income reaches the amount needed for expenses, it may be easier to win the game starting with lower-paying professions ("That's a hard one," Sonny told me when I picked the "airline pilot" profession card). This conveys the notion that it is not necessary to have a lot of money to be financially free; those who need less are actually closer to being rich. As Matías put it when explaining the game, "Kiyosaki says that if you have the intelligence to play the game and win, it doesn't matter if you have lots of money. If a person receives passive income to match her expenses, it means that she has the financial intelligence to get into big businesses."

Matías's point presents a counterintuitive but central definition of financial success that is shared by Cashflow players. Members of Rich Dad clubs usually complain that those who do not know enough about Kiyosaki's teachings tend to think that one's chances of becoming rich are related to the amount of money one has. This distinction between one's material conditions and one's chances of mobility is a defining feature of financial self-help, and Cashflow vividly conveys this point. Structural economic conditions are not seen as external limits. Therefore, the social class in which one is born affects the way one has been financially educated in the context of the family, but not the chances of financial success, since the latter depends on oneself. Social class is seen less as a position in society and more as a choice and a state of mind:

> We do our best to provide distinctions between how the rich, the poor and the middle class think . . . and then leave the choice up to you as to which way you want to think. After all, one of the benefits of living in a free society is that we all have the choice to be rich, poor or middle class. That decision is up to you, regardless of which class you are in today. (Kiyosaki 1999, 6)

Cashflow is meant to spur personal transformation. In a post-game discussion, Matías emphasized one of the goals of the game: "the key is to put my ideas together and realize how I have to train my brain to be able to visualize an opportunity and take it. It is a way of fertilizing the soil of my brain to be ready to jump on an opportunity." Matías also recognized that it is obviously necessary to have the cash to be able to take advantage of a good investment opportunity. But in his mind, that cash will always be within reach if the right mindset has been adopted. In more concrete terms, the thinking is that if you have a good idea, you will always be able to find investors for it. Financial intelligence is disentangled from financial wealth.

With this mindset, bad luck during a game of Cashflow cannot be blamed for a bad performance, because if one does not get the right cards, other players usually do, and the unfortunate can always move ahead by buying the cards picked by others (if one has the money) or with other players' money (if one gets and sells the good cards). In Cashflow, emphasis is diverted from the material conditions that shape one's financial success, and is instead fully focused on cognitive and emotional determinants of wealth: without financial intelligence, one will not even know how to recognize a good investment opportunity if it presents itself. Without the right attitude, one will be too afraid to jump and will always find excuses. Cashflow is a sort of therapy to cultivate these traits of risk-taking, self-reliance, and financial intelligence.

The disentanglement between money and financial knowledge is also represented in the game by the transition from the rat race to the fast track. When a player leaves the rat race and enters the fast track, he enters a different game. The fast track is where the rich invest their money, and it features very large investments, including factories, chain restaurants, buildings, oil investments, and so on. By turning the page of the financial statement to the one used by players on the fast track, the player finds a new form to fill out with his financial information. Now the passive income acquired on the rat race track is multiplied by one hundred, and that becomes the monthly cash flow with which a player starts his journey on the fast track. This is the only time in the game, which otherwise reveres and advocates accurate mathematical calculations and bookkeeping, when money multiplies for no clear reason. When I asked Matías during a game why the money was multiplied by one hundred, he replied,

> Kiyosaki says that passive income is multiplied by one hundred because the person who has achieved financial freedom has acquired the knowledge and training to do big business. It doesn't matter if he is a doorman, teacher, doctor, or

truck driver. If he has done it, he has the financial background to multiply that amount by one hundred. Why? Because he is already financially free. He understood the game of money. He can operate at a new level.

In other words, Matías argues that financial intelligence trumps any other social or economic determination, which includes, within the game, conventional mathematics. Players who demonstrate financial intelligence by getting out of the rat race can fast forward to the world of the rich, appropriately called the "fast track."

As exciting as it may sound to reach the fast track, it is in many ways a less thrilling experience than playing the rat race. For example, Gabriel, a player from Argentina, told me in an interview,

> The key is in the rat race, which is the day-to-day—the normal, everyday life of everyone. That's an excellent thing of the game, and I really like it. I didn't get out of the rat race in the three times I played, but I don't care. I didn't even want to get out of the rat race. I prefer to continue exercising in the rat race preparing for when I have the chance to be out. It's much more interesting. Why? I don't know, having three kids and being fired from my job . . . trying to think how the fuck to get out of that situation. . . .

Some players actually wonder if it was better to stay in the game's rat race even after achieving financial freedom. Raquel, a schoolteacher with whom I shared several Cashflow events in Buenos Aires, once invited me to play in her home with friends and family. In that game, she decided to remain in the rat race, even after her passive income had surpassed her expenses, because she felt she got more out of that experience than from the fast track. While the rat race has a more pedagogical goal, the fast track focuses on aspirations: how would it feel to be rich?

More than anything, the rat race establishes a mechanism that players try to replicate in their real, daily lives. Kiyosaki does not urge people to quit their jobs right away, but rather to plan their financial lives with the goal of achieving financial freedom. The game vividly shows players what that means in practice. With the meager savings a worker can squeeze from a monthly paycheck, one should try to use it to invest in properties, stocks, or businesses within one's reach (that is, "small deal" cards), instead of spending it on consumer items ("doodad" cards). Also, one will sometimes need to get rid of assets when their value is high, in order to accumulate more cash to jump on bigger deals that will bring more cash flow. As this process of investing and reinvesting unfolds, players are meant to realize that the proportion of their salary in their overall income is decreasing, to the point that they can quit their jobs and be completely financially free. Of course, obstacles can appear on the way. Some cards yield negative results (for example, damages to one's property forces owners to pay $1,000), or one can be downsized or have a baby. It is also possible to lose the game (by becoming bankrupt) if one has negative cash flow and lacks the money or assets to sell at half price to cover his or her expenses. However, while obstacles are part of the game, in practice they are not frequent occurrences (particularly bankruptcy).

As several scholars have shown, games are usually rich in meanings and representations (see Fine 1983; Geertz 1973; Goffman 1961; Henricks 2006; Sallaz 2008), and Cashflow is no exception. The game provides definitions of financial success, establishes a separation between wealth and financial intelligence, and helps players develop an idea of what financial advancement really means—financial freedom and passive income. In the next section, I turn to the technical calculative tools that players acquire playing Cashflow.

Acquiring Calculative Tools

The second form of learning that takes place during Cashflow is the acquisition of calculative tools. In this section, I focus on what Michel Callon (1998) calls the material reality of calculation. In the last decade or so, social scientists studying finances have taken inspiration from science and technology studies and approached the study of finances with a focus on the materiality involved in calculation. The financial intelligence advocated by Kiyosaki and cultivated in the game is, from the point of view of the growing field of social studies of finance, not an ability located inside human actors' minds but rather an assemblage of humans, techniques, and devices. Financial calculation, both at the highly complex level of financial derivatives and at the more basic level of popular investors, is an achievement aided by a variety of devices. As Donald MacKenzie emphasizes, "the properties of artefacts, technological systems, conceptual tools, and so on are not 'details' that sociological analyses should set aside: fully rounded analyses need to incorporate them" (MacKenzie 2009:3). The fact that "equipment matters" is one of the precepts of social studies of finance (MacKenzie 2009:13–16); the equipment used in Cashflow contributes to shaping the calculations that players are prompted to perform, both in the game and in their everyday lives. The financial statement used in the game, for

Profession ______ **Player** ______

Goal: To get out of the Rat Race and onto the Fast Track by building up your Passive Income to be greater than your Total Expenses

Income Statement

Income

Description	Cash Flow
Salary:	
Interest:	
Dividends:	
Real Estate:	
Businesses:	

Auditor ______

Person on your right

Passive Income= ______
(Cash Flows from Interest +
Dividends + Real Estate + Businesses)

Total Income: ______

Expenses

Taxes: ______
Home Mortgage: ______
School Loan Payment: ______
Car Payment: ______
Credit Card Payment: ______
Retail Payment: ______
Other Expenses: ______
Child Expenses: ______
Bank Loan Payment: ______

Number of Children: ______
(Begin game with 0 Children)
Per Child Expense: ______

Total Expenses: ______

Monthly Cash Flow: ______
(Pay Check)

Balance Sheet

Assets

Savings:		
Stocks/Mutual's/CDs:	No. of Shares:	Cost/Share:
Real Estate:	Down Pay:	Cost:
Business:	Down Pay:	Cost:

Liabilities

Home Mortgage: ______
School Loans: ______
Car Loans: ______
Credit Cards: ______
Retail Debt: ______
RE Mortgage: ______
Liability: (Business) ______
Bank Loan: ______

Figure 3.4. A Cashflow Financial Statement

SOURCE: Reprinted with permission of CASHFLOW Technologies, Inc.

example, works like a "prosthesis" (Callon 1998:51) that players acquire, which helps them configure their calculations in the financial realm.

Most calculations in Cashflow are relatively basic in terms of their mathematical sophistication. On a practical level, however, they can be cumbersome. Players have to write and erase their financial statements continuously throughout the game (hence the indispensable ubiquity of erasers on the game table), filling in information from the cards and constantly asking for help from others. The writing and erasing affects the pace of the game because each player has to wait for the previous one to finish his accounting before she can throw the die. In games with more advanced players, play usually continues and players do not wait for others to finish their accounting, making the game more dynamic and fast-paced. However, it is quite difficult to understand the mechanics of the game within the first few purchases of property, business, or stock.[7] During a workshop in Argentina with a dozen tables, I was asked to help coach players during a game session. There was a short session explaining how to play the game, but it was not enough. Every minute, I or one of the other three leaders had to run to another table to clarify doubts and explain the basics of the game. It was hard to explain quickly and effectively with the noise of more than sixty people playing in the same room. The first time that someone at a given table purchased an asset, I had to go through all the changes and calculations they had to make on their statement, while asking the other players to pay attention to the explanation. At times, while I was explaining at one table, I saw all of the hands at another table rise. It became easier only after the first hour, as some of the players were able to help others.

My participation as a coach made it clear how vital and labor-intensive this role can be, given the complexity of the game's rules and the difficulty of filling out the financial statements. Before starting to play, each person picks a random profession card and copies the information from the card onto his own financial statement, a preprinted letter-sized piece of paper with blank slots to fill in (Figure 3.4). Professions vary from lower-status jobs, such as janitor, to high-income professions, like airline pilot and lawyer. Unlike in such fantasy role-playing games as Dungeons and Dragons (Fine 1983), players do not "perform" their assigned identity; they only use its financial information, which differs mostly in terms of salary and monthly expenses (the added expense of having a baby, for example, is higher when the status of a profession is higher). Financial statements contain five sections: income, expenses, assets, liabilities, and a section in which the difference between "total income" and "total expenses" is calculated, resulting in one's monthly cash flow. This is the amount of cash remaining every month to be used for investments, and each player receives this amount every time she or he passes over a "paycheck" square. When the game starts, each player copies twenty-two separate numbers from the profession card to his financial statement.

Each time a player acquires an asset during the game, she has to copy all the information on the opportunity card (big or small deal) to her financial statement and return the card to the pile. For example, buying a rental property implies adding the following numbers to the financial statement: (1) down payment, (2) mortgage amount, (3) total cost of property, and (4) incoming monthly cash flow provided by the property. This triggers a set of recalculations in the financial statement, including total passive income, total income, and total incoming cash flow. Each player is likely to do this several times in one game. To make matters more complicated, every time a player decides to sell the property back to the market, she has to roll back all the calculations, and erase the asset from the asset column. Players sometimes team up to buy properties and divide the cash flow according to their negotiations, which makes the calculation even more complex. By the end of the game, the financial statement can be quite messy. The player to the right is supposed to be the auditor for the person on his or her left, although sometimes this rule is ignored. Most times, as I mentioned earlier, players receive help from other players to understand the procedures. It is not unusual that a player or his auditor discovers a mistake made in earlier turns that has affected all the calculations that came after, leading to a lengthy recalculation to fix it.

The financial statement is the most important object in Cashflow and a key tool in the process of financial calculation. One's ability to master the use of a financial statement becomes crucial both during the game and in everyday life on the path to financial freedom. During a game in New York, Sonny told me, "This game is not about real estate. It is not about stocks. It is not about business. It's about you and your financial statement." Game organizers encourage players to take the statement home and apply it to their own finances. Several players told me that filling the sheet out at home with their real financial information marked a major change in how they perceived their personal finances. On a few occasions during my fieldwork, participants suggested playing Cashflow using their real financial information instead of the one provided by the profession card randomly picked at the beginning of each game.

The financial statement encourages accurate bookkeeping—a skill that contributes to the self-discipline considered vital to financial success. Even the electronic version of the game, which is played individually on the computer, does not automatically place items in the right columns. A computer could easily do this automatically, but it is considered such an important skill that it is left to the player. But it is not just accuracy that players learn. By playing Cashflow, participants learn a means of organizing their personal finances and a particular way of understanding each expense and income item. During the game, players usually connect the significance of their transactions to their daily use of money. "Doodad" cards, for example, force players to spend money on consumer pleasures (dinner with friends, golf clubs, coffee, and so on). Usually players complain when they have to pick a "doodad," and some reflect on how they may spend that money in their everyday life without even registering it, draining the resources they could otherwise use to invest and generate passive income. A consumer expense now becomes a "doodad"—a frivolous good that stands as an obstacle between their current position and financial freedom.[8]

The financial statement does not contain any information about the player's cash savings. Instead, the game set includes fake bills in several denominations, and one player is supposed to function as the bank. However, bills are almost always replaced by a tracking sheet for each player in order to make the game easier and faster. Players keep count of how much money they have in their pockets by modifying the tracking sheet, which, as I often explained to new players when I was in charge of answering questions, is the equivalent of an online bank account in which one can see withdrawals, deposits, and balances. Thus, every time a player buys or sells anything, or passes a paycheck square, she has to add or subtract the corresponding amount on her tracking sheet. Many times, new players have a hard time identifying the function of each piece of paper (financial statement and tracking sheet) and what instances of the game will affect them. Cards like "doodads" will only affect accumulated cash (since players only have to buy a consumer good once) while landing on the "baby" square only affects monthly cash flow (by raising monthly expenses) without directly affecting the tracking sheet. The difference between the tracking sheet and financial statement is parallel to that between capital and cash flow and to that between having a fortune and financial freedom. In other words, one can have lots of money on the tracking sheet and not be financially free. Thus, a distinction between two material technical devices for calculation plays a role in reinforcing the central definitions of financial success.

Just as Robert Kiyosaki promoted in his books and other materials, the financial statement used in Cashflow distinguishes between assets and liabilities—a distinction that defies what most people learn in basic accounting classes. While a house or a car is usually considered an asset, they are regarded in the game as liabilities. For Kiyosaki, the distinction is straightforward: whatever puts money in one's pocket (generating passive income) is an asset, and whatever takes money from it is a liability. Santiago, age thirty-five, tried to emphasize the importance of this distinction to me during our interview:

> I changed my approach completely. From the beginning, the guy says that an asset is not what you have, but what makes money for you. He changes your idea from page one. Wait, but in high school I was told that my house was an asset! But your house doesn't give you money! While you live in your house, you have to pay bills, taxes. An asset is something that you buy that generates money for you. Do you understand?

This simple distinction, which moves certain goods from one section of the financial statement to another, has an impact on how players think about their expenses. Each expense (both in the game and in their actual finances) is classified according to this categorization. As mentioned above, "doodad" cards present consumer expenses, which are contrasted to money spent on assets. A house or a car, usually considered assets, are only categorized as such in Kiyosaki's framework if they are somehow generating positive incoming cash flow, for instance, as a rental property or taxi business. This distinction between assets and liabilities influences the distinction between "good debt" and "bad debt." Players are allowed to borrow money from a virtual bank at a 10 percent monthly interest rate. Such a high rate is not meant to discourage players from borrowing, but they are instead taught to realize that if they buy an asset, the incoming cash flow from that asset should be more than the interest paid for borrowing the money. Borrowing to buy assets is considered "good debt," while borrowing to buy liabilities, in contrast, is considered "bad debt." Players see themselves as having access to a secret that most people outside the realm of financial self-help do not yet realize. The ability to classify financial items in the correct column is seen as a central skill gained by playing Cashflow. Martín, age thirty-one, explained to me,

> I used to be orderly with my finances, but perhaps I didn't have a column for assets that would generate passive income. I didn't have one. . . . I was looking for it, but I never put it there. Now that I've seen that I can have passive income . . .

You see, that's what I learned. I realized that I was acting in the game as I do in real life, and that maybe what was missing was that column, which I now have, and the effort to rack my brains to figure out how I can generate passive income.

Here, Martín summarizes the importance of "the material reality of calculation, involving figures, mediums and inscriptions" (Callon 1998:4) in the configuration of economic subjects and the effect of a tool like Cashflow. By learning how to use a passive income column in Cashflow, and then transposing it from the game to his actual finances, Martín incorporated a calculative tool that will drive his real-life financial calculations and income generation. An apparently simple accounting tool, the column for passive income shapes subjects who frame their participation in the economy in terms of acquiring income generated by financial assets instead of working in the paid labor market.

Knowing the Self

Steve, the organizer of the New York Rich Dad group, always insists that you quickly realize that the goal of Cashflow is not to beat the other participants: "You are actually playing against yourself," he told me repeatedly. He says that through the game, players learn what their fears and tolerance to risk are and what kind of investors they are. As I explored in depth in Chapter 2, financial self-help demands a change in users' characters so that they strive for freedom and autonomy. Technical tools (what Kiyosaki calls "financial intelligence") are a necessary but insufficient condition. Most players do not regard Cashflow as merely a game. It is more like a crucial opportunity in which a person gets to know oneself, explore why he or she is still in his or her current financial position, and discover what work can be done on the self in order to move ahead. Sonny was fond of telling players, "The biggest thing you have to learn from that game is that *you* are your worst enemy." Although it may be nice to win the game, people play Cashflow to study and modify their attitudes and calculations in the financial world. Winning is usually less important than understanding what you are doing and learning, and players find it vital that they translate this knowledge into "real life."

Since winning is not a central priority, players tend to feel a general sense of cooperation and collective achievement during the game. When someone has gotten out of the rat race, applause from his table (and other tables) usually follows. The first person to leave the rat race is often praised. Sometimes, the organizer asks the first person who left the rat race to describe his decisions during the game so that others understand the process. In general, players frequently give and take advice from other players, and help others in understanding the calculations on their balance sheets. Many times, players collaborate and make joint ventures into investments when they do not have enough money to take a deal by themselves. The game can be very long, and leaving the rat race, not to mention winning the game, is not easy. There is a general sense of pride in leaving the rat race—an event in many ways more rewarding than winning the game in the fast track. Several of my participants remember precisely how many times they made it to the fast track in recent games. But the meaning of winning the game should not be overstated. In more than one-third of the games I attended, the session had to be stopped due to time limitations or it spontaneously faded when people started to network, talk about their own businesses, or exchange business cards. For Cashflow participants, the end goal is less about finishing the game and more about the lessons learned while playing.

There are, however, instances in which competition becomes more important during Cashflow games. These are usually instances in which players can demonstrate their bravery in investing or acumen in negotiation. In other words, competition is heightened when a player has a chance to prove his or her potential to succeed in the contemporary era of financial capitalism. When a player picks an opportunity card and she is not willing to use it (because she does not have the money for the deal or because it does not seem attractive enough), she can sell it to another player or auction it to all players. Herein lies another important message of the game: there should be no excuses or claims to being the victim of bad luck because one can always find creative ways to use other players' cards if one's own cards are not promising. Conversely, if a player gets a good card but does not have the money, one can find ways of making something positive out of that circumstance, either by selling it to the players who have money or partnering with them. Although card trading happens quite often, this is an exceptional situation in the game, since all other transactions (buying and selling stocks or real estate) are done in the context of "the market" and not between players. This is one of the very few transactions in which game money flows between players. When a player offers the card and someone is interested, the buyer has to pay the seller a price for the right to use it. After receiving the card, the buyer will then proceed to invest the money as if she had picked the card in the first place. New players often find this procedure difficult to understand. Several times, I saw organizers, who have the task of translating the game into "real life," explaining that the transaction was like giving a piece of information or a tip to someone else: "John rewards you for giving him a tip about a property for sale. And now John will use your tip to buy the property for himself. How much do you think your giving the tip is worth?"

Because this is the only value that is not provided on the cards, a value for the card has to be established, and it depends entirely on the negotiations between players. For players who have enough money but have not been lucky enough to land on "opportunity" squares, buying cards from others is a smart way to keep investing. The seller, on the other hand, is receiving compensation for a card that he would not have used anyway. Experienced players usually quickly agree on a value and move on to make use of the card. However, inexperienced players usually find it harder to establish a value. All players, of course, will try to get the most out of a negotiation, but there is no clear scale for determining how much a card is worth. If a card is not traded, then it goes to the bottom of the pile and no one receives any benefit. For inexperienced players—and occasionally for others—this negotiation is about their own value as negotiators. In a game in which you are supposed to discover features of your personality and your adequacy in the world of business and investing, no one wants to be perceived as a weak or gullible negotiator and accept a price that reflects badly on oneself (see Wherry 2008). The following fieldnote describes an interaction in New York in which an experienced player, Robert, was explaining the game to a rookie named Theresa:

> Theresa had a deal but didn't want to take it because it required too much money. Once she rejected it, Robert offered $25 for it. Although she didn't want the deal, she felt that Robert was taking advantage of her poorer situation in the game. She said, "I want $1,000" (which seemed off scale to me). He said that her request was unreasonable considering that the down payment for the deal was about the same amount. So she came down to $800, which was still extreme and far from the $25 Robert was offering. She asked how much money he had. So Robert explained, "In real life, this is what you get, an offer. Can you look at me and know how much money is in my bank account?" She said, "Of course not." Robert said that it didn't matter how much money he had since she wouldn't know that anyway, but just if the offer was good for her or not. Finally, she decided to abandon the deal and put the card under the pile (not selling it to Robert). George (who was observing the game) and Robert explained to her patiently that what she had just done was a mistake. George insisted that she

could have negotiated for $50 or for $75, but that throwing the deal out was just like throwing that money away. Robert told her that with her criteria, he would feel that she wanted to screw him over—no deal for me, no deal for you—and that in the future, he would not want to partner with her. She lost money and a potential partner.

In this case, Robert and George taught Theresa the value of mastering her emotions in order to become an effective rational economic actor—in two senses. First, she could have received money for free that she could have used later for investment.[9] Second, a low price for the card could have been an investment in networking, cooperation, and future partnership, which is considered crucial for success in financial self-help circles. Robert and George pointed out that Theresa was not identifying the indirect social benefits of this transaction.

Although Cashflow players value the calculative skills that they may gain by playing the game, it is not only technical skills that they need if they want to attain financial freedom. Sociologist Paul DiMaggio called attention to J. M. Keynes's forgotten idea of "animal spirits," "the emotional feeling-states that shape economic behavior above and beyond what a purely cognitive, rational model would lead one to expect" (DiMaggio 2002:79). While these emotional feeling-states are usually regarded as an obstruction to adequate economic action, in Cashflow and financial self-help they are what make economic action possible. The game pushes players to work through their internal fears and their gut feelings about money and risk. They explore their inner selves to determine whether they have "what it takes" to be successful investors who not only have the information to rationally evaluate investments but also the guts to leave aside the fears that accompany their "poor mindsets" and jump bravely into new financial opportunities.

Cashflow players use the game both to get to know their financial selves and to start developing new ones. In the first financial freedom workshop that I attended in Argentina in 2007, Ramiro, one of the organizers, lectured on the basics of the game for a few minutes before participants went to the tables to start playing. He strongly advised players not to let others drive their actions in the game. Listening to others' opinions is fine, he said, but since the game reflects who we are, it is better to think for oneself. However, the idea that being oneself is the best way to play Cashflow is also contested. Rolo, another game organizer, acknowledged that new players are often overly cautious in their investment decisions, and told participants, "Don't play as if you were playing in real life. Pretend to be someone else, be bold and take more risk. This game is about changing your mindset, so start doing it now." He later told me,

> Ninety-nine percent of players are very conservative at first. I see it in how they play and how they talk. I told a guy once, "The five times you played, you sat in the same spot." "Yes, and I lost all five times, never won," he told me. "Do you realize that you are doing always the same thing? Why don't you play *not* being you? This is a game, if you haven't invested anything in your personal life, here you should invest everything. Just to see what happens. Take risks." Because partly the idea of the game is creating a habit that you don't [currently] have.

Josh, a player in New York who was reflecting on the four games he had played so far, said that the first two times he played, he was very cautious and studied each opportunity and his ability to take it carefully. He behaved as he would have behaved in real life. "I did almost no deals, and eventually life caught up: I landed on baby, downsized, and so on," he said. The next two times he played, he decided to be bold and take more risks. "Life caught up again, but this time I was ready." Cashflow is seen by players as both a chance to learn about their selves and an opportunity to start assuming the economic identities of bold successful investors to which they aspire. Most important, it is not only a matter of acquiring the tools that make them rational economic actors, but also of working on their selves in order to align them with those tools and acquire the courage to take the risks deemed necessary for financial freedom.

Bending the Rules, Adapting the Game to "Real Life"

A game organizer in Argentina liked to adapt the motto of a cable movie channel, "It happens in movies; it happens in life," to Cashflow. He would start sessions by saying, "It happens in the game; it happens in life." For practitioners, the whole point of the game is to incorporate their experiences learned during the game into their financial lives. Despite the parallel to the cable channel motto, much of the game is not as immediately applicable to "real life" as players would like to think. Players deal with inconsistencies, such as the odd money-multiplying transition between the rat race and the fast track, and actively interpret and modify the game to make it functional. This engagement is crucial not only to make Cashflow generally possible, but also to make it usable in different national contexts.

Although it was originally developed in English for the American market, Cashflow is played in several countries. In spite of national differences, the basic process people follow when they play is the same: they learn goals, they acquire tools, and they work on their inner selves. All the transactions represented in the game, although abstract enough to be understandable in any capitalist context, come from the American economy. Argentine players usually commented (and often asked for my input) on how easy things seem to be in the United States if the game reflects the actual U.S. economy and investment opportunities. In the game, mortgage down payments and interest rates are ridiculously low by Argentine standards, and returns for investment in rental property are too high. Also, Americans are generally far more used to owning and trading stocks than Argentines. Many times, Argentines joked about local economic disasters and how the game would reflect them (especially in relation to the country's 2001 financial crisis and the *corralito*, when all bank deposits were frozen by the government). Frequent comments about the game's lack of realism are contested by the idea that realism is perhaps not so necessary. Ruben, for example, told me,

> Some people I played with . . . they don't understand that this is an education process, and they lean more towards saying, "It would be great to have an opportunity like these." The game itself, regardless of what is said about it, even if it has some things that are a bit unrealistic, is precisely about getting rid of the mindset that says, "Opportunities are for some people only," and to say instead, "Why not?"

Argentines had a harder time adjusting the specific examples from the game to their surrounding reality, and in this regard, their use of the game was different than its use in the United States. However, it is a difference of intensity, not of nature. At each step of the game, players everywhere contrast the Cashflow game with reality and try to determine what the game is telling them and what they can make of it, regardless of how realistic it is or not. This active engagement, which I call *translation*, is what makes the American game work in different national contexts. Players actively translate the game to make it fit their context. This local translation is what makes it global.[10]

It is for this reason that rigid rules are not a strong presence in games. Rather than reading a rulebook, most people learn Cashflow's basic rules by playing with others who have played before. Once the essential mechanism of the game is shared by all players in a given session, what is allowable and what is forbidden are decided by contrasting the transaction in question with what would make sense in "real life." I rarely saw a rulebook, and I never saw a player or an organizer consult a manual to figure out how to solve a complicated situation. In this sense, players are not passive consumers of the game, but rather *practitioners*, as philosopher Michel de Certeau (1984:29–42) preferred to call consumers due to the active and productive character of the use of cultural products. As much as Cashflow players respect and sometimes worship financial self-help gurus, they use what de Certeau defined as *tactics* through which they change the game. In a territory defined by the product Cashflow (de Certeau's *strategies*), players make small modifications, but, in a strange twist, they do not aim to subvert the original idea of the game, but rather to perfect it. The success of a tool like Cashflow depends in part on the robustness of the rules governing the game, but mostly on "how well participants translate the imperfect fit between contextual norms of the simulation and the reality it is based on" (Hoffman 2006:172).

Players call that reality "real life." Most games are coordinated by a facilitator who teaches the game, answers questions, and, most important, provides meaningful translations between the game and real life. For example, consider a situation in which a player had the chance to purchase stock at one dollar a share and then someone picks a card offering forty dollars a share to whoever owns the stock. This is the most profitable deal in the whole game, and it will probably enable the lucky stockholder to leave the rat race (if she bought a substantial amount of stock beforehand). Multiplying $3,000 into $120,000 in a few rounds seems a bit unrealistic. However, usually "translators" pose examples of companies like Google or Microsoft, or of angel investors who invest early on in a company startup, to justify such profit. This sort of "real life" is not the life of the average Cashflow player. Instead, "real life" is a constructed notion of a world with multiple financial opportunities available. The idea is that opportunities exist, and only one's fear or lack of financial intelligence can be blamed for not seeing them. The construction of this world of limitless opportunities is a collective effort, since all players contribute in matching the game to reality, but in practice, translators have a more definitive role in shaping the collective definition of reality. Translators provide imaginary access to the rationality of a world of financial opportunities, regardless of their actual "real lives." Of course, each facilitator may have more or less experience in business and finance, but what matters is the success of his or her performance as translator.[11]

Because of these ongoing efforts to connect the Cashflow game with real-ity, I observed several instances of rules being bent, ignored, or rewritten. In New York, where I played for the first time, partnering for deals is common practice. As mentioned earlier, the deal cards usually state that if a player does not want to use the opportunity (perhaps because he does not have enough capital), he can sell it to another player or auction it off among interested players. If the player chooses to sell the card, he ends up with some additional cash for future deals (instead of investing in a business that would generate incoming cash flow). In addition, players can take opportunities by partner-ing with others, usually dividing investments and returns equally, although sometimes that distribution may be subject to negotiation between the play-ers. On one occasion, I became part of a joint investment with almost every player on the board. When I played for the first time in Argentina, however, no one on my board even considered partnering. At the next game, I looked for a business partner when I needed one. In the post-session, I was asked to explain to the rest of the tables what I had done, and an organizer praised me for innovating. I later read the actual rules and found that partnering is for-bidden, which incidentally makes the game more competitive and less coop-erative. Some players told me that it did not make sense to ban such behavior because this would be a good business practice in real life when a good op-portunity is too large for one investor alone. The idea of *practicing* the game is generally taken from a free-market approach to rules: regulations should not strangle business creativity.

Another innovation that I only recognized as such after a while was that, in New York, most games are played with two dice. Thus, players go over "pay-check" more often, putting money in their pockets faster and thus speeding up the game. In Argentina, games were much longer because only one die was used. When I asked Ramiro, a game facilitator, why they did not add a die to make it faster, he said that such innovation places the game farther from reality, making it seem too easy to get out of the rat race. He did not invoke the rules, just the contrast with "real life."[12]

The first time I played in one of the games organized by Financial Freedom Argentina, I noticed a card that was new to me. It said, "You join a network marketing company." I was surprised because this card had never come up in New York games. It resembled very closely the rest of the cards, but there was a slight difference in how it was printed. When I told Alejandro, a member of the group that was in charge of my table, that the American game did not have that card, he was not surprised. "We added that card," he said. Nineteen-year-old Nicolás, excited that a card matching his own activity in "real life" had come up, completed Alejandro's sentence, " . . . in order to fit reality better. I have one of these businesses!" Alejandro added, "If you read Kiyosaki's new writings that haven't reached Argentina yet, he pays a lot of attention to the network business. So the game is somewhat outdated." Alejandro was referring to *Rich Dad's The Business School* (Kiyosaki 2005a), a book that at the time was not published in Spanish and in which Kiyosaki recommends that readers join multilevel marketing companies (like Herbalife, Amway, Mary Kay, and others). As I describe in-depth in the next chapter, Financial Freedom Argentina members are also part of a network marketing company (which they usually invite participants to join), so they adjusted the game to reflect the recent book, but also their own activities and interests. Later, Alejandro told me that his group was going even further than adding cards by developing an entirely new game to fit the Argentine context. Darío, an active member of an online forum that frequently organizes small gatherings, went as far as developing a new set of Latin cards, inspired by actual examples from players in Argentina, that seeks to adapt Cashflow to the conditions of Latin America.

Another rule that often goes ignored is one that prevents players from borrowing money from each other. All players are allowed to borrow money from a virtual bank, paying 10 percent interest monthly (an operation that further complicates the financial statement and the subsequent calculations). However, on many occasions, this limitation is ignored and players offer loans to each other. Sometimes, creative loans are offered, such as variable-rate loans with a low rate for a number of turns and a higher rate thereafter. The practice of lending is extended to players already out of the rat race who have, as I mentioned earlier, artificially multiplied their income by one hundred. The flow of money from the fast track to the rat race, which is not allowed according to the rulebook, nonetheless happens sometimes during games, generating many sorts of financial arrangements and promises of loan repayment when the player still in the rat race finally makes it out.

Cashflow players see their development as economic actors as an active pursuit. While play is usually considered a space where reality is suspended, in Cashflow, an imagined real life is always in the background and contrasted with game play. That connection with an imagined future overpowers the structure and rules of the game, and players actively engage in their own innovation.

·   ·   ·

Santiago's words, which I touched on earlier in this chapter, perhaps best summarize a distant observer's view of adults playing board games and the difficulty inherent in taking them seriously: "My friends are all grown-ups, married. 'Look, I have the little rat game, you have the black rat, I have the red, he has the orange, the little cheese. . . . ' They would think I'm insane." Santiago is an avid player, yet he empathizes with the casual observer who might see the game as a waste of time or as a meaningless regression to childhood. Cashflow, however, is both "just a game" and "more than a game." The fact that there is neither real money nor real financial risk involved makes it a farce, a simulation without consequences outside a colorful board. Yet for players it is a tool used for transforming the self, a practice that serves as a mirror placed before one's financial self in order to reveal the work needed to be successful.

Terry, a New York cab driver with whom I played Cashflow a few times, kept repeating to himself throughout his first game, "I need to play this a lot, man, every day." Day after day, thousands of financial best-seller readers perceive the transformation of their economic performance as a profound, transcendental experience. They read books, look for online resources, attend workshops and seminars, and play board games. By playing Cashflow, people change their definitions of mobility and financial success, acquire calculative tools that adjust to those definitions, and attempt to change themselves. Players of Cashflow may joke and have fun during the games, but it is nevertheless serious business.

Cashflow illustrates a number of dimensions that act concertedly to shape the type of subject that financial self-help gurus advocate for in their books and DVDs. These three processes—reconfiguring goals, acquiring new calculative tools for accounting, and working on the self—operate together to produce a neoliberal subject adjusted to financial capitalism. Cashflow also shows the collective dimension of financial self-help. It is technically possible to play the computer version of Cashflow alone. However, Cashflow is a powerful collective activity, in which fans meet each other, learn from each other, energize each other, and sometimes end up doing business with each other. The collective logic of the world of financial self-help is what I now turn to.

Creating a World of Abundance

4

TO A GREAT EXTENT, financial self-help is an *individualist* enterprise, since the burden of financial success is entirely on the individual. However, it is not an *individual* enterprise. Financial self-help is a collective endeavor—a set of collective practices, techniques, social theories, and beliefs through which people engage with others (others they know, others they do not know, and others they get to know). Whether driven by a desire of getting motivated, meeting like-minded people, or receiving training, or done simply for the more mundane goal of being exposed to potential partners and business opportunities, engaging with others is a strong maxim of financial self-help. As illustrated by David's assertion in Chapter 2 that one's income will likely be an average of those of the six closest people in one's life, books and other motivational materials often urge readers and attendees to expand their social environment so that it is more encouraging of their newly discovered project of achieving financial freedom. Participants I interviewed often complained that people in their more immediate social circle were too comfortable with the idea of working for their money. Ruth's story is a telling example. I first met her at a Cashflow game held at a coffee shop in Buenos Aires, and I interviewed her a few weeks later. At the time, Ruth worked in the IT area of a large supermarket chain, where a workmate had loaned her the book *Rich Dad, Poor Dad* two years earlier. Looking for business opportunities, she later enrolled in an online forum and started buying brand-name clothing from another forum member, which she would sell to other contacts in the retail business. Although this budding business was a major part of her life, Ruth admitted that she only talked about her financial projects with a few select friends because "some of them don't understand. They are people with the mindset that Kiyosaki describes . . . of having a position, a job, in a good company and that's it." She added, "Few people I know are on the same wavelength, of looking for opportunities, or investing and generating extra income. Most are . . . at least the people I know, are just working." Participants such as Ruth engage in activities in order to meet others who will not be discouraging of their new endeavors and who may also become part of their "team." In the same Cashflow game meeting in which I met Ruth, organizer Rolo alerted players that in addition to the benefit of playing and learning, they might happen to find the "right fit": a person that does or has exactly what they are missing in order to make a business or investment project blossom and thrive. This chapter analyzes the logic by which participants engage with each other, as well as with leaders, organizers, and book authors. I argue that a conflation of economic interest and disinterest governs this logic.

We often think of self-interest and generosity as two contradictory principles for action. Someone may behave *either* with self-interest *or* with disinterest in economic gain, but not with both simultaneously. Recognizing the presence of self-interest in a given behavior or attitude signifies, at the same time, a lack of generosity. There is no simpler way to refute someone's altruism than by mentioning their ulterior motivation of self-interest. We tend to believe that generosity is authentic only if it appears in pure form, uncontaminated by self-interest. In the financial self-help world, however, interest and disinterest cohabitate quite peacefully. In fact, participants generally do not expect others to behave solely according to one or the other, but rather to employ a combination of both in their daily lives. The main argument of this chapter is that financial self-help is neither a world composed of individuals acting solely with self-interest in mind (as we often think of actors in markets), nor a world in which self-interest is rejected outright (as we often think of antimarket worlds such as charity or the arts). The key to understanding the moral order of financial self-help is in the notion of "a world of abundance."

I adopted this phrase from Steve, the organizer of the New York group that met monthly to assist and motivate members, and I later realized that the term eloquently captured the logic underlying much of the moral order of financial self-help. Steve consistently encouraged people in his group to freely share ideas, support, and time, starting with his own. In my informal conversations with other group members after each meeting, participants often praised Steve for sharing so much of his business knowledge, much of which he acquired in seminars costing thousands of dollars, and which he now made available for free. In the meetings, he often repeated a motto when encouraging people to help one another: "Live in a world of abundance, not in a world of scarcity." The logic of this recommendation was to assume not that we live in a zero-sum world, but that everyone lives in a world in which there is plenty for everyone to be rich. According to Steve, if one lives in a world of abundance, one is already a rich person: opportunities, ideas, and promising opportunities will flow your way. However, if one relies only on self-interest, one is sentenced to social worlds of people with the same attitude, that is, the poor. People with a poor mindset, this rationale suggests, let their fears of insecurity and scarcity govern their minds. Generosity is not seen as contradictory with financial gain and self-interest; rather, it is embedded in the meaning of being a financially successful person. The idea is that by reshaping themselves to "think like the rich," practitioners can frame giving as an integral part of becoming a financially successful person, instead of as a hindrance to their financial progress.

In the next section, I employ the work of Pierre Bourdieu and of Viviana Zelizer to explain the theoretical argument of this chapter: that in financial self-help, the vision of a utopian world of abundance inhabited by the rich (that everyone should strive to inhabit) makes people blur the contradictions between interest and disinterest. In the section that follows, I then illustrate this argument by analyzing what authors and users of financial self-help say about the fact that people (gurus in particular) make a profit by helping others to become rich. Finally, I analyze the case of a network marketing company that was entangled with one of the groups with which I did fieldwork in Argentina. This organizational form offered a glimpse of the utopia of abundance of financial self-help.

Interested and Disinterested Action

One of Pierre Bourdieu's greatest contributions to economic and cultural sociology was to demystify the idea of *disinterest* that appears to govern certain fields in which economic interest is not the main logic. The artistic and literary worlds, for example, reward disinterest in economic gains. The most respected artist is the one that does not care for economic success, and engages in art only for art's sake. For Bourdieu (1998:110), in those worlds, "commercial success may even be a condemnation" raising suspicion that the artist is trying to please audiences instead of committing to authentic artistic creation. The same can be said, for example, of scientists, educators, or social workers—members of fields in which economic gain cannot be stated legitimately as the main goal. These fields thrive on the collective misrecognition that people do not act with the intention of obtaining benefits. However, individuals do obtain objective benefits from their disinterested behavior. For Bourdieu, the divorce between this objective reality and the subjective (individual and collective) understanding of that reality is crucial. For example,

> The religious enterprise is an enterprise with an economic dimension which cannot admit to so being and which functions with a sort of permanent negation of its economic dimension: I undertake an economic act, but I do not want to know it; I do it in such a way that I can tell myself and others that it is not an economic act—and I can be credible to others only if I believe it myself. (Bourdieu 1998:115)

This misrecognition is what makes fields not based on purely economic gain such as the arts, volunteer work, or religious organizations possible. As can be seen in the quote, Bourdieu is careful in excluding pure cynicism from his account. It is not that people know the truth but do not say it. Actors in fields organized around disinterest have acquired dispositions that make it impossible for them to recognize the economic returns of their actions.

The world of markets and business, on the other hand, seems much simpler for Bourdieu. Because the economic field is explicitly based on an interest in financial gain, actors in this realm need not undergo this complex and arduous work of repressing interest in economic gains. In this sense, the economic field seems more transparent than any other field. For Bourdieu, the economic field needs no misrecognition:

> The emergence of the economic field marks the appearance of a universe in which economic agents can admit to themselves and admit publicly that they have interests and can tear themselves away from collective misrecognition; a universe in which they not only can do business but can also admit to themselves that they are there to do business, that is, to conduct themselves in a self-interested manner, to calculate, to make a profit, accumulate and exploit. (Bourdieu 1998:105–6)

Thus, the economic field is radically different from other fields (and especially from what he calls "anti-economic universes" such as art and religion).

It is the only one in which self-interest can be openly admitted by the actors, without regrets, without misrecognition, without the extensive collective work of covering it up. For example, in 2011, Alessio Rastani, an American trader interviewed live on the BBC TV channel, stunned the show's anchors when he confessed he did not care much about the economic measures the Eurozone was taking to contain the financial crisis. Rastani said,

> Personally, it doesn't matter. I'm a trader, I don't really care about that kind of stuff. If I see an opportunity to make money, I go with that. So, for most traders, we don't really care that much how they're gonna fix the economy, how they're gonna fix the whole situation. Our job is to make money from it. (BBC News 2011)

Rastani then confessed that he dreamed every night of another recession in Europe, because a recession would bring new opportunities to make money for those prepared to do so. Rastani's confession embodies the logic by which the economic field works, in which agents can explicitly admit that their actions are governed by self-interest. Rastani's sin was perhaps sharing that admission with people who did not participate in his world.

Bourdieu's distinctions between economic and anti-economic universes may be useful in understanding the difference between, for example, the world of investment banking, in which actors participate to make money (and no one need deny that fact) and the worlds of art or care work, in which actors usually show how little they care about their economic self-interest. He clearly separates the economic field from other fields. But as sociologist Viviana Zelizer (2005) suggests, the long-standing intention of many scholars to clearly separate the economic from the non-economic, money from intimacy, and self-interest from solidarity, does not reflect how those distinctions often work in reality. Here, she summarizes this view as "separate spheres" or "hostile worlds":

> A sharp divide exists between intimate social relations and economic transactions. On one side, we discover a sphere of sentiment and solidarity; on the other a sphere of calculation and efficiency. Left to itself, goes the doctrine, each works more or less automatically and well. But the two spheres remain hostile to each other. Contact between them produces moral contamination. (Zelizer 2005:22)

The world of financial self-help defies these sharp distinctions. The model Zelizer calls "hostile worlds" and "separate spheres" does not help explain how financial self-help fans behave with one another. Two principles that we often consider to be mutually exclusive (economic interest and disinterest) actually coexist harmoniously. For Zelizer, although a "hostile worlds" type of analysis is misleading, people often invoke distinctions between interest and solidarity or between money and social relationship as a way of establishing or maintaining boundaries (2005:28).[1] However, financial self-help participants explicitly reject the hostile worlds model, refusing to see economic self-interest and disinterest as opposed and incompatible.

Financial self-help is a world in which the idea of pure economic disinterest (like in the arts or philanthropy) is deemed suspicious. It would not be logical or expected for a person to display constant altruism on the quest for financial freedom; after all, people do want to make money. However, that does not mean that financial self-help is a world of pure self-interest—what Zelizer would call a "nothing-but" account, according to which only one principle of action is present. In financial self-help there is a constant negotiation of interest and disinterest. Financial self-help is a conceptual encounter between investment banking and volunteer work. The selfish ideal of just making money would be unacceptable, while the altruistic ideal of just helping others would not be believable. In many cases, financial self-help followers understand the act of helping others and making money out of it as not contradictory but complementary goals.

The Cashflow game reflects this conflation. One of the squares on which one can land in a Cashflow game is "charity." When a rat game piece lands on the "charity" square, players have the option of donating 10 percent of their total income to charity. At first, I was surprised by the inclusion of charity in the game. "If Cashflow is a tool to learn how to think in order to become financially successful," I wondered, "then what is this square doing on the board?" Giving to charity would reduce a player's capital and hence put him or her farther from the goal of achieving financial freedom. What is the act of giving to others doing in a game in which the ultimate goal is to accumulate incoming cash flow?

But this altruistic action comes with its perks. For the next three turns, the player who donates to charity has the option of using an additional die. This will help the player go faster, passing over more "paycheck" squares, thereby increasing her capital at a faster pace. One would normally expect charity to be motivated by generosity, and in fact during Cashflow games, players generally mention that this should be the main reason for giving to charity. But according to the rules of the game, players benefit from giving to charity. They do not obtain a direct financial benefit from it—in other words, they do not simply receive money for giving money. The benefit they obtain is not immediate (it applies throughout the next three turns), or direct (charity will increase one's speed on the board, which indirectly will earn one more paychecks), and it is not completely guaranteed (you may always roll low dice numbers in those turns, effectively suppressing the benefit). Although the returns for giving disinterestedly are distanced in time from the act of giving (Bourdieu 1990:105), they are by no means erased or misrecognized: players know that giving to charity will eventually bring tangible financial benefits. It is not a secret: this fact is clearly written and visible on the "charity" square on the game board.

Players offer two explanations for why one benefits from giving to charity. One is more mystical and the other is more instrumental. The first is based on a maxim central to financial self-help: you should give if you want to receive. The mystical notion that financial outcomes are related to individual actions in some mysterious way is popular not only in financial self-help but also in other forms of self-help, religion, and everyday life (the saying "give and ye shall receive" is used often in everyday parlance, for example). The book and DVD *The Secret*, published globally in 2006, popularized the notion of the "law of attraction," according to which the visualization of wishes has much to do with their realization in the future (Byrne 2006; Ehrenreich 2009:59–73; *The Secret* 2006; see also McGee 2007). According to the law of attraction, people attract positive outcomes by positive thinking. By giving to charity, players may get something back in the future. Earning something in return one day is not a specific and observable effect of the giving, but because of karma.

This belief in the law of attraction is closely related to the notion of a "world of abundance." When players are short of funds, they may be tempted to pass on the offer of giving to charity and preserve their savings instead. But that would mean living in a world of scarcity. No weak financial position justifies the decision to not donate to charity. If one lacks the mindset to donate, that means that one's mindset is still that of the poor. The game encourages people to adopt the mindset of the rich, so most players choose to donate to charity when they pass these squares on the board.

The second explanation is slightly more mundane and instrumental. In one of my early games in New York, there were, as usual, a number of new players. When someone landed on the charity square, several observers standing around the board (who arrived too late, when there was no more room to play) tried to explain what options the player had. Jim, who seemed to have a lot of experience in the game, and who was eager to translate it into "real life," told the new players, "When you give charity you make relationships, so you get a return on your new relationships; that's why you get two dice." Giving to charity (or helping people in general) means an increased involvement in one's community. By knowing new people, one will expand and enhance one's network, which will eventually lead to more business opportunities. This explains why acting on an attitude of disinterest in personal wealth and giving to charity eventually brings back benefits.

Charity is a good example of the interplay between interest and disinterest. While Bourdieu would expect the objective gains of generosity to be denied and repressed in the act of donation, in this case they are accounted for and made explicit. That does not mean, however, that financial gain should be the only reason for donating: in the world of financial self-help, one can care about others and make money off of that caring without these being contradictory goals. In fact, the rationale of giving in order to receive is quite useful for social interactions. People can always assume that others helping them may be following the maxim, which makes acts of generosity seem less suspicious.

Ultimately, in financial self-help circles, showing good moral character means thinking and behaving like the rich, which involves seeing the world as one of enjoyment of money and endless possibilities. Those who do not understand and incorporate this mindset into their lives are poor, not just financially but in spirit, because their mental picture of the world is poor. Financial help gurus claim that the poor do not understand that because there is enough for everyone, interest and disinterest are complementary rather than contradictory attitudes. In her advice books to women, Suze Orman also emphasizes how reconciling with money—seeing it as an entity that helps oneself, and that enables instead of limits oneself—will produce the greater good for everyone. For Orman, if we frame the world in terms of abundance, money will not be the divisive element that we usually consider it to be. Echoing Viviana Zelizer's analysis of money as a vehicle for meaningful social relationships, Orman sees money as a means to bring everyone's interests together. She urges women to be self-interested as a way of helping those around them: "When you change your behavior with your money, it enhances those that you love, it doesn't take away from them. You can just see that by giving more to yourself (financially speaking) you can give more to everybody else" (Orman 2007b). Caring about oneself and caring about others are the same thing. The utopia of a world of abundance, in which our possibilities are unlimited because there is enough for everyone who tries hard enough, dilutes the contradiction between interest and disinterest.

Is Financial Self-Help Just a Gimmick?

Most people I meet who do not participate in the financial self-help world react to my mention of it with a degree of suspicion. Many nonreaders of financial self-help are usually aware of its existence, and even if the majority of people likely haven't heard about the Cashflow board game, many have seen popular books conspicuously displayed in airport bookstores, seen their titles in best-seller rankings, watched some commentary on the media, or perhaps have a friend who was at some point enthused about the ideas in a best-selling book. But most outsiders keep a skeptical distance from it. That distance is frequently expressed in a simple question: "Isn't it just a way for the authors to get rich?"

Behind the honest questioning of an often shady industry, outsiders often automatically consider the financial self-help world a giant deception. But although fans of the genre obviously do not consider financial self-help a giant scam, most are not as naive about it as outsiders may think. Although the dangers of deception are present in the financial self-help world, followers manage these hazards in a very different way from outsiders. For example, the fact that authors make millions by selling books and conducting workshops may be reason enough for outsiders to discredit this world. Insiders, however, see this fact in a different light, reframing it either as trivial or even positive.

The fact that Kiyosaki has a hugely profitable business at his fans' expense is not taboo. In the Rich Dad online forum in Argentina—a forum inspired by Kiyosaki's ideas and created by his fans—people openly discuss the ethics of his industry. When I interviewed Luis, the creator and main administrator of the forum, he said the following about a forum section on Kiyosaki's validity and ethics:

> Luis: I created a section in the forum called "Kiyosaki: Messiah or devil?" It is a section for the people, because even when faced with the book, there are people who say that Kiyosaki is a swindler.
>
> Daniel: Really?
>
> Luis: Well, not himself, but the book. . . . [Imitating other people:] "Everything is a lie, he's a swindler, and if he defrauded us on this, who knows . . . [what else]?" A lot of things! Well, it's logical, people get passionate. Something Kiyosaki achieved was to make people passionate, both in favor and against. That's not up for discussion. In fact, he wrote books before that utterly failed. If you read his acknowledgments in *Rich Dad, Poor Dad*, you have two pages of people who he thanks. All professionals!

Marketing, sales, consulting, everything. Obviously, everything he says doesn't come out of his head 100 percent. It comes out of people that he put together. That's excellent! I'm not criticizing him.

Daniel: Are there people who get disappointed by this?

Luis: Because the story of the rich dad is a lie [referring to the fact that Kiyo-saki didn't actually have a rich dad figure in his life]. So people say, "He made a fortune selling the book to us. Thanks to us!" But other people wonder, "Does it matter? He wrote a book, and created a story to transmit you a message. That message, does it help you? Can you apply it in your life? That's the only important part. The rest is just packaging so that you buy it and to reach people. It's a business. Does the rest matter?"

This excerpt from my interview with Luis encapsulates the problem I assess in this chapter: financial self-help, in addition to providing advice to people on how to think in order to achieve financial success and financial freedom, is it-self a mechanism for financial enrichment. Financial self-help is a multimillion dollar industry in the United States and worldwide (Olen 2013). Many people, and especially the gurus themselves, obviously benefit from this. Yet most fans do not see this as a reason to feel cheated. Several discourses and practices neutralize the idea that "helping others" and making money as a result are essentially contradictory. In countless instances, participants in the financial self-help world negotiate the relation between interested action and disinter-ested action. While people like to separate these principles of action, this world forces users into a more nuanced view.

Luis created the section in the forum in response to several member-initiated threads critical of Kiyosaki. He recognized that Kiyosaki's books helped him at the beginning, but after the first book were increasingly repetitive, offering little additional wisdom. A forum member accused Kiyosaki of caring too much about selling products (interest) instead of providing good material for his read-ers to advance financially (disinterest). When the debate heated up, Luis told me that he initially thought of deleting the anti-Kiyosaki posts, but that he realized that there was great value in this critical discussion. Luis decided to only censor overly aggressive messages, and posted this message in the forum:

Every debate that is useful to learn Kiyosaki's philosophies better, or to analyze how to apply them to local realities, will be welcome. We can healthily debate our points of view, but I won't accept messages like: "Kiyosaki thief," "All of Kiyosaki's books are the same," "Kiyosaki doesn't explain anything concrete,"

"All I achieved by buying his books was to make him rich." All of these statements are losers' statements, poor people's statements. We have to learn to think like rich people, expand our concepts.

In spite of Luis's warnings, the discussion continued with open hostility, gathering hundreds of replies. A few users complained that Kiyosaki was just rewriting and rebranding some of the classic financial self-help books. For those users, the enterprise was nothing more than a marketing scheme designed to make Kiyosaki, not the readers, a millionaire:

> Kiyosaki became too ambitious, after the first two books, the rest look like thick brochures or catalogues of what he is selling. But it seems that his only income is from the little books and the board games, because he repeats, repeats, repeats, repeats, almost to the point of brainwashing the person until they say, "The books of the little Japanese man are the best in financial education; I'll have to buy all his books, board games, and all the other trinkets. That's the only way I'll leave the rat race."

This criticism, which may not be unfamiliar to those outside of self-help, is repeated throughout the forum in several ways. However, most fans who participate in the forum or those who I met in my fieldwork do not seem bothered by Kiyosaki's repetitions or by the fact that the *Rich Dad, Poor Dad* story may be fictitious. There is no dispute of the fact that Kiyosaki makes good money through his product sales. While he asserted several times publicly that these sales are actually a small part of his income, and most of his wealth comes from other investments, the suspicion that this is false and most of his financial success is the result of his financial self-help business is quite irrelevant for enthusiasts. The forum member suggested that Kiyosaki "brainwashes" readers into buying more material, yet this "brainwashing" can also be interpreted by readers as positive, and even desirable. While we usually understand brainwashing as an uncontrolled intervention on the will from the outside, many readers reinterpret brainwashing as important work on a poor, uninformed self that needs reinventing. After all, they are indeed trying to change their mindsets. Joaquín (age twenty-one) posted to the online forum, and explained that they have voluntarily subjected to this brainwashing:

> Kiyosaki obviously has his business, and he's going to squeeze it until the last drop. Anyway, that's his problem, not mine. The issue here is that those books shook the minds of many. Today, if it wasn't for him, this forum wouldn't ex-

ist or it would have a different name and I wouldn't be here. It's true that the books seem like a brainwash, but the question is: What's wrong with a brainwash? Today I face situations in which my "employee side" and "self-employed side" clash with the "business owner" and "investor" sides. The idea is to start changing that mentality, perhaps it's a brainwash, but the truth is that by playing Cashflow, reading the books, looking at the website, etc. my mind changed a lot. It annoys me to read and reread the same concepts over and over, but honestly, in the case of Kiyosaki, that repetition recorded concepts and ideas in my head that I would have forgotten if I had read them once only.

Far from being regarded as a dubious technique for selling more books, repetition is reinterpreted by fans like Joaquín as a technique to work on the self. If many books say slightly different things but essentially reproduce the same idea, he posits that it is because that idea does not hold easily. Similarly to sports training, repetition plays the role of making ideas and actions embodied and unconscious (Wacquant 2003). Work on the self is based on repetitive exercise, and reading similar ideas in different books or playing the same game over and over is seen as a useful practice. The notion that one can voluntarily subject oneself to repetition and brainwashing as part of the path to financial freedom also restores the idea of individual autonomy. While fans never cease to be consumers who add money to the guru's account, they frame their engagement as a free and willful subjection. In another comment, a forum member reinforces that the proper approach is not to resist but to fully subject oneself to the "brainwashing," emphasizing the autonomy of the individual in that decision. This member offers four reasons as to why this brainwashing is welcome:

1. Kiyosaki doesn't defraud anyone. Whoever wants to buy his books and games, buys them. Whoever doesn't want to, doesn't.

2. He NEVER says that his books will make you rich. He says MULTIPLE TIMES, in ALL HIS BOOKS, that the important thing is FINANCIAL EDUCATION, and that includes finances, accounting, investment, sales, leadership, etc. etc. He's quite clear, I don't know why people doubt.

3. He clearly says that he doesn't teach anything new, that these are MILLENNIAL SECRETS to become rich. He recommends reading *Think and Grow Rich* and *The Richest Man in Babylon*.[2]

4. For those who say that he's repetitive, actually he is. That's the most effective way to record it in your head, so that your brainwash is complete and goes deeply. WE HAVE TO WASH OUR BRAIN, and remove all the fears

of investing and progressing. I want to read his 10 books in Spanish once again, in spite of them being repetitive. Of course, without neglecting my new readings, the financial education that will allow me to create businesses.

Although this user defends Kiyosaki from misrepresentations, the meta-discussion on the ethics of self-help is sometimes seen as a waste of time. Concentrating on the authors' shortcomings or their ethicality is viewed by some fans as diverting attention from the real goal of financial self-help, which is to transform oneself to achieve financial freedom. Another commenter intervened in the discussion suggesting members stop looking elsewhere to explain their failures:

I think that many people should do some reflection, because it's very easy to blame an author or a neighbor for your failures and your poor life, instead of realizing that the only one to blame is yourself. It's time to mature and be responsible for your own life, and stop blaming others and call them liars and cheaters.

In other words, a core idea of financial self-help, that individuals have to become responsible for themselves, is used to interpret critiques of financial advice authors. Another popular argument that I frequently encountered was that the fact that Kiyosaki (or any other guru) has managed to produce such a successful enterprise actually shows how (financially) intelligent he is:

If it's true what they say, that this guy became rich with the books he wrote, then he's the best!!! It means he found a business that gave him returns for 10,000% for copyright sales. Is it or is it not an excellent business?!!

In this argument, readers identify with and admire the guru. In the art world, or other fields governed by a logic of disinterest, an admired artist who becomes wealthy by selling products to their fans may pose a conundrum, in that the purpose of making money appears to be more important than producing authentic art. Much of the success of the artist lies in authenticity and disinterest, and economic success often puts that in question (Bourdieu 1983:320–21, 1998:110). But in financial self-help the success of the producer actually confirms how well-suited he or she is for the job. This line of reasoning suggests that it is not problematic for someone to make money from their followers, but in fact, this actually shows how consistent that person is. Financial self-help gurus perform the successful financial self that they promote—in essence, they practice what they preach. Kiyosaki had an idea and created a successful business with it that provides him with incoming cash flow via sales, royalties, franchises, and so on. Participants of financial self-help recognize that economic self-interest is at the core of this world, and the interested actions of others may very well be used as instructive examples. In the following comments, three different forum members dismiss the idea that Kiyosaki's wealth from his book sales somehow diminishes him morally. Quite the contrary, his wealth is proof of his sagacity and serves as an example to emulate:

> Yes, you are right, but why didn't you do it? The guy made money like this, he had an idea, he put it in practice and he did well. That's undeniable. You are in this forum, that's also undeniable, and you're not here by chance. So Kiyosaki could be as much a devil as you want to portray, but the guy learned to make a business, and thanks to him we are all gathered here. So I don't think this discussion makes much sense. In a book I read: "What is the truth? The truth is what works for us."

> First of all, Kiyosaki created an excellent business, which is surely coherent with his philosophy.

> Kiyosaki for better or worse made his enterprise with his books. If it was that easy, why don't we do it ourselves? Many people see the negative side of something, but they don't know the work that he had to do to make his works bestsellers. Whoever says that it's a fraud, make a series of books equally successful and you will win my admiration. Meanwhile I keep waiting. . . .

Evident in these discussion posts is the perspective that people do not need to misrecognize or repress self-interest. Financial self-help fans transform economic self-interest into a positive and noteworthy feature that can also have positive effects on others. As the remarks by forum creator Luis demonstrate, the fact that Kiyosaki compiled a team to develop a successful financial self-help business is not seen as reason to suspect his authenticity or sincerity, but rather as a sign of his business ability. Financial self-help authors are actually showing how financial freedom is done. While some practitioners merely disregard or minimize suspicions that would turn an outsider off, others openly praise the fact that authors make lots of money selling books. For them, it confirms that an entrepreneurial attitude will lead one to success. It proves that success is attainable by anyone who takes action and thinks properly, and it shows that authors walk their own talk. Another forum user posted approvingly,

> Kiyosaki does his business (and pretty well, by the way) writing books, giving conferences, and selling games. . . . Rather than criticizing him, we should be

admiring the guy. He makes his dollars (quite a lot) identifying a need and satisfying it (the rule of any profitable business).

Kiyosaki's financial success, to this user, is a sign of his business acumen
satisfying a market demand and another reason to follow his suggestions. Another comment also reflects this point, while also dissociating the author's own
intentions from the text themselves. Sharing ideas about obtaining financial
freedom and making money off of it are not seen as contradictory. For this
reader, even if Kiyosaki's honesty is questioned, he provides "lies that work":

> Mr. Kiyosaki discovered a way of obtaining financial freedom and he wants to
> share it, in exchange for some money. It's another way he found of expanding his
> income. Even if he called a world press conference and said, "I have been scam-
> ming the world and the gullible who bought my books; it's all a lie, stop looking
> for an easy way out, get a good job and save for your retirement, your house is
> your main asset and I'm a liar," that doesn't mean anything. If what he wrote in
> his books are lies, they are lies that work. And I also take my hat off to him for the
> way in which he compiled ideas from other authors and put them in an easy way
> in the books. Did he make his fortune selling books? CONGRATULATIONS.

The bluntness of the acceptance that financial self-help is a business in itself makes authors (and everybody involved) more credible. The fact that the
Rich Dad books and other products and services are a significant source of
Robert Kiyosaki's fortune is not regarded as a secret that has to be hidden from
the public, but rather as confirmation of his shrewdness and success. According to a forum member, "they [Robert Kiyosaki and coauthor Sharon Lechter]
are carrying their mission of elevating the financial knowledge of humankind.
And they receive money for that." A goal as altruistic and universal as elevating
the financial knowledge of humankind is not contradictory with the goal of
making money. The author himself is not shy about the profitable character
of his enterprise. In a short presentation he gave during a seminar to promote a
coaching program to succeed as a book author, Kiyosaki said,

> The message is: I'm not an author, I'm an entrepreneur. I build businesses be-
> hind books. I build businesses behind games. I am a real estate [investor]. I am
> what I say I am in that book. . . . I made the game $200, and I wrote a book to
> sell the game, and to this day it's still going. I've been six years in the *New York
> Times* best-selling list, only two other books have done that. And that's because
> I'm not an author—I'm a business man, I'm an entrepreneur. Am I clear on that?

There is a big difference in that. I'm a best-selling author, not a best-writing author. . . . When I released the book I had studied sales and marketing, psychology, why people buy, marketing, you know, things like this, what does my cus-
tomer really want [sic]. I'm not an author. And the problem with most authors
is that they are really boring, they write boring books. (Harrison and Bradley
Communications Corp. 2006)

Robert Kiyosaki often uses his own Rich Dad business as an example of
successful entrepreneurship and business creation, regardless of the fact that a
generous portion of his income comes from his own readers and consumers.
He illustrates such notions as passive income, cash flow, business systems, or
franchises explicitly using his own success selling the very DVD that the consumer is watching. However, while as in the previous passage he often emphasizes his being a businessman and a salesman, in other instances he conveys the
notion that it is all about helping others. In a book Kiyosaki coauthored with
Donald Trump, suggestively called *Why We Want You to Be Rich*, he says,

In Teach To Be Rich, a product I created to assist our CASHFLOW Clubs in
teaching others to be rich, I talk about how some people do not want to give
people fish or teach others to fish . . . instead they sell people fish. Many of these
people are stockbrokers, real estate brokers, financial planners, bankers and insurance agents. They are in the business of selling . . . not necessarily teaching
or giving. When you put the two words, *sell* and *fish* together, you get the word
selfish. And even though most people in the business may not be selfish, enough
are to make the word ring true. I use it here to emphasize the importance of
staying on your guard to be aware of the differences between those who give—
the teachers—and those who sell. (Trump and Kiyosaki 2006:49)

In this passage, Kiyosaki excludes a number of activities from the logic of
the world of financial self-help. Those who are *only* salespersons, such as brokers or insurance agents, are interested in selling instead of helping others. This
statement comes from the same guru that, as I discussed earlier, has little problem recognizing that his books are a business and being a best-selling (not best-
writing) author is his main goal. The notion of a world of abundance reconciles
this apparent contradiction. In the preface to the book, Sharon Lechter, who
collaborated with Kiyosaki on several of his books, says,

Both men [Trump and Kiyosaki] are teachers, not because they need more
money. They are both teachers because they are concerned about the fate of you

and your family, this nation and the world. Rich people who want to make a difference typically give money to causes they believe in. But Donald and Robert are giving of both their time as well as their money. . . . Instead of just writing checks to help the poor and the middle class, Donald and Robert are teaching them to fish. In addition, a portion of every book sale will be donated to other organizations that also teach financial literacy. (Trump and Kiyosaki 2006:4)

In the two previous passages, the authors emphasize their own disinterest in further financial gain. They suggest that only because *they do not need more money* can they act on their concern for others in a way that other people cannot. Because they live in a world of abundance, Trump and Kiyosaki are in a position in which they can be perceived as generous and self-interested at the same time. This merging of interest and disinterest appears not only in how Kiyosaki presents himself and in how his fans judge him—this logic of interest and disinterest is also embedded in one of the most frequent activities many fans undertake: multilevel marketing. On one level, this practice offers fans an economic activity they can pursue as a way of "taking action" in real life. But more important, multilevel marketing is an economic activity structured so that participants can see interest and disinterest as complementary rather than competing.

Multilevel Marketing and Financial Self-Help

After reading books, attending seminars, or playing Cashflow, financial self-help enthusiasts are confronted with what to do in "real life" to pursue financial freedom. Followers learn that they have to reframe their goals, work on changing their mindsets, educate themselves financially, and learn to recognize opportunities and jump on them, but the most popular books do not provide a definitive answer as to exactly where to jump, except for the somewhat vague suggestions to benefit from real estate, the stock market, or business systems. For example, a workshop participant told me in a brief conversation before playing Cashflow, that "it is like a diet, they tell you how to balance different foods, what kind of nutrition you need, but what you eat is up to you."

Readers learn in Kiyosaki's books and in seminars inspired by his ideas that they have to find some way to start moving from the employee quadrant to the business or investor quadrants in Kiyosaki's scheme of economic positions, even if this transition takes many years and a great deal of effort. In order to accomplish this goal, readers need to find alternative ways to initiate investments within their means that can increase their capital and cash flow, bringing them one step closer to financial freedom, just as the mechanism of the Cashflow game suggests. The nitty-gritty details of starting a business, investing in someone else's enterprise, acquiring property, or trading in the stock market are of course much more complicated in practice than the model suggested by the Cashflow game. Hence, for many participants, multilevel marketing (MLM) or network marketing becomes an attractive alternative, given its relative simplicity, comparatively low cost of access, promises of high returns, and the prospect of receiving support from other members. Network marketing companies are essentially businesses that function on the basis of a network of independent distributors or representatives. They are the most frequent organizational form of *direct-selling* companies. Distributors of direct-selling companies do not work as employees for a corporation or receive a salary, but they join a network and earn commissions for selling or recommending the products or services offered by the company (from cleaning supplies and well-being products to vacation packages). While few direct-selling companies reward their distributors only for their individual sales, most operate as MLM businesses, rewarding individuals for the recruitment and sales by members associated with them in a network (Cahn 2011:6). My fieldwork and interviews with participants of workshops organized by Financial Freedom Argentina who also joined an MLM company called Vacation Express illustrate how the idea of a conflation of interest and disinterest described earlier materializes in an organizational form. I will demonstrate how participants attempt to translate and reinforce what they learn in financial self-help books, seminars, and games in the context of a specific business practice.

Although not every fan of financial self-help participates in or has a positive image of network marketing, there are strong affinities in the ideas and social interactions promoted by MLM and financial self-help. Like financial self-help, network marketing is primarily about something other than making money, although that is an important part of it. Anthropologist Peter Cahn, who studied distributors of the MLM organization Omnilife in Mexico, notes that "devoted direct sellers almost never understand their charge in strictly financial terms. For them, a primary component of their work is to promote internal change through a reshaping of mental states" (2011:6). In fact, while many people I met were driven to network marketing by their participation in financial self-help groups, others learned about Robert Kiyosaki's books and Rich Dad groups only after they became distributors in an MLM company. The main affinity lies in the fact that MLM members are seen as independent entrepreneurs who can manage their time and dedication autonomously. According to sociologist Nicole Woolsey Biggart, "unable to give a paycheck, direct selling organizations offer distributors something employers cannot give: a socially valued independent status. They turn housewives and truck drivers into 'entrepreneurs.' They make teachers and secretaries 'businesspeople'" (Biggart 1989:162). Like financial self-help, MLM companies provide a discourse that stresses ideas of independence, entrepreneurship, and individual success coupled with a diagnosis that the old model of work in corporations is obsolete (Biggart 1989; King and Robinson 2000). In fact, Robert Kiyosaki himself published a book supporting network marketing in 2005 (Kiyosaki 2005a).[3]

I first heard about Vacation Express in my first Cashflow game in Argentina. When I arrived there in July 2007, I started looking for games or events about financial freedom in which I could start doing field research. My experience entering the field a few months earlier in New York had been very smooth. I showed up on a Thursday evening at a game held in a meeting room of a small bank branch (this was Steve's group, which also met on Saturdays for general advice and discussion), and I told the game facilitator that I was doing research on readers of financial self-help. Soon thereafter, I was playing Cashflow for the first time. During that first game, I met Sonny, who ran one of the boards, and who offered to add me to his e-mail list so I could receive notices about the games he organized every other week or so. I was expecting that the Argentine online forum that I had been reading for months before moving (and which I thought at the time was the only Rich Dad group in the country) would organize similar informal games that I could observe and where I could meet people. However, although the forum was quite active online, with new posts and topics every day, there was no word about organizing Cashflow meetings in the first month following my arrival in Buenos Aires.

After some more online research, I found a different webpage announcing a game a couple of weeks later in the city of La Plata, one hour from Buenos Aires. This website was quite different from what I was expecting. In the online forum I had been reading, games were normally organized informally by forum members, inviting people to play in their apartments or making a deal with a restaurant or bar to get a prix fixe menu and let them meet to play Cashflow in their establishment. In contrast, this website seemed to belong to a more formally organized group. It was so well-polished that I found myself questioning whether it was an official branch of the American Rich Dad company in Argentina (I later learned that it was not). The website announced the creation of several chapters of their club in several provinces. They called themselves Financial Freedom Argentina.

The game I read about on the site was announced as a full-day "financial freedom" workshop, held in a hotel, with breakfast, lunch, and several presentations. To sign up and reserve a spot, there was no option for electronic payment (one had to make a deposit in a bank account), so I called the event's organizer, Omar, to ask him if I could pay the fee the day of the game. I told Omar on the phone that I was a sociologist doing research on Rich Dad clubs. He enthusiastically told me that I would have the chance to meet the leaders of Financial Freedom Argentina, who were traveling from Buenos Aires to run the workshop. His name-dropping made the group look more organized and professional than what I expected. The groups I had seen in New York up to then seemed much more casual.

The workshop was a very different experience from the one I had during my fieldwork in New York. While in the New York groups (and in other Cashflow meetings I would attend later in Argentina) a Cashflow game was a rather informal meeting, this was a one-day event with a formal schedule. In New York, one or two organizers facilitated the game by bringing a couple of boards and materials. They acted as translators (described in Chapter 3), but that was largely the extent of their supervisory role. In contrast, this Argentine group was well-organized, presenting movies and slides, giving a brief explanation of the game, and lecturing on some of Kiyosaki's core concepts, including financial freedom. It was more "top-down" than my previous experience. Later Alejandro, one of the organizers who also imported and sold original games across Argentina, told me that the group was traveling all over the country and facilitating these workshops. Soon after, the members started wearing distinctive shirts during the games and events.

At the hotel, we played Cashflow for about five hours. After the games were over, there was a lecture about different ways of leaving the rat race.[4] According to the speakers and the PowerPoint presentation, there were only four ways to leave: (1) investing in the stock market; (2) starting a business; (3) investing in real estate; and (4) getting involved in network marketing. The event's main speaker, Ramiro, reviewed one by one the disadvantages and difficulties that made most of these roads to financial freedom difficult in the beginning. Entering the stock market and real estate require substantial knowledge to avoid quick failures, and real estate in particular demands a high volume of capital. Real estate, Ramiro said, was a good option at a later stage on the road to financial freedom but an unlikely one as a starting point, given the amount of cash required. Starting a business was also very difficult, as the rates of success are allegedly very low. Ramiro said that roughly 95 percent of new businesses fail in the first year—a figure I heard over and over in Financial Freedom Argentina seminars as well as in MLM companies' presentations. These leaders argued that starting a business is too risky, since one stands alone against the world and too often becomes a slave to the business. Network marketing, however, was presented as a much more feasible option than the other three because it offered the advantages of a large corporation coupled with those of owning your own business, without having employees or being an employee.

Ramiro later showed a video in which Robert Kiyosaki himself praised the advantages of multilevel marketing: he argued that these networks offer low startup costs and a company that works with you so that you get the skills that will make you rich. He called it "the perfect business" because members generate income, but mostly because working in this organizational form would help them develop the right skills. Network marketing was framed as *the* business that would provide the skills and the time for people to make the transition from the employee quadrant to the business owner quadrant. As I discussed in Chapter 1, Kiyosaki strongly recommends that followers work to become a "B" (business owner), but also warns that the transition is hard because many people lack the skills and the emotional control to do it successfully. An apprenticeship in somebody else's business, as Kiyosaki allegedly did himself with his own rich dad, is not available to most people. So he recommends network marketing companies as a way to own a business without the need to create one, which would be an easier and smoother emotional and cognitive transition to the "B" quadrant. Unlike when being self-employed or starting a new business from scratch, Kiyosaki argued, these companies provide vital support and training.

In his presentation, Ramiro compared the advantages of entering an MLM company with the downsides of opening a *locutorio*. The locutorio, a small shop containing a number of telephone booths for public use, has become an Argentine icon of small business. Thanks to the decrease of formal employment and the privatization of telecommunications in the 1990s, many Argentines invested in locutorios (some of them with money from severance pay after being laid off from their regular jobs). Alejandro, one of the workshop organizers, and his wife, Valeria, were one example. They recounted their story to me one afternoon in their home, while sipping *mate*.

In August 2000, seven years before I met them, Alejandro and Valeria decided to open a locutorio in their neighborhood. At the time Valeria had an administrative job in a small company that distributed auto parts. The recession that began in 1998 was beginning to take a toll on their lives. In December 2000, Valeria's employer demanded she take her annual two-week paid vacation two months earlier than expected—the company had no work for her. When she showed up at work after the forced time off, she was not allowed to enter the plant. After eight years with the firm, she was fired without notice—and with a backlog of three months of unpaid salaries. The locutorio remained the only activity that generated some income for their family. However, it was not enough to cover their needs. They had to pay the debt incurred to start the business—they only had $8,000 of the $20,000 needed to open the locutorio and had used credit cards to finance the store furniture. Business ownership was a new experience for them. Alejandro told me that, not having been exposed to financial self-help at the time, he later realized he did not have any kind of solid business plan, so he and his wife did not expect to make substantial profits in the first year or so. Alejandro and Valeria did not know what to do, so they kept the business open but decided to offer bill payment services (*pagofacil*) in addition to the phone booth calling services. In Argentina, most people pay their utilities and other bills in banks or in small shops like locutorios, drugstores, or pharmacies that obtain a license from payment processing companies like *pagofacil* or *rapipago*. Although this decision involved managing relatively large amounts of cash in a housing project on the edge of the city of Buenos Aires, where crime was high, they decided to go ahead with the expansion of their business. Since there were no banks or *pagofacil* branches located within several blocks, they hoped that the addition would surely attract more customers. Yet, while both worked long hours at their locutorio, numbers never quite added up. Like many locutorios in Argentine cities that became a smorgasbord of services, Alejandro and Valeria kept adding services to survive. They added a post office branch and an Internet service by the hour, trying to keep the business afloat. In 2004, Valeria read an article in a national newspaper about *Rich Dad, Poor Dad*, and a few months later remembered it when she saw the book in a bookstore. After bringing it home, Alejandro read it right away:

> The feeling was . . . anguish. I thought it was written *for me*. I haven't read it in
> a while now, but I recall the sorts of businesses Kiyosaki knew that may have
> worked thirty years ago, people who grasp on to their businesses, almost behind

bars. They go on because they don't know what else to do, and I saw myself [in those stories] . . . I said, "Shit I'm thirty-something, with this business." And I saw my neighbors, who've been [working] twenty years or more in their business . . . and that routine of opening the shop in the morning, closing at night, going home . . . "I don't want that for me," I said.

By 2005, they had decided to close the locutorio. In the workshops run by Financial Freedom Argentina, locutorios were often used as a comparative case in order to show how difficult and frustrating it was to start one's own business, and especially to illustrate that small business owners are entirely on their own. Network marketing, in contrast, allegedly provided immediate training and support, something that one would never get anywhere else (unless one wanted to remain an employee and receive training from a corporation, which would entirely defeat the purpose). In the video shown during the workshop in La Plata, Kiyosaki presented network marketing as an elegant way of supporting oneself while making an emotional, mental, and physical transition to the rich side of the quadrant.

Omar, the local organizer, told participants that he would contact them by e-mail or phone later that week to tell them about the business opportunity to which Ramiro referred during his presentation. That was the first time I heard the name of the company that the group was promoting, Vacation Express, about which I learned more and more throughout my fieldwork in Argentina. To enter the business, one had to pay a considerable entrance fee (about $1,300US) to earn the right to receive income in two ways. One was by recommending travel services to others. This way, members would earn about 40 percent of the commission that travel agents receive, just for having the customer give their pin number to the travel agent. The second way of receiving income was by "building teams," or in other words, recruiting new members. Associates would receive $100 for each member recruited, or recruited by their recruits, according to certain rules and limitations. Earnings would be received after the thresholds of three, five, and eight new recruits.[5] An additional benefit was that members, as part of the tourism industry, would receive significant discounts for their own travel.

As an outsider who paid to attend, I was initially a bit offended by the fact that the workshop seemed to be an excuse to promote a business in which the group had a personal, vested interest. Everything—the Cashflow game (which organizers had amended by adding home-made cards about network marketing), the lecture on the four ways to leave the rat race, the videos—seemed to be eight hours of preparation to recruit people for a network. I felt that this was closer to late-night infomercials from U.S. television than to the more horizontal and cooperative groups I had met in New York. As an ethnographer, one has to be suspicious of one's first reactions. While I initially expected others at the event to feel the same way, that was not the case at that event, nor in the rest of my experience with network marketing. Attendees seemed enthusiastic to learn more about this business opportunity, and unbothered by the way organizers attempted to profit from an event that appeared educational. While I assumed interest and disinterest to belong to different realms, in financial self-help they can cohabitate peacefully.[6] I later learned that the group had only recently gotten involved in network marketing. Ramiro, who entered the network in his native Colombia, had arrived in Argentina a few months earlier. He came across Financial Freedom Argentina's webpage, contacted founder Matías, and presented the business opportunity to him. Matías told me that he respected Ramiro's shrewdness for business: "In his vision or business ability, he understood that by sponsoring the leader of a Rich Dad group, he would reach a lot of people, and that's what happened." Matías entered the network under Ramiro and let him work with Financial Freedom Argentina, recruiting members for Vacation Express.

Two weeks after attending the workshop, I traveled again to La Plata to interview the organizer, Omar, who had enthusiastically joined Vacation Express after he met Ramiro at a Cashflow workshop in Buenos Aires. Omar gave me two tickets for a company event the following week in a luxury hotel in downtown Buenos Aires, and insisted that I go as his guest and bring a guest along if I wished.[7] The event was called "Night of Stars," which did not give many clues about what to expect as an attendee. When I arrived at the hotel on a Thursday evening, the room was completely full and I estimated that no less than a thousand people were there. While many already belonged to the network, others, like me, were invited by members to get a sense of an organization they could potentially join. Alejandro and Valeria told me that many people were there because of Financial Freedom Argentina.

The event started with a welcome by a man who sounded like a professional TV or radio announcer, and who was a member of the network. He introduced a woman in her sixties, a school principal whom, he told the audience, he had considered like a mother ever since he met her eight months earlier through Vacation Express. They both asked for a show of hands of those who were attending for the first time and asked everyone to join them in a round of applause. Next, the lights went off for a video featuring the company's executives, including the CEO and founder, welcoming the audience from the company's headquarters in Miami. In the video, the founder of the company was presented as a visionary who wanted to lift Latin Americans out of poverty.

The two presenters then welcomed Adrian, another network member, who humbly said that it was the first time he was speaking in public. He said that slowly, with the help of others, he was overcoming his fears and improving his speaking skills. He recalled when the company had started in Argentina the previous year, with just a dozen people meeting in a bar. Adrian assured the audience that he had distrusted the company at first, but his distrust only made him waste time and delay his entrance to the network. "What was the point of not trusting Vacation Express," he said, "when you can see evidence of the success of the people all around?" A father of a six-year-old, Adrian said that he had quit his job as an account executive for a telephone corporation, where he could not spend as much time with his daughter as he did now as a distributor for Vacation Express. Like other speakers after him, Adrian repeatedly highlighted the camaraderie and collaboration of members (especially compared to his previous job). He said that being part of Vacation Express was as much about money as about personal development and that the company was in search of business entrepreneurs, not employees. He and other speakers mentioned Robert Kiyosaki's books, especially *Rich Dad, Poor Dad* and *The Business School* (the latter is specifically about the benefits of network marketing) as their inspiration for getting into the business.

The main speech was given by Eber, one of the top network members, a highly charismatic and entertaining speaker from Ecuador. He repeated Kiyosaki's ideas about the differences between the industrial age and the information age, the changes to the retirement system that should shake people out of the illusory idea that they have financial security, and the downsides of working for corporations. In the midst of applause, cheers, and music, Eber invited several people to the stage who used to have conventional jobs and were now happy to have joined Vacation Express. In thirty seconds each, about a dozen men and women of various ages, including Omar (the member who invited me), shared their experiences with the audience. They all spoke emotionally about how their lives were changing and about the size of the checks they were receiving, and each testimony was followed by raucous cheers and applause. After the testimonies, Eber declared that not everything would be "a bed of roses." There is no magic: network members would have to work hard, but unlike in traditional corporations, they would see rewards according to their efforts and not their position in the company. Eber reminded audience members that they would have to face and overcome their fears, but they should not worry too much, because they would get all the support they needed to be successful.

Adrian and Eber both explained the specific benefits of belonging to the network. As Laura, a fresh member in her mid-twenties, echoing the company's official discourse on its compensation plan, later explained to me:

> Vacation Express is a personal franchise in which you have three different ways to receive benefits. One is saving money on travel; you may very well choose to travel only. You could also recommend tourism products, being the intermediary between agency and customer. So the business is not only the network, there are other things that make up the business. The network is one alternative, obviously it's the one that generates the most money. Each person chooses. For example, I know a lady who entered only to get travel discounts.

Like other members, Laura emphasized that there were several options for members, but that recruiting was the most profitable. It took me some time to understand the functioning of Vacation Express's compensation structure, but it soon became clear to me that most if not all of the income came from recruiting other members. While the amount of money possible in building teams was quite clear from the beginning, the commission amount for travel referrals was unclear, and a quick calculation could easily show that they were insignificant compared to the benefits of recruiting new members.

The fact that most of a person's income comes from recruitment rewards makes Vacation Express resemble a pyramid scheme. The distinction between multilevel marketing and a pyramid system is that the latter does not carry a genuine market product, sold to people outside the network (WFDSA 2013a). People obtain a benefit only for recruiting people. In the case of Vacation Express, members were able to earn income from commissions generated from tourism recommendations. The presence of a product gave the system an appearance of sustainability, but it seemed to be little more than a mask to cover what was mostly a pyramid scheme. For Omar, Laura, and others, the real business—and the real money—was in recruiting. Several members expected to earn income from tourism referrals in the future, only after they had established their network and had profited from its expansion. Multilevel marketing and pyramid schemes can be hard to distinguish in cases like this, in which the product is an excuse for a recruiting business (Competition Bureau of Canada

2009; Valentine 1998). But, unlike pure money pyramids (Verdery 1995a, 1995b), in which people deposit money and get more regardless of what they do, in this case they entered a world of practices similar to those of MLM companies that were not pyramid schemes.

People involved in Vacation Express rarely spoke of "recruiting members" but rather of "building your team." And this is crucial because, even in a pseudo pyramid scheme, they did enter a community of people that spoke a language of entrepreneurialism, financial freedom, and personal improvement. When I asked Omar whom he spoke with about his concerns with financial freedom before getting involved with Financial Freedom Argentina, and later with Vacation Express, he said, laughing, "Alone . . . alone like a nutjob. And the good thing about network marketing is that people speak the same language as you. People in network marketing are interested in financial stuff, in Kiyosaki." "Building your team," the preferred term for the practice of recruiting new members to Vacation Express, is not just a *euphemization* or a *misrecognition*—using Bourdieu's terminology—of the self-interested process of recruiting members to make money. In fact, recruiting a member is a complex action. It involves both receiving a financial reward for bringing someone new *and* extending the opportunity to that person to do the same once she or he entered the network. And, because of how Vacation Express was organized, many of those successive recruitments benefit both the recruiter and the recruit, who help each other.

Being successful in recruitment depends on developing particular skills that are regarded as necessary for achieving financial freedom: interpersonal relations, sales skills, team work, entrepreneurship, leadership, and public speaking. All those skills can be summarized in the skill of *selling*. Kiyosaki and other self-help authors deem selling the most important skill people need in order to be successful. In order to find investors, one will need to sell them one's project; in order to promote one's business or service, one will need this aptitude; even if one is not selling anything, one is always selling oneself. This elevation of selling is inscribed in the neoliberal mandate that individuals make an enterprise of themselves: "Individuals are solicited as allies of economic success through ensuring that they invest in the management, presentation, promotion and enhancement of their own economic capital as a capacity of their selves and as a lifelong project" (Miller and Rose 2008:97). Selling is vital in neoliberalism because individuals are seen as entrepreneurs of themselves, for whom every action is directed at increasing their "human capital" (Dilts 2011; Foucault 2008; Hamann 2009; Lemke 2001; Read 2009).

In building their selling skills, current members argue, the new member is not left to her own devices. Once she enters the network, she receives formal and informal training, motivation, and social support from the recruiter and other people around her. The new person enters a social circle and forges a bond with others in the network. Most people do not find it contradictory to help others (or provide them with financial opportunities and support) and make a direct profit off that help. "Building a team" is the discursive expression of the idea that entering the network is only the beginning of a long series of mutually beneficial practices.

Being part of Vacation Express means engaging in practices similar to those described by Nicole Woolsey Biggart (1989) in her classic study of direct selling, but also in the few available ethnographies of direct-sales networks (Pratt 2000; Pratt and Rosa 2003; Wilson 1998, 1999, 2004), particularly in the Latin American region (Cahn 2011 on Mexico; Casanova 2011 on Ecuador; Pedroso Neto 2010, 2014 on Brazil). Members attend several levels of training events that are common in direct selling and network marketing. They also conduct informal gatherings of the immediate network (usually called "home meetings," although sometimes they take place in public places); two- or three-hour training events about the structure of the company, its products, the compensation system, and advice on how to recruit effectively; larger charismatic events like the Night of Stars in hotel conference rooms in which potential recruits are invited to observe firsthand the workings of the company and its motivational power; full-day events in a farm outside the city; and international three- to four-day gatherings with members from several Latin American countries.

Members have to pay for the costs of these activities, although they could use their member discounts for travel to international events. Most of these activities featured presentations by charismatic company leaders who allegedly started like everyone else and who were currently making large sums of money. Events are also an opportunity to showcase the achievements of recently affiliated members and give some of them the opportunity to practice their public speaking skills. Keeping up with the activities of the company demands considerable effort. I had an interview once in a McDonald's in downtown Buenos Aires at 8:00 a.m. with Nicolás, the enthusiastic and committed Kiyosaki fan who was also adhering to a strict diet and exercise regimen. He chose the place and the time because he was already meeting with his immediate network beforehand (they regularly met at 6:00 a.m., before many of them went to their daily jobs).

Most financial self-help fans I met or interviewed who entered Vacation Express had three goals in mind that combined interest and disinterest. First, they wanted to make a substantial amount of money (much more than what they could make in a regular job) in a relatively short period (one to three years). Second, they wanted to learn skills, be exposed to experiences that would help them overcome obstacles and fears, and interact with other positive-minded people. Third, they wanted to be able to help others along the way.

A few months before I met him, Marcelo decided to quit his administrative job in an ice cream chain because he had had enough of it. He had worked for spells in McDonald's and as a stock clerk in a supermarket, before he worked for eight years for the ice cream chain, where he started as a delivery boy and worked his way up to various administrative positions. Coming from a humble family that immigrated to Buenos Aires from one of the poorest provinces of Argentina, he had always tried to save money from his jobs, but never using anything more sophisticated than term deposits. In 2003, a coworker convinced him to buy government bonds, which offered a generous interest rate after the Argentine government's default the year before. He later found a website for stock investing and put some of his savings in the local stock market. Although he quickly became interested in investing, Marcelo admits he did not have much of a plan. "I made good returns," he told me, "but not because I was good at investing, but because everybody who put money on it was doing fairly well." It was not until 2005 that he read *Rich Dad, Poor Dad*. "It blew my mind into five thousand pieces," he told me. "I liked it a lot. But they were concepts that I kind of had, but not so well elaborated. Very vague. My thought was very limited and the book rounded it out a lot." Marcelo knew before reading the book that he had to save some money every month and try to invest it to obtain a return. "But I never reached the conclusion, it meant looking much farther . . . that investments . . . the assets you have . . . [pause] I mean, your generation of passive income should be more than your expenses. And that's when you are financially free. And that's the concept of the book for me." He heard from another coworker about a Cashflow event, and soon after attending he joined Vacation Express, which he saw as a chance to generate much higher returns than the stocks he currently had:

> So, what I want is to generate a lot . . . a lot of money with the network. And after that, when that is already operating, and with an amount of passive cash flow—weekly, because my company pays weekly—in that moment, when I'm super cool, then I'll do what I like. I will learn very well how to invest in forex

and other investments. Then I'll go crazy with graphs and everything, because I won't need to devote time to the network.

Marcelo calculated that, after an initial period of high involvement effectively recruiting new members, he would be in a position to receive high passive income without devoting much time to the network (because the recruitments of many others in their "down-line" would benefit them). This would be a sort of "primitive accumulation" that would give him the capital and the cash flow to continue moving up to more challenging investments that required more knowledge. Marcelo's calculation is consistent with the dynamics of the Cashflow game. The first investments in "small deals" are meant to bring the money that will make investing in larger deals for passive income possible. In this sense, network marketing is seen as an attainable investment for most people, and hence the bridge from a small capital to a large capital that may allow larger deals (such as real estate investments) in the future. Laura had a similar idea of the potential returns of network marketing. I met Laura in a Cashflow gathering she organized in her apartment in Buenos Aires through the Rich Dad online forum. While she was not as enthusiastic as Marcelo was about some of the charismatic practices at events like the Night of Stars—"you have to clap all the time, raise your hand . . . I don't like that, it's ridiculous"— she quit her job as an accountant in a small firm when she entered Vacation Express a few months before I met her. She saw a clear benefit in the financial rewards of network marketing compared to a regular job:

> The idea is to acquire capital so that it generates a passive rent. In fact, with Vacation Express, or with any other network that you devote time to, you can generate the capital that eventually in the future will generate a passive income, so that you don't have to work. This is the idea Kiyosaki poses as one of the ways of generating passive income, one of the ways is marketing networks. So it's endorsed by him, he even says that if he had to start from zero he would start with network marketing, in order to make all the money he made. If you make a comparison between an employee or a business owner, and the marketing network, in this case Vacation Express, if you project income in three years, working minimally, you can see the difference.

But money was not everything to these financial self-help enthusiasts. Both Laura and Marcelo highlighted the nonmonetary aspects of participating in network marketing. Laura told me she did not quit her job (which she had held for a year) specifically because of network marketing, but that her exposure to the new business coincided with her being unhappy in her position, with her mind wandering away from the job. Before she left, she was asked to train the person that would be taking over her job. As she told me the story, she realized that helping someone else would be understood differently in an MLM company: "They did not pay me extra for explaining the job to someone else. . . . When you explain things in a network, you multiply what you know and you also receive from it . . . but here [in my old job], nothing. They don't pay you more for explaining, for staying later to teach someone." Laura was only beginning with network marketing, and while she was still not sure that it would work for her (she saw herself as shy, and was trying to overcome her shyness), she stressed how her work at Vacation Express could result in benefits for everyone involved in the network, since she was not forced to choose between herself and others. While Laura was still hesitant about the "brainwashing" aspect of network marketing, Marcelo welcomed the brainwashing:

> I would say that they [MLM companies] brainwash you. But being brainwashed is very useful for me. Because they brainwash you from all the garbage that people who work as employees think. . . . Network marketing teaches you to change many things in your attitude, in the way of thinking and seeing things. So we have many books about changing [one's] mentality towards abundance, towards an abundant mentality, and not scarce.

Marcelo highlighted his participation in network marketing as a way to work on the self in order to become a rich person. Being a rich person meant not just making the money, but mostly developing an *abundant* mentality. For him, employees are defined by scarcity and it is their scarce mentality that keeps them there. Participants in network marketing value not only the income it may provide and the personal change they may undergo, but also an environment in which helping oneself and helping others do not appear to conflict. He appreciated that for the same reason, unlike in the traditional workplace, there is a sense of collaboration among network members:

> There are many positive things in a marketing network, and the most important one that I see is that you are in a group of people who are all pushing towards the same goal. It's not like a job in which the person who works well is always fixing what others screwed up. . . . It's all people with an optimistic mentality and who help you because they are in the same situation as you. They are trying to develop themselves and achieve something better. . . . In a marketing network you can find a mentor, and you are surrounded by people who are not employees or

who are trying to stop being employees, and who are trying to progress. So it's a good environment for you to develop, you get training and a group of people who push you forward.

Members like Marcelo see collaboration and motivation as a main feature not just of the work in the network but of the recruitment itself, which is seen as an offer of opportunity, even when it benefits the recruiter. For Financial Freedom Argentina organizer Matías, recruiting for Vacation Express is neither selling nor deceiving; rather, it is showing the other person the opportunity he has, helping the other person "see what you saw":

> A very important thing in network marketing, perhaps one of the most important ones . . . is the issue of sales, because this is not a sale that you ring a bell and sell three pairs of socks for 10 pesos. You have to see the opportunity that I saw. You have to realize and see with your own eyes what I saw with mine, so that you realize that this is an opportunity for you. I have to transmit that to you. You have to see that.

Network marketing offers fans of financial self-help the possibility of belonging to a money-making enterprise while seeing themselves as autonomous, having "mentors" instead of bosses. Members see marketing networks as an alternative to the traditional corporation, in that they have full autonomy. For Matías, since they are not controlled by top management, success depends on "leading" and not forcing:

> The other important thing is the issue of leadership. When I had a regular business, I had 280 people working for me. And they did what I said because I paid them. If they stay later, they stay, because I pay. If we make a training session on a Saturday, I pay. What I did then was manage people. In network marketing, you have to learn to direct people.[8] Because it's your personal business. And you will participate in a network because you see that if you do something together with me, and with me leading you, you will get a positive benefit.

Matías articulates more explicitly the way in which in network marketing self-interest is channeled so that it is not contradictory with helping others. This is seen as a total contrast with the corporate business world:

> What's the best? That those on top are helping you, and those under you are helping you. Not like in the corporate world, in which you have to be careful of the handsaw [backstabbing] that's coming. You have to look out for the hand-

saw, because one day . . . it happens to all of us, it's human nature, each one will protect their own benefit. If worse comes to worst: "We're best friends, I really love you, but if I have to decide between my family and yours, I choose my family." I say this openly! Why? Because it's human nature. I can pay lip service and say "Hey, I'm never going to abandon you. . ." That's not true! One day I need something, I'm going to watch over myself and my family before you. Today. The day I become Mother Teresa, it'll be different. But today, that's my nature, like 99.9999 percent of people in the world. So, when you find that, in network marketing, people lend you a hand . . . If you are part of my network, besides lending you a hand because I want you to do well, because I want you to experience a change, it's not because I am a saint. The only way I have to win is if you win, too. If you don't win, I don't win. I have to be concerned about you earning money. You don't see anything like this in the corporate world.

For Matías, network marketing puts people in a position in which they have to help each other if they each want to succeed. He appears devoted to helping others, but there is no point in trying to "become Mother Teresa," devoting oneself to others with no regard for self-interest. His point is that one can have both interest and generosity and make them compatible, and that network marketing makes it possible. While for him the regular workplace brings only self-interest out in people, network marketing also encourages their cooperation. Like Marcelo, and in accordance with the mechanism suggested by Cashflow, Matías saw network marketing as a step to generate an income that would help him reach larger investments in the future. However, he said that the experience of working collaboratively with others was very important for him. Helping others may become so important that he left open the idea of continuing working in network marketing in the future, even after moving on to other businesses. Matías also emphasized that one has to participate to really understand how to be both self-interested and generous. My insistent questions to Matías about how Vacation Express worked led him to believe that I did not understand the concept of network marketing at all:

> Matías: Kiyosaki is very clear when he says, "the more people you help, the more you will generate." One thing is if I'm a consultant for a company, and I spend my day on that. Another thing is if perhaps I write a book on, let's say, generating commercial contacts with the Middle East (or anything), and I sell 150,000 books. Will I make more money? No doubt, and it's a way of helping. Another way of helping is network marketing. If

> you understood the concept of network marketing, *and I think that you*
> *in particular did not understand it* . . . if you understood the concept you
> realize that what I'm doing is giving you the opportunity so that you, in
> a short time, or in your free time, generate a cash flow that would alter
> your normal flow. If you're an employee, you keep being an employee, if
> you're a shopkeeper, you're still a shopkeeper. But you start developing
> skills and knowledge.
>
> Daniel: What do you think I don't understand?
>
> Matías: I say that because you, not participating [in Vacation Express] . . .
> there are things I understand as I progress. I'm not an enlightened genius.
> . . . At first I did it because Kiyosaki said, "do network marketing." And
> he's my financial dad. If Kiyosaki says it, it must not be useless, let's do
> it. But once you start, you realize it's an absolutely democratic way for
> people to obtain that which they couldn't obtain [before].

For Matías, I was still living in a world in which interest and disinterest were contradictory, a world in which people cannot be at the same time generous and self-interested. For him, I still had a poor mindset which saw the world as a zero-sum and not as one of abundance. Living in a world of abundance could only be crafted with participation, immersion, and social interaction with others who had that mindset. While participants like Matías and Marcelo insist that collaboration with others will ensure success in multilevel marketing, failure appears to be the exclusive responsibility of the individual. Given the help and support members receive, the only explanation available for failure is the individual. Laura, for example, explained to me why some people eventually quit multilevel marketing companies:

> There are those who quit because they don't do well, or perhaps because they
> didn't do what they had to do. Or because it didn't work for them, or they real-
> ized that their personality didn't fit these kinds of things, or because they didn't
> change something in them to be able to do it. Obviously, to enter a network, you
> have to have an open mind for selling and for accepting new challenges and new
> things, which perhaps you wouldn't see in a traditional environment.

Laura shows once again the affinity between the discourse of financial self-help and that espoused in network marketing companies. It is up to the individual to change oneself and take charge in order to succeed. An optimistic attitude is crucial. Once they enter, members become quite enthusiastic, and they usually start using a new language. It is difficult to find someone involved in a network who will say something bad about their company. Being positive is supposed to be one of the most important factors in success, so the mere display of doubt when representing the company could be a sign of lack of commitment. In an attitude that evokes Max Weber's analysis of the protestant ethic and the spirit of capitalism, expressing doubt can be a sign of the failure to be saved (Weber 2002b). People enter network companies partly to avoid the alienation of traditional corporations, in which the employer may be "the other" who is making money out of his or her workers. Complaining about one's network company, in contrast, would amount to complaining about oneself. I routinely asked interviewees if there was something they did not like about network marketing, but I rarely received concrete answers. In online forums, the mere mention of a company usually launches long discussion threads with extreme polarization. Some people question specific companies (or the whole notion of multilevel marketing) for being a complete scam, a Ponzi scheme, while others angrily accuse the haters of not having an open mind to understand a business that has changed the lives of millions. People do say bad things about other network marketing companies—that they are a cult, that their compensation scheme is not generous, or that their products do not sell well. I heard negative comments about Vacation Express only from a member, Alejandro, who quit after a conflict with another member about where in the network to locate a recruit who they had both been courting. Alejandro was one of the leaders of Financial Freedom Argentina and was disappointed that the group had become too much of a recruiting tool for the network. He believed the group had lost its essence since they got involved with Vacation Express, and they were now seeing every person as a potential recruit and nothing else. He also admitted that money was made only by recruiting and no one was really referring tourism. I asked him if he thought differently while he was inside the network (in my earlier interactions with him, he seemed to be sincerely enthusiastic about the company). He answered that then he had been too excited about the novelty of network marketing to realize this. On the other hand, those still inside the network told me that Alejandro left because he did not understand that this was a business in which everyone could make money together, and that he mistakenly thought that where to place the new recruit made any difference—that someone else was going to benefit at his expense. In other words, that he did not belong in a world in which his interest and those of others could be one and the same.

·   ·   ·

An hour before the start of the regular monthly meetings of Steve's group in New York, new members have a brief orientation in which Steve tells them what the group is about. He always comments that people find it strange that he holds these meetings for free. So once he explained it:

> I really discovered that my passion is not real estate, my passion is helping people. So that's why I do this, and that's why I do this for free. Like if you play that game, you know, the Cashflow game, and you land on charity, and you get to roll an extra die for a couple of turns. Giving back I believe is a big part of successful people, because they live in the world of abundance as opposed to the world of scarcity. And so, this is part of my giving back. People always ask, "I can't believe you do that for free! There must be some ulterior motive. What do you want?" You know, skeptical New Yorkers . . . And so, no, it's just part of my giving back, because I really enjoy helping people.

Steve used the charity square in Cashflow to illustrate the logic of his genuinely generous and quite remarkable sharing of knowledge and mentorship, suggesting that, like in the game, he hoped to eventually receive some reward in the future. But in an apparent contradiction with his enjoyment of helping others, Steve started that same orientation meeting by telling new members, "You're here because I'm selfish." He said he had selfish reasons for starting the group, in order to build a supportive network of positive, like-minded people around him who would help him achieve his financial goals. As he went on with the group, he discovered his vocation of helping, which was not contradictory with the selfish reasons that motivated him to start the group in the first place. It was free of charge and open to anyone, and Steve seemed to me quite generous in sharing his time and expertise with the people he considered his community. Yet new members were welcomed with an explanation of selfish reasons that gave meaning to the group. Financial self-help is a field that works by making interested and disinterested action compatible.

Steve also said that giving to others is a crucial part of seeing the world from the point of view of the rich and successful. In a mythical world of abundance, according to the world of financial self-help, there is so much for everyone that there is no need to choose between acting with self-interest and with disinterest. In the world of abundance, caring for oneself does not take anything away from others, and in turn caring for others rewards the person helping. The world of network marketing proposes an organizational structure in which people can live this utopia. People involved in network marketing see themselves as shielded from the everyday life of the corporate economy in which employees have to compete with and backstab each other for a promotion. Network marketing is popular in financial self-help circles not only because its discourse has many affinities, but also because it provides a glimpse of the utopia of a world of abundance in which all can be winners.

In the financial self-help world, participants treat relationships with others as an important part of their larger project of crafting a neoliberal self. Changing oneself means also changing how one relates to others and vice versa. "Thinking like the rich" is a mandate in the world of financial self-help not only in terms of investing savvy but also in terms of replicating an attitude toward abundance and scarcity. "Living in a world of abundance" encapsulates financial self-help's mandate to look inward and work on the self. Consistent with the main tenets of financial self-help, failure is always internal: it is failing to change one's attitude toward abundance and scarcity. The logic that the way one thinks shapes final outcomes, and that failure can only reside in the self and can never be blamed on external conditions, is mobilized with particular intensity by Argentine fans. The economic conditions they face are dramatically different from those American users face, yet they use the same products to transform their selves.

American Dreams in Argentina

5

IN ONE OF MY FIRST ENCOUNTERS with Sonny, the most active Cashflow game organizer in New York City, he showed interest when he learned that I was from Argentina. "Kiyosaki says that the United States will become Argentina," he told me during a game, as if providing me with a revelation. "Didn't you have a financial and currency crisis there?" he added. I was intrigued. Sonny insisted many times on the bleak future of the U.S. economy, even before the beginning of the 2008 financial crisis. He pointed me to *Rich Dad's Prophecy*, a book in which Kiyosaki warned about the next big crisis of the American economy in the mid- to late 2010s, prompted by the retirement of the baby boomer generation. In the book, published in 2002, Kiyosaki made a small reference to Argentina as an example of where the United States was headed, and which Sonny remembered well:

> *The Next Argentina?*
>
> Many Americans hate being compared to Japan. Many economic scholars in America say that what is going on in Japan will not go on in America. I tend to agree. If anything, Argentina is a better example of what might happen to America in the future. Argentina, only a few years ago, was a rich industrial powerhouse with a fantastic standard of living. It was a rich land, a favorite place for many Europeans. In many ways it was more European than South American. But in just a few years, this very rich country became a poor, debt-ridden, bankrupt nation with a weak currency. Money has left and so have the rich. Taxes are high and the currency has collapsed. Corruption is everywhere. If the problems are not solved, real anarchy could erupt. Could that happen to America

in twenty to thirty years? Most Americans think not. Unfortunately too many Americans have come to expect that government will solve their problems, and I am afraid rather than solve the problems, an older America will vote for more government and higher taxes. With Social Security the most popular act ever passed, I am afraid that those who depend upon Social Security (soon to be a major voting bloc) will vote once again that the younger workers take care of them. If that happens, taxes will skyrocket. While it took hundreds of years for the Roman Empire to finally collapse, with today's speed of money transfers, the great American Empire could fall pretty fast. (Kiyosaki 2002:113)

This passage offers only a vague, detached view of Argentina and its economic problems, but it covers enough to satisfy Kiyosaki's American readers about the parallels to this faraway place. However, many Argentines would agree with Kiyosaki's apocalyptic view. Argentines usually like to complain about the decadence of the country and the failed promises of its governments. There is a long-standing tradition, in Argentina but also in the foreign press, of narrating the history of the nation as an inexplicable decline, as a country that had great chances to be an economic powerhouse but somehow squandered them all.[1] Nonetheless, Sonny's reference to *Rich Dad's Prophecy* was more an exception than the rule. In the New York Cashflow groups, members do not have Argentina and its economy on their radars. When I occasionally mentioned I was doing research in Argentina in addition to the United States, often people were just surprised by the fact that there were groups playing Cashflow there, too. In contrast, Argentine financial self-help fans do have the United States in their minds because almost all financial success books they use are American imports.

This chapter analyzes how Argentines deal with the fact that most financial self-help products are made in the United States. Up to now, I have for the most part analyzed the world of financial self-help without specific attention to location. I have drawn from ethnographic and interview material from both the United States and Argentina, focusing largely on how both cases illuminate the rationale and practices of financial self-help in general. As I showed in Chapter 1, Kiyosaki offers a social theory of the transition from industrial to post-industrial societies, arguing that individuals continue to consider school and work as a viable means of social mobility simply as a result of inertia, while major transformations have actually done away with the securities offered by the welfare society. In that regard, it is not hard to explain the acceptance and success of the financial self-help genre in Argentina. Like many other countries,

Argentina made a transition from an industrial period of labor stability, strong unions, and upward mobility through work between the 1940s and the 1970s to market-oriented modes of development. Much of the larger context of privatization, flexibility and instability of work, and the increasing power of finances is indeed similar in both countries to a large extent (although on a different scale). This does not mean that the particular forms neoliberalism has taken are equal in both countries. But the general trends are sufficiently similar to make Kiyosaki's diagnoses about the United States and world economy resonate well enough in the Argentine context. There are, however, obvious differences between the United States and Argentina to which I turn now. These differences introduce another dimension to my analysis of the world of financial self-help.

One difference stands out: Argentina's economy and financial system are significantly less stable than those of the United States, and are perceived as such by financial self-help participants. While the timing of my research coincided with a few years of recovery from the most devastating financial crisis the country has ever experienced, the economic chaos of 2001–2002 is still ever-present in the background of all things economic in Argentina. Even considering the effects of the catastrophic financial crisis that hit the United States in 2008, Argentines are much less confident in their financial institutions and the overall predictability of their country's economy than Americans. Yet American-made financial self-help has enjoyed remarkable success in Argentina, leading to the emergence of groups of fans around Kiyosaki's books and board game. This success may mislead us to think that the products are passively adopted by Argentine fans, without much attention to the fact that they were originally created for a very different context (such as the U.S. economy). The first time I played Cashflow in Argentina, Lorena, a new player who was quite enthusiastic about the game, said to me in a somewhat contemptuous tone, pointing at the board game: "This is *very yankee!*" Her recognition of the American character of the game, however, did not stand in the way of her interest in it. Like Lorena, users of financial self-help in Argentina are fully aware that Kiyosaki's products are quintessentially American, designed for a more predictable economy with a stronger and more stable financial system (regardless of Kiyosaki's continued warnings about its bleak future). They are not naive in this regard, but this knowledge does not stop them from taking up the challenge of making the books and game work in the Argentine context.

It would be easy to describe the deployment of American self-help in Argentina and around the globe using familiar narratives of cultural imperialism.

However, I show in this chapter that the Argentine use of American resources and ideas defies these narratives. Scholars in consumption and globalization have widely criticized notions such as *McDonaldization* (Ritzer 2004) and similar descriptions that oversimplify reception of American culture in Third World countries. The notion that consumption is a process of active self-construction has been mobilized to debunk images of peripheral countries as *passive receivers* of American cultural influences (Sassatelli 2007:174–82). This debunking, however, has often been replaced by a view of consumer practices in the periphery as *active resistance* to globalization and American culture. Financial self-help represents a third alternative. It is neither a case of passive acceptance nor one of active resistance, but a case of "active adoption." Financial self-help is partly a case of Americanization, in that imagined American cultures and lifestyles are indeed disseminated throughout the world.[2] Yet that dissemination is not possible without the active engagement of users, who help connect foreign financial self-help with local contexts.

Users have to insert "the local" into "the foreign" in order to make financial self-help rhetoric and resources global at all. Ironically, the incorporation of the local does not necessarily entail resistance. Given the different economic contexts of the United States and Argentina, an unmediated application of American financial self-help in Argentina would easily fail: often users' first reaction is one of doubt about financial self-help's local applicability. It is only through reflection, collective work, and active translation of the tools that financial self-help starts to make sense in such a different context. This engagement is the opposite of resistance; it involves actively working to accept these principles, and thereby furthers the global success of financial self-help.

Yet another factor complicates this process of active adoption. As I mentioned, users in Argentina plug their complicated economic context into American ideas and techniques to make them locally meaningful. But at the same time Argentine fans embrace core ideas of (American) financial self-help as a condition to begin the work of translation. The very project of adopting American financial self-help in Argentina becomes possible only if they refuse to regard the structural context as a more important factor than the individual self. Fans work through the differences between the United States and Argentina because they do not want to let those differences discourage them from wanting financial freedom. Also, they use Kiyosaki's general definitions about financial crises to interpret the local unstable context in a way that encourages them to acquire more "financial intelligence." In other words, users actively adapt

American financial self-help products to the local context, but ideas from those products also simultaneously frame their active adaptation.

The first part of this chapter describes the context of the Argentine economy and the succession of massive crises that have shaped the relationship between Argentines and finance, particularly the 2001–2002 crash. This generation has truly become accustomed to living with the constant fear that their life savings could disappear from banks overnight, permanently. Many countries, including the United States, undergo economic crises, but not many people have experienced tidal wave after tidal wave of economic crises with the strength and frequency Argentines have in the last four decades. The second part delves into Argentine fans' understanding and use of financial self-help in that context.

The Experience of Financial Instability in Argentina

Books such as *Rich Dad, Poor Dad* have been top-sellers in Argentina since at least 2003 and for longer than any other best-seller, just like in the United States.[3] Robert Kiyosaki's books started to be published in the aftermath of a devastating recession and financial crisis that sunk the country into economic chaos. At the time of my fieldwork in Argentina in 2007–2008, the economy had been in recovery for a few years, since 2003. However, a recovery for Argentines is usually little more than a buildup for the next crisis. For reasons that combine long-term structural problems in the country's development, recurrent policy mistakes, and a severe distrust of government and financial institutions on the part of citizens, Argentines famously expect a crisis to hit the nation every decade or so. The injuries from these crises, and particularly from the 2001 economic collapse, are still present in Argentine culture and its economy, even more than a decade after that unforgettable year.

Before 2001, three eras of financial collapse are still vividly remembered by Argentines who lived through them, and are often evoked by younger generations who heard the stories circulate through their families (D'Avella 2014). The first one is called the *Rodrigazo* after the name of the minister of economy in 1975, Celestino Rodrigo. In the midst of a huge political and economic crisis, the government abruptly devaluated the local currency and increased several state-controlled prices overnight, unleashing an inflationary crisis. The second era is that between 1977 and 1982 (Fridman 2010). In 1977, the military government launched a reform that liberated the financial system and in a short time exposed Argentines to a wealth of financial investments. The financial system expanded to areas of cities and towns that had never been reached before, in order to attract the savings of millions of Argentines. The era became known as *la plata dulce* (the sweet money) and was later immortalized in a critical comedy film about the new taste for financial gains (*Plata Dulce* 1982). This second era ended with two successive crises. In 1980, several large and small banks failed, leaving thousands of depositors complaining in front of the banks' doors (the state, however, eventually bailed out depositors). The 1977–1982 financial fever came to a final close in 1982 with another currency crisis frequently evoked by Argentines. The minister of economy of the military government, Lorenzo Sigaut, attempted to drive fears of devaluation away by saying, "Whoever bets for the dollar, loses" (*el que apuesta al dólar pierde*). The attempt was unsuccessful, and a violent devaluation confirmed that the dollar had been the safest bet all along. The third era well remembered by Argentines was in 1989–1990. In 1989, inflation rates reached over 3,000 percent, forcing incumbent president Raúl Alfonsín to resign in the midst of lootings in several cities (Gerchunoff and Llach 2003:497; Pucciarelli 2006; Sigal and Kessler 1997).[4] Incoming president Carlos Menem (who had to be sworn in six months before official inauguration day) ended up a year later unilaterally replacing depositors' certificates of deposit over a certain amount for long-term debt bonds.

As a result of these recurrent financial earthquakes, by the 1990s bank failures had become part of the Argentine popular imagination, even making their way into pop culture. The blockbuster movie *Nueve Reinas* (Nine Queens 2000) included a climactic scene in which the main character arrived at a financial institution to cash a check, only to discover a crowd in front of the bank. As people violently protested in front of the glass doors, news correspondents covered the event. The financial institution had abruptly failed that very morning and the check was now useless. This image was central to the landscape of the Argentine economy. A few years later, an American remake of the movie was made called *Criminal (2004)*. Like all remakes, it slightly altered several parts of the script to make them work with American audiences. One of these changes was notable. As the main character arrives to the bank to cash the check, everything looks normal. The American script implies that there was something illegal about the man's check because the branch manager asks him to step into his office, while the police come to arrest him. The film suggests that the check will probably land him in prison, yet nothing is wrong with the bank itself. While an abrupt bank failure with crowds complaining outside made sense in the plot of an Argentine movie, it did not fit the script of its American remake.

When the movie *Nueve Reinas* was released in 2000, the major financial crisis the country would experience was yet to come. After the 1989–1990 crisis, Argentina abruptly went from being one of the world's highest-growth economies in the early 1990s to suffering the most acute recession a national economy had experienced in times of peace since World World II (Gerchunoff and Llach 2003:452). That recession started in 1998 and would have devastating consequences. In 1991, the government had established a system of pegged currency in which each unit of local currency (the *peso*) was worth one dollar by law. This system had put an end to inflation and stabilized the economy, but the fear of an inflationary relapse loomed so much that both political elites and the Argentine public opposed going off the currency peg, even when it began faltering in 1998. Argentines suffered from collective trauma brought by the previous crisis (Levit and Ortiz 1999).

By 2001, three years of recession had put a strain on even the most simple of financial transactions. By mid-year, Argentine provinces had been authorized to issue provincial bonds to cover their deficits, as the national government had an increasingly harder time getting foreign loans while the currency peg prevented it from expanding the local monetary circulation. Thousands of provincial public employees received bonds, which were to be used as money, in lieu of their salaries. Soon there were sixteen different provincial *quasi-currencies*. Only two bonds circulated nationally, but the rest were limited to each issuing province. Some stores accepted local bonds while others did not, or if they did, they valued them lower than the official rate of exchange with the peso. It was truly a monetary chaos that prevented serious long-term financial calculation, given that there were so many different currencies, each changing value over time and according to each local store. By 2003, about half of all circulating money in Argentina was made up of bonds (Luzzi 2010a; Obradovich 2006; Schvarzer and Finkelstein 2003).[5] In the meantime, impoverished Argentines in several provinces started creating barter clubs to be able to trade without cash (González Bombal and Luzzi 2006).

Provincial bonds replacing national currency as well as a cash-less economy were some of the most serious financial effects of the recession, in addition to increasing poverty, unemployment, and social unrest. But there was more. In December 2001 the government installed a new rule to keep money within the banking system: citizens could not take more than 250 pesos/dollars a week in cash from their checking or savings accounts. Very quickly, Argentines started calling this policy *el corralito* (the playpen). Debit cards were still not a common form of payment, and much less so the lower one descended the economic ladder. Soon cash started to seriously dry up. The informal economy suffered. The scarcity of cash, added to the long-term crisis and the budget cuts in formal welfare programs and informal patronage politics, was too much to take for people already living in poverty. In several provinces, and especially in the outskirts of Buenos Aires, the poor started looting supermarkets and small shops (Auyero 2007). Following protests in major cities and a general state of chaos, President Fernando de La Rua resigned and had to leave on a helicopter, leaving a trail of more than thirty deaths in the last few days of his presidency. Four different presidents (counting two interims) succeeded De La Rua in the next two weeks. It was unclear what the future held, and it was even less clear what the value of the local currency would be and what would happen to the money deposited in the financial system.[6]

Early in 2002, it became clear that depositors would not see their bank savings, at least not immediately. Depositors were given two options. The first was to turn their bank savings nominated in dollars into pesos at a 1.40 rate, and have access to those pesos in cash only according to a schedule established by the government (between six months and a year). Of course, street exchange rates were much higher than 1.40, which meant effectively losing much of their savings measured in dollars. Their second option was (similar to what happened in 1990) accepting a long-term bond in dollars, through which the state committed to paying their savings and interest over a period of ten years (Bermudez 2002). As expected, depositors were not happy with the choice they were offered (a reduced amount of not immediately accessible cash or a bond that would be immediately traded at a very low rate). Walking through the financial district of Buenos Aires in the first half of 2002 was a surreal experience. Every morning, hundreds of depositors would gather in front of banks with their pots and pans. Soon they started to bang them against the bank doors. They later changed pans for hammers. Banks became fortresses with sturdy metal coverage in front of their glass doors, and depositors insisted on banging them with their hammers. After all, they had deposited real money, and now the banks said that they were unable to return what had been *their* money. Graffiti covered banks' exteriors, accusing bank owners and CEOs of being crooks and thieves (Abelin 2012; Luzzi 2008, 2010b, 2012).

The crises of 1975, 1977–1982, and 1989–1990 were surpassed in intensity and consequences by the one in 2001–2002. The general feeling in Buenos Aires after the collapse was that Argentines would never again put their trust in financial institutions (D'Avella 2014; Luzzi 2010b). The majority of middle- and working-class Argentines with savings were affected in some way by the *corralito* and its consequences. People used to ask each other casually, "Did you get trapped in *el corralito?*" *El corralito* was part of the daily lives of Argentines, for whom local economic disasters are usually a favorite topic of conversation, together with soccer and political corruption. The protests of depositors naturally dwindled with time, but the effects of the financial crisis remained. As anthropologist Nicholas D'Avella (2014:177) argues, "Argentines are not only invested in pesos, dollars, gold, and real estate. They are also invested in the past." "Sick" currencies (Neiburg 2010), recurrent inflation, confiscations of bank savings, and even the temporary emergence of multiple provincial currencies mark an existential relationship between Argentines and finance that forces them to be distrustful of sophisticated investments. Having had the rug pulled from under them so many times, Argentines with the capacity to build their savings often rely on a primitive form of savings: cash. Argentines famously keep savings "under the mattress," relinquishing potential interest but also shielding them from unpredictable crashes (D'Avella 2014:184). Moreover, these savings are largely kept in dollars in order to protect them from currency fluctuations. Always wary of the advent of the next crisis (Visacovsky 2010), ordinary Argentines are often more worried about losing the value of their savings than about expanding them through investment practices.[7]

Adapting Tools to the Argentine Context

It is not surprising that Argentine readers are initially skeptical about Robert Kiyosaki's books and resources, and American financial self-help in general. *Rich Dad, Poor Dad* and other books are direct translations of the originals in English and contain references and examples from the American economy. They are written with American society and its financial system in mind, and obviously not in light of the realities of the Argentine economy and its rocky past. The Spanish version of Cashflow not only has American cultural references (players can choose as their dream, for example, a private fishing cabin by a Montana lake), its main reference is the credit system, stock market, and real estate of the United States. Financial self-help books constantly mention the structure of retirement planning in the United States. The expression "401k," which means something specific for most employed Americans, is meaningless for Argentines.[8] These resources are not only applicable to a more stable financial system, they also represent an imagined "American Dream" of individual social mobility. Financial self-help is a distinctive American cultural product, developed with an American audience in mind. Yet these financial self-help resources thrive in places like Argentina and other countries for which they have not been originally designed.[9]

Argentine financial self-help participants know that they are dealing with American products; they know that these products speak largely to a different audience in a different cultural and economic context; and they know that many of the financial opportunities that the books promote are unfeasible in Argentina. For example, Sergio, a twenty-four-year-old employee and engineering student who had been practicing stock trading online for a few months, reflected on the differences between Argentina and other countries:

> Imagine the differences between the United States and Argentina. The guy says, "I had $10,000, took out a loan, and I paid it back in ten years." In Argentina that doesn't exist. When I played Cashflow, I won in just a couple of rounds. I had a salary of 1,600, a down payment of 5,000, and a loan of 45,000. Here, try buying an apartment with 5,000 pesos. You should be thankful if you buy a car from 1980. I think that here, playing Cashflow may be useful to manage your money. I mean, you can't apply it here in Argentina, because the relation of numbers is different, it's too slow. But, well, that's what attracted my attention and I started to find out how to generate money . . . assets. . . . Perhaps, for someone in Europe who reads this book it would be easier to achieve it [financial freedom]. But here in Latin America, it's very complicated with the issue of the possibilities that banks offer you to give you a loan, the super high interest rates. . . . It's not like in other countries, where they have fewer requirements and perhaps more benefits.

Sergio was initially skeptical of the opportunities suggested by the Cashflow game and quickly determined that they are not for Latin Americans. His diagnosis was the most common reaction by fans. Raquel, a forty-year-old math teacher, said that her first reaction was equally skeptical. Again, the absence of accessible credit as found in the United States was a major concern. She first asked me,

> Yeah, great, but I ask you: is it so easy to get loans in the U.S.? Because here, when you try to get a loan, you are practically asked for a DNA sample! And even so, you still may not get it!

When she first read Kiyosaki, Raquel immediately thought that his ideas were not applicable in Argentina. She later thought that it was part of a prejudice.

At the beginning, I thought it was very idealistic. Besides, the idea of saying, okay, you can apply this in the United States, not in Argentina. How does it occur to the guy that this can be applicable?! Remember that he said that the context didn't matter, you always find a way. This guy is crazy! In the United States they have different rules, a different kind of legislation. It can be done. Not here. With that preconceived notion inside me.

Raquel initially mocks the idea that the context should be irrelevant for the project of financial freedom. Yet in the end she treats that reaction simply as a preconception. She came to think that the problem was with herself and not with the book's proposals. Gastón (age thirty-five) had a similar reaction, and he was still not sure that Kiyosaki could be "applicable" to the Argentine context:

I think [doing what Kiyosaki suggests] is the right path. Now, well, the great unresolved business is how to apply it in the local market. That is, how to apply all this kind of theory to the market as it is in Argentina. I think that there are possibilities, but it's pretty difficult, it changes a lot. I think it's more adapted to Europe, North America, and not so much Latin America, Brazil, Argentina, Chile maybe. . . . The economic conditions are different, there's not as much freedom as in other countries, I think it's very conditioned. . . .

Gastón had been working for fourteen years as an administrative staff member in a company that provided maintenance and cleaning services to buildings, and he had studied foreign commerce in college. He was interested in economics, and he liked to analyze the Argentine economy. Gastón complained about the instability of the Argentine economy, which made the financial freedom project very difficult. Throughout our interview, he repeatedly brought up each financial disaster the country had undergone, and how he was truly worried of taking risks in an environment in which things could change abruptly:

If you play a game where the rules are clear, you play the game. But if you start the game, and they change the music in the middle of the dance, then it's like . . . you get scared. Imagine investing money. You leave, because you don't like it: "Hey, you said it was like this and now you changed it. . . ." It's a trick. Like the classic "whoever bets for the dollar, loses." We all paid attention, give me pesos! We ended up all upside down. That is changing the rules in the middle of the dance. That's why I don't see that there's much . . . reliability is the word. There's no reliability. You can't trust. The most absurd thing is preferable, thinking like in the Middle Ages, put your money under the mattress . . . right? Unless you start investing in foreign markets, United States, Europe . . . that's different.

Gastón was ten years old when the minister of economy, Lorenzo Sigaut, promised that "whoever bets for the dollar, loses." Yet he brought up this 1982 example to illustrate the instability of the Argentine currency. Gastón was ambiguous about whether what he was learning from the books and the game was "applicable." The memory of financial disaster seemed to make him wary of jumping into investing, yet he told me that he was gathering more and more information, with the intention to "go for it." Like Gastón, Susana, an accountant in her fifties whom I also met in a Cashflow game, contrasts her image of the Argentine economy, quintessentially unpredictable, with that of the United States:

> Not because I know a lot, I tell you, there's a lot I still have to learn, but you have to be alert. In the United States it's surely more stable, and if you get a loan, interest rates don't change a lot, you know how much you will pay ten years from now . . . and the dollar is stable. Here, you don't know. At the end of the year, there will be elections, and you don't know what they [the government] will do! Maybe they take the dollar to, I don't know, 3.30, or maybe it goes down, no one knows! Maybe those in government know so that they do a nice business. . . . So you have to be aware of all that. In the United States, perhaps not. It's much more stable, more quiet. . . . Here you can't get distracted.

The credit, real estate, and stock markets are the bases of Kiyosaki's more technical advice, but they are exactly what Argentine practitioners bring up as the greatest differences between the United States and Argentina. Iván, the professional economist who became a writer on personal finance, explained to me what he considered an enormous difference in how the stock market operated in both countries:

> In the Argentine stock market, the strategy of "buy and hold" is useless. If you look at the numbers, for example, Grupo Financiero Galicia and Banco Francés's [two leading companies] stocks were, before 2000, six dollars and eleven dollars, respectively. Today, after the explosion, the *corralito*, everything we lived and all the later recovery with Chinese growth rates for three or four years, Francés's stock is nine pesos, or three dollars, as opposed to the eleven they were before. Galicia's stocks are less than a dollar. After the recovery. The same happens with the Merval [the general index of the Buenos Aires stock market]. Its record was

in 1992, when it reached 850 points. When the dollar was one to one, that is 850 dollars' worth. Now the Merval is 2,000 points; if you divide it by 3.20 [the currency rate in 2007] . . . it means that fifteen years later it hasn't gotten to the maximum level of 1992. So, the strategy of buying and holding doesn't work. In contrast, in the American market, the maximum was before the World Trade Center attack, 11,400 points. Then there was the crisis, but this year it reached 14,000 points. In the American market, buy and hold works. There you have a large difference in terms of the potential investments that an individual investor without much financial knowledge can make.

Iván brings up a crucial difference between the United States and Argentina. Currency devaluations (either gradual or abrupt) may erase the value of investments and savings in the long term. While stock market values in Argentina have tripled as measured in local currency, that growth is meaningless when the currency value in comparison with the dollar is taken into account. Gabriel, who was studying economics at the time of our interview and organizing Cashflow games and an investment club with Rolo, said,

The macroeconomy of Argentina sucks. I mean, Kiyosaki tells you, "Get a loan, pay the mortgage, and rent it out so that the property pays itself." That's impossible to do here. So it's impossible—Kiyosaki's theory about credit is impossible to apply in Argentina. It's impossible because numbers and interest rates don't add up! So that you understand, interest rates are 18 percent here, and 4 percent in Italy. . . . It's what we are used to in Latin America. Here Telefónica [a European-owned telephone service company] charges you 35 bucks plus [exaggerating] $200,000 for the calls, and in Spain it's just 20 euros and you can call everywhere in the world for that money!

In spite of Gabriel's and others' reflections on the difficulties (and even the impossibility) of "making it work" in Argentina, they were still committed fans and participants in financial self-help groups and activities. For many fans, their quest is to prove that what they have learned in the books *can* be applied in Argentina. When I first heard about Robert Kiyosaki, I did a preliminary search for online material. One of the first things I found was an online forum thread from 2004 in which a user said what many of my interviewees told me: that the ideas seemed to be fantastic, but he wondered if they would work in developing countries. Another user, who I later learned was the founder of the first Cashflow group and one of the first fans to bring the game from the United States, answered that he was trying to demonstrate that it would work, and invited the doubting user to the Cashflow meetings he was organizing. In fact, many encounter financial self-help groups in Argentina precisely because of their doubts about applicability. They search online and quickly find groups, webpages, forums, and advice from people convinced that it can be done and whom they can meet in organized activities. Sergio is an example of this:

> What caught my attention was how to apply it in my country, how all this works in my country. What I did . . . the first thing I did was to find out through the Internet if there was any place here in Argentina where . . . to avoid reading in English, finding something in Spanish, to start reading things. He recommends that you start instructing yourself—the first step is to instruct yourself towards financial education. So I started looking for places where I could study all about financial education, until I reached the webpage of Financial Freedom Argentina. There I started to look for information about courses and short seminars in order to start taking the first steps.

Similarly, the problem of applicability led Raquel, the math teacher who initially thought the books were nonsensical, to Financial Freedom Argentina. After reading the book, she wondered if there were things that "could be done here" and followed online links until she signed up to attend a financial freedom workshop. Argentine readers can easily find a network of social support after reading a book by themselves. The local groups of financial self-help produce the social environment that makes American imported resources more believable. In reality, the social life of financial self-help is as important as the resources themselves. The more this world develops, the more "applicable" those ideas become. In fact, the launching of the Rich Dad products in Argentina was not accompanied by any significant advertising strategy. The users themselves unintentionally organized a formidable local marketing campaign, independent from the central Kiyosaki company. It is thanks to the work fans engage in to solve the problem of applicability that these American products become exportable. The products are not inherently global; they are made global by local active engagement.

In the last decade, local books on personal finance and popular economics started to be published at a higher rate in Argentina, in part as a result of financial self-help groups. At the time I conducted fieldwork in Argentina in 2007–2008, there were barely any local authors of financial self-help. Although there were local promoters, leaders, Cashflow organizers, motivational speakers, and investment experts, the core material was, and still is, based on American ideas and American resources. In financial self-help circles in Argentina, there were frequent mentions of Kiyosaki, Donald Trump, Napoleon Hill, Robert Allen, and even Warren Buffet, but no local books or role models. Although a few books on personal finance and investment already existed, they did not come up in the activities I attended or interviews I conducted.[10] Mario's words perhaps best illustrate the reaction to the idea of Argentine-made financial self-help. Mario reviewed self-help and personal growth literature for a website, so he was a connoisseur of the world of self-help and success literature. When I asked him to name a local self-help author focused on finance, he said,

> National authors? [he thinks for a few seconds]. I'm thinking . . . If I'm thinking, it's because it's hard, otherwise I would drop a name easily. I think . . . like everything, right? If I tell you, "Let's go to watch an action movie." If I don't say anything, let's go watch an Argentine or an American movie. Which one do you want to see? A yankee. Why? Because it's better. If I invite you to watch a movie about soccer, would you watch an Argentine or a yankee? You would go for the Argentine.

For Mario, advice on financial mobility is as American as action movies. It is seen as what, for better or worse, Americans know how to do well. Yet, while enthusiastic, as I have previously shown, fans are frequently left with doubts after reading American best-sellers. This led to the publication of a few local books trying to fill those gaps. This is a result of the local success of American authors, which opened opportunities to reframe those narratives with a more local flavor and examples that catered to the Argentine context. These locally published books are also tied to the international growth of personal finance expertise as a practical field connected with increasingly respected scholarly fields, such as behavioral economics, experimental methods, and cognitive psychology. Local books have not become successful best-sellers like American books, but they are taking up increasingly more space in bookstores. Economist Iván told me in 2007 that the field of personal finance was practically unexplored in Argentina, and since then he became a columnist and book writer on personal finance. Although he never participated in any local Rich Dad groups, he wrote extensively about Kiyosaki in his books and columns, particularly defending the validity of his ideas in Latin America (but attending to the different contexts). A few other local financial experts and economists started publishing books on personal finance in the last few years, trying to find a niche in response to the perceived lack of relevance of American authors in Argentina. Although he does not mention Robert Kiyosaki, financial planner Marcelo Elbaum (2008) named his book *Hombre rico, hombre pobre* [Rich Man, Poor Man], presumably to benefit from the success of the Rich Dad series. Another financial consultant, Mariano Otálora, has published several books about investment and financial planning since 2010. His first book was called *Del colchón a la inversión: Guía para ahorrar e invertir en la Argentina* [From the Mattress to Investment: A Guide to Saving and Investing in Argentina] (Otálora 2011). The title evokes Argentine fears of finance, which leads them to keep savings in cash, literally or figuratively under the mattress. The cover of the book reads: "A 100% Argentine book for Argentines." On the first page, the author writes,

> Do you think that an Argentine can apply the recipe of Robert Kiyosaki's *Rich Dad, Poor Dad*? Impossible. Millionaires never confess "how they do it," and they do not tell us about the obstacles. All those stories have no place in Argentina. We have political, cultural, demographic, normative, and idiosyncratic differences that prevent us from following the examples of the international gurus of finance. So, what to do? That's the question I asked myself when I started writing this book. *Del colchón a la inversión* is a 100% Argentine book, written for Argentine readers.

As I mentioned earlier, this declaration of impossibility is a common reaction on the part of Argentines when reading Kiyosaki and international gurus. However, it is usually a preface to an even more forceful declaration of the potential of those ideas and the conviction that it is worth facing the challenges to try to attain financial freedom. After hearing an interview with Mariano Otálora on the radio in 2011, Matías, the leader of Financial Freedom Argentina, teamed up with sports journalist and TV celebrity Rafael Agüero (who had been attending Cashflow meetings) to write their own book evoking the ideas of Kiyosaki and disseminating the experiences of their club's participants. Their quest was to prove that Kiyosaki's ideas can be used in Argentina. They considered that Otálora's judgment meant that he did not truly understand (or even read) Kiyosaki's books. The book project began the day Matías called Rafael to tell him to quickly turn the radio on to hear Otálora's live interview. As Rafael writes (in first person) in the book coauthored with Matías,

> As the interview went on, his arguments were less and less convincing to me. So I thought that the author hadn't read much about the Rich Dad, Poor Dad philosophy or, if he had actually read it, didn't understand it. Or worse, if he indeed

read it and understood it, perhaps he never tried to truly apply it. And most important, he never mentioned the philosophy behind the financial advice of Kiyosaki. Those of us who have studied them, know that his message and concepts are useful for any individual seeking not just financial growth, but also personal growth in all areas of life. In that moment, the idea of this book was born.[11]

This excerpt suggests a fundamental way in which fans manage to overcome their initial skepticism about the applicability in Argentina of American financial self-help. The authors critique Otálora for not realizing that the practical financial advice is only one part of Kiyosaki's contributions and thus suggest that fans disentangle the essence of the philosophy from the more practical issue of applicability. What they suggest in the book is what fans often do to work through the many suggestions that sound irrelevant in the Argentine context. Argentine readers see Kiyosaki's teachings as a set of essential ideas and tools that do not imply a strict recipe for their application. Achieving financial freedom becomes for them the challenge of finding specific localized investment practices that will work in their own national context. They do not think that Kiyosaki bears that responsibility and they only take away "the philosophy." Matías, for example, thinks that Kiyosaki's advice is not particularly useful only if one wants to replicate his strategy of investing in real estate. Other aspects, he argues, are indeed applicable. In fact, for Matías the Internet has made it possible for people to invest in global markets from anywhere in the world:

> Many people think that Kiyosaki has to do with the United States. But that's because all his business strategy, or at least what he puts in the books, has to do with real estate, with purchasing real estate with a low down payment, like they do in the United States. That's not possible [in Argentina]. Day trading, you can do it in the U.S., or here, investing in bonds, or stock, or knowledge, you do it in the U.S., or here. In the local stock market, or in any stock market. If you want to invest in Frankfurt, or in the Nikkei, you just do it! No one tells you that you can or cannot. . . . Business systems, you do it here or there. Franchises, they work here and there.

Matías reduces Argentines' second thoughts about Kiyosaki to many readers' fixation with his real estate model of buying with credit to rent out for cash flow, which is not easily applicable in Argentina. But for him other investments are. Similarly, for Luis, the creator of the Argentine online forum, people often get caught up in the demand for specific advice, which is harder to translate from the U.S. context, instead of using the basic concepts, which do not vary from country to country:

> If you read Kiyosaki, he never ever says, neither in the books nor in interviews that I have read, "I'm going to make you rich and I'm going to teach you to become rich." But the publicity he gets, directly or indirectly, makes people think that. Now, the question is, can you apply it or do you have to change it? He teaches core techniques and ideas. I ask you a question: Is it the same in the United States or in any other country, or here, an asset and a liability? Understand that if you buy a car to go out on the weekend that's a liability because it takes money out of your pocket, but if you buy it as a taxi and you hire a driver, you get money and it's an asset. The concept is the same in the U.S. and here. Nothing changes. Here is the dilemma. Kiyosaki gives lots of examples about how he or other people did it. Where? In the U.S., because he talks about the U.S. And there you have different laws, a different lifestyle, culture, society, where it is much easier to do *those* things. So people pick up the book and say, "Oh, but he goes to the bank, gets a loan with no down payment, and rent is always higher than the mortgage, you can't do that here! This is only for the U.S.!" . . . The problem is that people want everything to be easy, they want to be told exactly what to do. And there are things that you can do there and not here. But the central philosophy, the central idea to me is the same. . . . These people, all they want is to be told exactly what to do and how, perhaps be given the money to do it, and also to have the revenues delivered to their door! Really, a lot of people are like that.

As illustrated by Luis's words, separating the more abstract ideas from the concrete investment advice is one of the ways in which users in Argentina make sense of American financial self-help. But, as Luis also suggests ("people want everything to be easy"), the individual self and not the national context are blamed for failure to succeed financially in Argentina. This is crucial, since users mobilize a core idea of financial self-help that I have explored throughout this book: individuals should be responsible for themselves and they can never blame structural factors. For Luis, the complaints about Kiyosaki's lack of applicability only show how lazy some people are, and how they do not truly seek or want financial freedom.

Financial self-help practitioners reject being discouraged by the obvious differences between the United States and Argentina, because for them giving up would show more about themselves than about the economic context of the country. Omar, who is heavily involved in the network marketing company Vacation Express, thinks that the differences between countries are more about the self than about the country's conditions:

> There are many people who think that what works in the United States wouldn't work here, like network marketing. They say that in the U.S. it can work, but not here. I don't think it can't work here. What doesn't work here is the people, I tell you. There are many people here with a closed mentality, with employee mentality. Employee for life. Here, a person who is . . . say thirty-five, that has been an employee for the last twenty years, or ten, or five, or fifteen, whatever, will want to study more in order to get a better work position. But not in order to see if they can have their own business. Out of ten people, nine will want to study to get a better job and one will think that he can make his own business.

For Omar, what seems to be failing is not the context or the financial stability of the country, but Argentines themselves. For a philosophy that places all the weight of success on the individual, it is not surprising that national differences are first recognized but then regarded as irrelevant. In fact, an important message that users take from financial self-help resources is that they should not accept defeat in any form. Capitulating to structural conditions of any kind is just relying on excuses. According to this mentality, the more people see that the local conditions in Argentina are preventing them from achieving financial freedom, the more they are showing the power of their fears and their "poor self." Financial success essentially comes from the inside, not from the outside. For example, Martín reflected during our interview,

> I talked with people that [say], "No, because of the context, because of Alfonsín,[12] inflation got me. . . . " They say, "Tell that yankee to come to live here!" I think they are negative people that do not take the essence. They don't take the inside, the message. They see the package and start their rant. Because one of the books I read talks about how you escape from success. You escape success. And I think it has to do with knowing yourself.

Martín regards inflationary crises like the one that happened in 1989 as excuses that reveal one's negativity and fear of success. Others see in the instability of Argentine finances not a disadvantage but a sound justification for applying Kiyosaki's advice. They see Kiyosaki as more important in Argentina than in the United States, because in a context of a volatile economy, one has to be even more prepared. Matías, for example, returns to the notion that people have to take the essence of Kiyosaki's advice and not the specific recommendations about specific markets. Essentially, if they are financially educated, the ups and downs of the economy should not affect them:

> Daniel: What about the volatility of the Argentine economy?
>
> Matías: Fabulous! That's even more in favor of what Kiyosaki says—that you have to be educated. If you are more educated, you are more prepared. . . . The great majority of people say that here it's not possible. That what Kiyosaki raises is not possible, because they are based on Kiyosaki's strategy. They see the form and not the essence. The core is "educate yourself financially." The core, the matrix, the spine of the philosophy is "educate yourself financially." If you're financially educated, you will do well here, in the United States, in the Congo, or in South Korea. You will do well anywhere if you are financially educated. The issue is if you are financially educated. Then you are prepared to cope with the ups and downs of the economy.

I interviewed Matías in a coffee shop right before he was meeting his friend Luciano, a Christian minister who ran his own church with a special focus on businesspeople, and who occasionally participated in Financial Freedom Argentina. Luciano arrived early and joined us. As Matías was telling me about being prepared to cope with a volatile economy, Luciano interrupted:

> It's a little bit like what happened in Argentina with the issue of the *corralito*. Tell me what politician or businessman was trapped. None of them. They were all informed, they were all in the loop. It caught those of us who were uninformed.[13]

The crisis of 2001–2002 is often reinterpreted through Kiyosaki's framework by financial self-help followers: not only can people avoid being hit by a crisis if they are financially educated, but they may also expect to benefit from a crisis if they are well prepared. For Rich Dad online forum leader Luis, recurrent financial crises are a good reason to embrace Kiyosaki's ideas:

> There's a reality: in the crisis of 2001, December 2001, 2002, Kiyosaki says—and many people say—there's no better time to make money than in crises, it's when the most money is made. You have to be prepared. It's not that you have to a have a crystal ball and say, "Look, there'll be a crisis." You have to be prepared with your knowledge. Honestly I'm not prepared today; I'm not prepared yet, neither economically, nor in knowledge and experience. Not in the slightest. I try slowly every day to learn with my experience and that of others. But you have to be prepared. There's a reality in Argentina. . . . And people should know

it, financially and economically, what we are. Even if it was an extremely large crisis, the reality is that we have a crisis every seven years, historically. The reality is that in Argentina we know that there's nothing safe. And we know banks, governments, and everything, what they are . . . People should know that. Perhaps they know it but don't pay attention.

This point about being prepared for a crisis because it can create financial opportunities was echoed in the meetings I attended in Steve's group in New York in the aftermath of the U.S. financial crisis in the fall of 2008. Contrary to my expectations, very little changed in the group's discussions as a result of the collapse. If anything, the crisis confirmed the adequacy of Kiyosaki's ideas in the eyes of participants. There was of course concern about the recent events, and mainly a need for answers, given the technical complexity of the crisis. In the first monthly group meeting after the fall of Lehman Brothers in September 2008, Steve gave a thorough explanation of the causes of the crisis. But he was also forceful in reminding the group that what happened should not change a bit the plan he had been motivating members to follow: buying rental property, starting a business, and achieving financial freedom. "All of this creates for us opportunities," he said. He added that it was very important for him that the group be prepared and insisted several times that money does not disappear, it only changes hands. If anything, the crisis confirmed that trusting the security of one's job was a serious mistake. Steve reminded group members that those suffering the crisis the most were the financially uneducated, who thought that the roof over their heads was really an asset (a basic notion that, as I showed earlier, should be easily debunked by acquiring the right calculative tools). Following Kiyosaki's teachings, crises are seen as large transfers of income between the poor and the rich, and those with the adequate financial intelligence will find multiple opportunities to make money. "Don't miss the boat! It's about to leave the dock! I need you to get on it!" Steve enthusiastically encouraged. In several sessions of the group, Steve put his hand in his pocket and took out a thick pile of credit cards, which he called "my boys." He insisted that he was still getting credit card offers in the mail and that opportunities and money for investment will be there for those prepared (obviously, the credit cards should be used to acquire assets, not consumption debt). The housing foreclosure crisis suggested that more people would be renting, and property values would go down, which would create excellent opportunities for those investing in cash flow. In the financial self-help world, crises are data from reality and as such simply a part of one's financial intelligence, but never an excuse on which to put the blame for one's failures. The first meeting after the Lehman Brothers fall ended, as usual, with an oath that all participants recited in unison: "If I! Do not buy! A property! By December 31st! I ought to be! Ashamed of myself!"

For Argentines, the sudden financial crisis scenario has been part of the landscape for decades. Economist and teacher Iván gives a more technical explanation than Steve for why crises are opportunities to make money, which puts Argentines in a good position to take advantage of American financial advice:

> From the point of view of investment, we live in a very volatile country, in which you have a crisis every ten years. But even the concept of crisis is something that can be seen from the point of view of personal finances. And it's very interesting. Kiyosaki and many other people talk about crisis as the transference of money from the mid-lower class to mid-upper class. When there's a crisis, those who are in the Employee quadrant are those who suffer the most. Because their income is tied to a company, and their future is tied to the results of the company. So, when there's a crisis scenario companies first reduce their budgets, reduce the staff. Many employees end up on the street, they have to sell their properties, downsize, etc. And people who are operating in other quadrants—self-employed, investors or business owners—they take advantage of those situations to increase their assets. If you are a stock holder, when a company fires people, the stock price goes up, because they are cutting costs. . . .
>
> I know many people and students in the classes we give in the magazine who, in the worst moment of the crisis, in 2002, would go to beach resorts and buy land for 5,000 pesos. They would bring dollars from abroad to buy land. And they increased that investment by 400 or 500 percent. You have to have a culture above average. If you have little financial culture, you'll tend to sell land for 5,000 pesos, because you will be scared because the apocalypse is coming, or because you need money because you were fired, etc.

Like Luciano, Iván brings up the *corralito* in his classes on financial coaching to show how being in the loop and being financially educated shields investors from financial crises. During the crisis, people with financial knowledge were able to "jump" government restrictions using legal means. While most depositors could not take their investments out of the country, Iván said that many people bought stock from firms that were cross-listed in the Buenos Aires and New York stock markets. Stocks of Argentine firm Pérez Companc, for example, artificially inflated due to these operations. Investors would then sell the stocks in the American market, hence "jumping" the *corralito* by using loopholes that only financially savvy people could benefit from.[14] Iván sees the instability of Argentina as an advantage for using American advice:

> I think that many differences [between the United States and Argentina] are given mostly by the development of capital markets, by the development of the financial system, the loan system. . . . But those differences do not necessarily make things harder in this country; they sometimes might make them easier, right? In moments of volatility and turbulence, those who are well prepared have many advantages.

Similarly for Gabriel, the key in an economy like the Argentine is simply to be ready and "get on the train" at the right time, in order to benefit from crises:

> We've had two booms and busts in like twenty years, it's impossible. What you have to do here is trying to get on the train in the earlier round. I mean, get all the money you can in the bonanza so that when everything falls apart you can buy houses for two bucks, you can buy taxi licenses for 3,000 pesos, as they were in 2001, and today they are over 50,000, that's how you do your business. You enter one round early. Otherwise, you'll always be in the same place.

While Argentines often complain about the country's economy, accepting American financial self-help does not mean that they erase or reject their own experiences dealing with it. People in Cashflow games often half-joke about how prepared Argentines should be, given their ability to survive financial disasters. During games, players often suggest adding Argentine variables to the game (like inflation, *corralito*, government restrictions, and so on). "Argentines would immediately get it, just like that!" said one player while snapping her fingers. Indeed, Darío, an inventive small business owner and forum member, created an ingenious set of cards that he sold in online forums, and which included actual experiences of investments, obstacles, and "doodads" from local players, including sudden changes in government regulations. It reflected, for example, the manipulation of inflation rates by the Argentine statistical office as well as my own story of having to purchase a new recorder for my interviews because the one I had did not comply with my new computer's operating system. Rolo, a game organizer, said that Italians did not understand the *corralito* when he went to Rome on vacation. The fact that Argentines have gone through so many crashes should make them more resilient and ready for the next one. Rolo mentioned that in a Swiss university they study the Argentine economy, simply to figure out "how we do it." He said that Europeans praise Argentines' "waist," figuratively referring to their agility and ability to duck the punches and survive in an unstable economy. "We have waist, and we don't apply it," Rolo said. "We have been through everything, and we don't take advantage of that."

.   .   .

Rolo's words reflect a positive valuation of some features of *argentinidad*. He thinks that Argentines, having been exposed to so many seismic financial crises, have developed the flexibility and shrewdness that succeeding in business and investing requires. For Rolo, Argentines have only used those traits to stay afloat, but have not fully taken advantage of them. The project of adapting American advice to the Argentine context is shaped by Argentine fans' refusal of structural economic conditions as influential enough to prevent them from embarking on the quest for financial freedom. American financial self-help can travel across different economic contexts in part because users mobilize its own core ideas and techniques to make them applicable. Once one understands that industrial society and its securities are gone everywhere, calculative tools (financial intelligence) and work on the self (toward financial freedom) are all that one needs to move ahead. Argentine fans suggest that the national context may require altering particular investing techniques or giving up on some of them, but it cannot become an excuse to indulge in one's fears.

Conclusion
Financial Self-Help and Beyond

THE HISTORY of the success and expansion of neoliberalism is to a great extent an account of large-scale structural changes. When we think of neoliberalism in the last three decades or so, we often think of a history of dispossession and imposition. We think of multilateral agencies such as the International Monetary Fund and the World Bank, of think tanks that disseminate neoliberal policy recommendations, and of economists trained in monetarist theory in American universities. Neoliberalism makes us think of the privatization of public services and anti-union policies, and of global changes in the worlds of work and trade. It makes us think of fiscal austerity and deregulation of markets.[1]

This book tells a story about neoliberalism that does not contradict the one about large-scale transformation, but it offers another angle from which to view those changes. There is another side of the story of neoliberalism—a side that allows us to see the tribulations of people living not only under new structural economic conditions and policies, but also exposed to popular books and other tools that provide them with a diagnosis of those conditions, and recommendations on how to deal with them. Most important, those recommendations are fundamentally about changing oneself to survive and thrive in a neoliberal world and becoming an entrepreneurial subject that strives for financial freedom. The story of neoliberalism I have described in this book is one about subjects in the making—a story that I suggest is no less important to investigate than the macro-level changes of the last three decades.

This is also not a story of resistance to neoliberalism but, rather, one of embracing it. In this book, I showed how the large-scale transformation of labor, government, and policy has been accompanied by popular forms of expertise and practices that are used to cultivate neoliberal subjects, who are expected to adapt successfully to these transformations. What began in the 1970s and 1980s on a global scale was a shift not simply in state policies but also, as Michel Foucault and others argued, more fundamentally in how the state governs subjects and in how individuals think about and govern themselves. This book shows the pervasiveness of neoliberalism, extending beyond governmental spheres of economic and social policy expertise into the apparently mundane realm of everyday people trying to achieve "financial freedom" in a financially unstable world—users of financial self-help literature and media.

Money is at the center of financial self-help. Participants talk about money, exchange ideas on what to do with it, try to find investors for their business ideas, play a board game to simulate how they use it, or attempt to control their wasteful expenses. In this world, however, finances are both something to be mastered technically and a vehicle to work on the self. All the practices that enthusiasts undergo—from reading a book or attending a seminar to carefully recording one's expenses or buying stock—are practices of the self, directed to attain freedom, both from the dependence of a job and from the fear of taking risks. Financial self-help practitioners learn that the way one behaves with money reflects who they are as a person.

In these circles, money must become a vehicle to motivate an entrepreneurial self, for whom a job, regardless of its income, is a source of dependence and an inhibitor of one's entrepreneurial qualities. One of the sparks that prompt participants to seek out financial self-help activities in the first place is being uneasy about earning a living in a salaried job. But even many who look back at their jobs regret the feelings of security or stability (if they were lucky) that those jobs may have provided. These feelings are reframed as a trap that keeps people inside the "rat race." Income from a job and income from investments are framed as qualitatively different in financial self-help because each represents a different relationship of the individual with the world and with herself. Of course, the work on the self involved in financial freedom requires quite a lot of sacrifice. But that sacrifice is seen as inherently different from the sacrifice of going to a "9 to 5" job every day because it is the sacrifice of a virtuous entrepreneurial self in the making—the only one worth pursuing.

Besides being a popular genre in itself, financial self-help is reflective of larger trends in societies that have undergone neoliberal transformations and increased financialization. In this conclusion, I would like to venture a little bit outside the world in which I have focused throughout this book—that of committed fans of financial best-sellers who participate in activities inspired by them—and suggest that what I have learned in financial self-help is important to understanding recent public and civil society efforts to improve the financial literacy of the population and increase financial inclusion throughout the world. I will do so by examining a recent controversy surrounding a financial education program initiated in Argentina.

In 2010, the ombuds office of the city of Buenos Aires reviewed a complaint presented by parents at a local public elementary school. The parents objected to an educational activity organized in the school by the local chapter of an international nonprofit organization called Junior Achievement. The activity was called "Beyond Money" and was meant to educate children in basic financial skills for their future, including learning the fundamentals of money and how to manage it, how to be an intelligent consumer, and the benefits of having a personal bank account. According to the NGO, the activity was meant to complement content covered in social studies and math courses offered by the school, and relate it to the students' household economy and the market at large. The ombuds office agreed with the parents that the activity was problematic. The office reviewed the guiding principles for the activity and found them too narrow, suggesting that they should be paired and even confronted with other frameworks that would "contribute alternative views about social reality and the workings of the financial system and consumer society, and also warn about the risks of idealizing them." Among other objections, the ombuds office's resolution took issue with the presence of Robert Kiyosaki's *Rich Dad, Poor Dad* book among the few readings suggested by the study materials used in the classes. Professionals from the Area of Education, Culture, Childhood and Youth of the ombuds office carefully reviewed *Rich Dad, Poor Dad*. Quoting the book extensively, they concluded that much of the framing of the Beyond Money program was connected to and inspired by the principles found in the book. The professionals judged Kiyosaki's story of his two dads and their different attitudes toward money, dependence, and mobility to be based on stereotypes discriminatory against the poor and preconceptions that tied the financial well-being of people to their mindset while ignoring other factors. For the ombuds office, while the activity was presented as an attempt to explore math content and its relation to personal and familial life, it was "inscribed in a hierarchical and stereotypical vision of social reality, from which students are presented with models that appear to be ideal, unitary, universal, and even 'successful' representing the world of work, education, business, finance, consumption, and class relations." The resolution ended with a "warning about the implicit assumptions of the framework used" and "leaving the question open as to the significance for the students of learning 'financial abilities' supported by that theoretical framework [*Rich Dad, Poor Dad*] and with the educational ends for which the activities have been thought" (Defensoria del Pueblo de la Ciudad de Buenos Aires 2010). In other words, the ombuds office was concerned that students were not simply learning financial skills but acquiring certain ideas inspired by Kiyosaki's book.

Although the resolution was passed in November 2010, news outlets only started picking up the case a year later (Tiempo Argentino 2011), and particularly in 2012, when the (right-leaning) government of the City of Buenos Aires complained about activities on "problem resolution" organized in city schools by *La Cámpora*, a partisan group with strong ties to the (left-leaning) federal administration of Cristina Kirchner. In response to these activities, the city government established a hotline for parents to denounce external political interference in local schools. Federal government sympathizers objected that they had not heard similar complaints when Junior Achievement taught free-market and entrepreneurial values to the same students. An editorial in the newspaper *La Nación* (2012) claimed that the parallel was ridiculous, accusing those who compared the two cases of

> putting on an equal footing the ideological work and partisan propaganda executed by the group [La Cámpora], with the educational work of non-partisan Junior Achievement, consisting of the diffusion of technical knowledge about economic life, business plans, commercialization, finances, human resources and production. . . . There is nothing wrong with children receiving technical concepts about various issues relevant to their future life in society."

The Junior Achievement director for Argentina also protested what was to him an unfair comparison of "an ideological workshop, part of a political campaign, with an activity to teach students how to start their own business" (Videla 2012).[2]

The story of Beyond Money illustrates two important issues. First, it exemplifies the expansion of resources like Robert Kiyosaki's books beyond the porous confines of the world of financial self-help enthusiasts I researched in this book. The last decade or so has witnessed an expansion of policies by governments, international organizations, the banking sector, and NGOs aimed at enhancing citizens' "financial education," "financial literacy," or "financial inclusion," particularly for those people struggling with poverty. These policies are often well-intentioned, in that lack of access to financial institutions and lack of knowledge about finances have become additional indicators of inequality in societies in which finances play an increasing role. These programs attempt to provide practical knowledge about basic financial issues, from interest rates to the importance of insurance and adequate management of personal finance, spending, and savings, and generally try to raise the level of "financial literacy" of the population (Lusardi and Mitchell 2011). Sometimes those initiatives are targeted to children, and in some countries schools have incorporated financial education to their curriculum. Sometimes they involve partnerships between financial institutions, government, and NGOs. Beyond Money is but one example of an expanding field.[3] Unlike Robert Kiyosaki and the groups with which I conducted research—who aggressively advocate financial freedom, replacing paid work for passive income, and moving to the "investor quadrant"—the field of financial education at first sight simply appears to provide technical tools and information. Yet as the example of Beyond Money illustrates, Kiyosaki's framework is used to support activities not necessarily targeted to his readers.

Second, the controversy over the school's workshop illustrates a larger issue: the difficulties of separating the technical aspects involved in efforts branded as financial education, financial literacy, or financial inclusion from the ethical orientations embedded in those efforts. Defenders of Beyond Money claimed that the aim of the activity was simply to provide students with technical information relevant for their lives. But is it so easy to separate the technical from other dimensions, such as the ethical or the emotional? Are modes of calculation not entangled with questions of who one is and who one wants to be?

This anecdote about one school's attempt to incorporate financial literacy into its classrooms illustrates what I see as one of the main insights of this book. I have defined financial self-help by the presence of a sociological component, a technical component, and a motivational or emotional component. Explanations of the social and economic structures, financial calculative tools, and techniques of the self all work in conjunction to produce the subject of neoliberalism, who sees himself or herself as the only one responsible for his or her financial destiny, and who embarks in a voluntary process of self-transformation. The configuration of (neoliberal) economic subjects is a process in which all these dimensions interact. In my analysis of Cashflow, for example, I demonstrated how goals, calculative tools, and work on the self overlap and connect.

As with financial self-help in general, it would be easy to dismiss an activity like Beyond Money as simply a masquerade of an ideological mission. However, both show the inseparability of techniques and ethical orientations. One of the most important insights of Actor-Network Theory (Latour 2007) as well as the economic performativity approach (Callon 1998) is that objects, including techniques, formulas, sheets, and so on, are in many ways crucial political artifacts. A great deal of the success of neoliberal economics is that it is not just an ideology, but rather, it has become embedded in calculative tools.[4] Despite the claims of technical purity by defenders, in teaching practical tools to deal with the financial world, Beyond Money inevitably pushed particular goals and a particular way of being and behaving. The presence of Kiyosaki's ideas, besides indicating the extent of his impact, is a reflection of the intertwining of calculation and goals like financial freedom. Calculating is a constitutive part of the self. As Peter Miller has argued, in order to understand neoliberalism and the impact of economic thinking, we have to look at "the material reality of calculation," but without losing sight of the political rationality it carries:

> Callon's (1998) important and well-timed call to arms, and his injunction to examine the interrelations between the economy as a thing and economics as a discipline, has had a very positive effect on what can broadly be termed economic sociology. But this "technological turn" in writings about the economy, with its emphasis on the material reality of calculation, has not been matched by a similar concern with the "programmes" or "ideas" that articulate, animate and give significance to particular ways of calculating. (Miller 2008:53)

By bringing together the literature on governmentality and the literature on performativity, in this book I have examined the ways in which neoliberal subjectivities are sought out and adopted by fans of financial self-help through the combination of social theories about the economic and social world, forms of calculation, and a reconfiguration of the self. But I suggest that these combinations can also be seen outside the world of financial self-help fans. As individuals increasingly contend with finances, and financial logics apply to "almost everything" (Chiapello 2015; Leyshon and Thrift 2007), individuals also shape themselves (with the aid of whatever cultural resources they can get) into particular forms of subjectivity. The toolboxes used in financial literacy initiatives may help citizens deal with the banking system, which is a worthy goal in itself, but they already contain technologies of the self. Financial education inevitably suggests processing one's emotions and desires, controlling oneself, and crafting goals that align well enough with the economic world in which we live.

In the case of financial self-help, the "programmes or ideas that articulate, animate and give significance to particular ways of calculating," as Peter Miller put it, are represented by the specific idea of financial freedom. Financial freedom means cultivating a self that rejects dependence and shows an inclination to being entrepreneurial. It is at this point that financial self-help most clearly intersects with the broader, increasing insistence on the entrepreneur as the legitimate subject of today's world. The almost constant celebration of *entrepreneurship*, a much larger phenomenon than the world of financial self-help, represents the same notion Kiyosaki espouses of disparaging salaried labor as a sad alternative for people who have not managed to forge a spirit of freedom and adventure. But even those who wish to remain employed are urged to cultivate their entrepreneurial traits. Entrepreneurship has become less a particular activity than a condition of the self. Regardless of what a person does, they are increasingly required to be entrepreneurs of themselves.

Fostering the entrepreneurial spirit of citizens (that is, changing the self) has become a serious policy proposal to ameliorate poverty, underdevelopment, inequality, and unemployment. For example, in 2011, the World Economic Forum organized roundtable meetings on entrepreneurship education in Latin America as part of its Global Education Initiative. The meetings resulted in a manifesto for entrepreneurship education in Latin America, which stated,

> Entrepreneurship is not always viewed positively in Latin America. The first step in building support for entrepreneurship education is therefore to promote entrepreneurship more broadly to change society's perceptions of what it means to be entrepreneurial and to be an entrepreneur. Greater awareness and access to role models and success stories (international, national and local) are needed to encourage young people to pursue their potential. (World Economic Forum 2011:5)

As the manifesto shows, changing perceptions and spreading awareness of entrepreneurship have become key goals associated with global development.

The report from the meeting also called for formal and informal education to help develop "entrepreneurial skills and mindsets." Like financial self-help, it stressed the fact that schools do not provide skills for social mobility:

> The informal education discussion group concluded that there are no set models to teach people how to be entrepreneurial. Participants noted that school systems do not incorporate the interest of the students in developing a curriculum and that school systems do not teach students skills needed to get out of poverty. (World Economic Forum 2011:19)

Finally, the report highlighted the need to create an entrepreneurial culture in the region, and explained some of the challenges Latin America faces. It said, for example, that "fear of failure is an important barrier to overcome in the region" and that "job insecurity and expectations about public sector jobs for life dampen entrepreneurship, but the group agreed that this is changing, especially among younger people" (World Economic Forum 2011:25). Unlike the Beyond Money activity in Argentine schools, this report does not cite financial best-sellers like *Rich Dad, Poor Dad* despite its striking similarities. While the links are not always explicit, the alignment between the goals of policies promoting entrepreneurship, financial education programs, and the ideas and practices I explored in this book are worthy of closer scholarly attention.

Methodological Appendix

This book is based on participant observation of financial self-help activities; interviews with participants and organizers; and content analysis of online forums, books, and other audiovisual material. I conducted fieldwork from April 2007 to June 2007 in New York, from July 2007 to February 2008 in Argentina, and from July 2008 to July 2009 again in New York.[1] The bulk of the fieldwork took place in various Cashflow clubs (mainly one in New York and two in Argentina), where I participated in Cashflow games and other activities organized by or around these clubs (workshops, talks, and formal and informal meetings).[2] In addition to Cashflow games and workshops that contained Cashflow sessions, I participated in other connected activities. In Argentina, I attended training and information sessions for Vacation Express, a network marketing company connected with Financial Freedom Argentina, and three classes of a financial coaching course organized by a magazine in Buenos Aires. Almost all of my fieldwork was carried out in the Buenos Aires metropolitan area, with the exception of a workshop in La Plata (one hour from Buenos Aires) and two events in Mar del Plata, a coastal city five hours from Buenos Aires. One of the events in Mar del Plata was a one-day workshop by Financial Freedom Argentina. The other was a three-day annual conference on entrepreneurship in which Financial Freedom Argentina offered a short session of Cashflow to introduce conference participants to the game. In New York, the bulk of the non-Cashflow fieldwork occurred in monthly support meetings organized by Steve, in which group members were trained and shared their ideas and advice about real estate and other investments for about five hours. I also attended a few other activities connected to this group, such as real estate training workshops, as well as free workshops advertised on TV about stock trading software and real estate training. I routinely took notes, and I also audiorecorded most of the events I attended, in order to be able to review them later. Normally, people did not care much about my use of a recorder, although in a few instances I felt (probably mistakenly) that the recorder was going to make people uncomfortable so I did not record. I did not notice any particular difference between the times in which I recorded and those I did not. In Cashflow tables, for example, players were so engaged with the game that the small recorder became one more item on the table amidst a flurry of notepads, pencils, erasers, cell phones, drinks, and plates of food.

I also conducted fifty in-depth interviews with people I met in games and work-shops or through online forums. I recruited interviewees in games or other events, ask-ing directly if they would help me by meeting me for an interview. I contacted them later on to arrange a time and place. Ethnographers often recommend waiting until one knows people well before interviewing them. In some cases I followed this recommen-dation (for example, I interviewed most game organizers well into my fieldwork). With participants, this was not always possible, since I did not know if each person would show up to multiple Cashflow games or not. So I interviewed several people whom I had only met once or twice before. I tried to achieve a balanced sample to cover a range of people with varying degrees of experience with financial self-help, men and women, leaders and lay participants. I conducted interviews mostly in public places like coffee shops as well as in interviewees' homes or offices. The average length of an interview was one hour and forty-five minutes, ranging from sixty minutes to three hours, depending on how much time the interviewee had, and how much he or she wanted to talk. On a few occasions, I stopped the interview and resumed it on a different day, meeting up to four times in one case. While I had a guiding questionnaire and took care to ask a few core questions of all interviewees, I generally let conversations go to topics interviewees considered important, to make sure I did not constrain the kinds of issues that might emerge. I usually started interviews with a broad question about how the interviewee became connected to a financial self-help group, leading to them recounting their biog-raphies as well as insights about their readings, activities, finances, and personal strug-gles. Besides formal interviews, I had many more informal conversations as part of my fieldwork, about which I took notes afterward.

In addition, I used material from an online public forum of Argentine fans of finan-cial self-help (particularly in Chapter 4). I registered in the forum at the beginning of my fieldwork, and I read it regularly for two years, although I rarely participated myself (only to confirm my attendance to a Cashflow game or some other event organized by a forum member, for example). Given that many of the interactions in financial self-help happen online through the forum, it made sense to pay attention to what people said there. Obviously, online writing is not the same as everyday speech, and users may prepare posts with different levels of care. Yet this lack of spontaneity was not disad-vantageous for the purposes of my research. Online forums provide a space for people to share their stories and opinions, which is similar to what in-depth interviews try to achieve.[3] Finally, books, CDs, DVDs, websites, and other written and audiovisual mate-rial provided the data to round out my understanding of the nature of the discourses and practices of financial self-help in the United States and Argentina. I did not select a sample of books at the beginning of this research. Instead, I read books and accessed other resources as I advanced in my fieldwork, hearing what participants in the groups I followed read and recommended. Triangulation from fieldwork, interviews, and texts allowed me to reconstruct a set of ideas, practices, and experiences that are widely shared by people who participate in the world of financial self-help.

Ethnographic research ought to tell us something about the specific world under scrutiny as well as something about larger sociological questions. Ethnographic observations or interview materials are not data by themselves. They are turned into data by theories. There are various views on how developed the theoretical framework of the ethnographer should be prior to going to the field. My position is that an ethnographer who does not go to the field with a few more or less clear theoretical ideas will need to record absolutely everything that happens in the field. Theories (either explicit or subconscious) inform ethnographers so that they know at least where not to look. But ethnographers cannot go too far down a path constricted rigidly by one theory. Ethnography is a delicate equilibrium because researchers must remain open to new possibilities. They have to be ready to discover patterns and trends that they did not contemplate in the research design. So, contradicting the previous dictum, ethnographers are interested in almost everything that happens in the field. Too many times, ethnographers do not really know why they are observing something, and have no idea if those observations will become data or not. Many times, I told people in the field that I was interested in anything they did related to money and financial education, and asked them to please let me know of any activity in which I could join them. As such, ethnography is undoubtedly quite an inefficient and time-consuming enterprise. Research in general, but ethnographic research in particular, demands a back and forth between theory and data, throughout the process of data collection and analysis. Ethnographers have to re-read what they find in the field in light of the theories considered before going to the field and new ones that better illuminate new data (Becker 2009). During my fieldwork, I let theory guide me, but I did not allow it to overly constrain my observations.

I presented my research in a style close to what John Van Maanen calls realist tales:

> Realist tales swallow up the fieldworker, and by convention the text focuses almost solely on the sayings, doings, and supposed thinkings of the people studied. Materials are organized according to topics and problems relevant to the fieldworker's conceptual and disciplinary interests. The presence of the author is relegated to very limited accounts of the conditions of the fieldwork. (1988:47)

For Van Maanen, the realist ethnographer vanishes from the descriptions, and that is partly what I sought to do. I included myself in the narrative in this book only insofar as it was necessary to convey a certain point or to make clear an image from the field. My goal was to focus on others, not myself. This was due not so much to an epistemological choice, but rather a stylistic one. I did not want this book to be a story of a sociologist; I do not feel that I am more important than, or even equally as important as, the people I studied during my fieldwork. While any research is inevitably a story that involves the researcher, I preferred the researcher not to be the main actor in readers' minds. However, being able to remove myself as much as I could stylistically does not mean that I believe that the ethnographer can remove himself or herself epistemologically from the ethnographic account. Hence, I also tried to avoid the deceiving image of a world that appears to be studying itself (which leads researchers to abuse the passive voice instead of openly saying "I"). I readily acknowledged throughout the book that I was present as observer, participant, and interviewer.

Most scholars today recognize that ethnographic research is essentially a study of an encounter between the researcher and the worlds she studies. An ethnographer is not a tabula rasa that receives stimuli from the outside and converts those stimuli into field notes. Yet the ethnographer works hard to be objective and to be able to trust the validity of his findings. Objectivity to me is the committed pursuit of issues that appear to be different from the ethnographer's previously held ideas, hypotheses, and even moral values with equal or more strength than those that fit the previous notions the researcher held. Hence, since I stylistically left myself out of much of this book's narrative, in the next few pages I would like to make up for that and write about my experiences in the world I studied. Rather than an act of academic narcissism, I want to recognize the relational character of qualitative work because I think the reader can learn more about financial self-help by learning about my place in the research process.

While ethnographers often try to blend into the worlds they study, by definition their participation is different from that of any other person in the field. Ethnographers can spend time with people, live in the same places, do the same things, participate in people's lives, and even in some cases experience the same physical pain, but as researchers, they still take notes, and at some point they leave the field and write about their observations and experiences. They might at times feel so included that they may even forget that they are researchers at all; yet whether they feel it or not, they are conducting research. Although people in the field eventually may treat ethnographers as "one of us," that is never quite the case, and often some fortuitous event makes ethnographers realize that their insider status was an illusion. At the end of his book *Body & Soul: Notebooks of an Apprentice Boxer*, Loic Wacquant (2003) narrates his only official boxing combat, as part of the Chicago Golden Gloves tournament. After he felt the taste (and the pain) of a real fight, which was much more severe than his already intense training, his coach told Wacquant that he hoped that the sociologist had collected enough material for his book. The coach was seriously concerned with Wacquant's physical integrity, and he had never forgotten that the sociologist was participating ultimately to write a book. Another ethnographer, Mitch Duneier, confessed that as he was listening to tape recordings of his field sites, he heard what his subjects actually thought of him. By that time, Duneier thought that he was much more integrated into the lives of his subjects (street book vendors) than he really was (Duneier 2001:333–58). For Duneier, it is not necessary to "go native," or to be considered one of the people you are studying in order to produce knowledge. The idea that ethnographers can blend in unseen is no more than a fiction.[4] In general, but particularly in the world I studied, an ethnographer is a peculiar species. I approached a world in order to study it and write a book about it. That is already quite different from the way we normally interact with the world in our everyday lives. I studied people who were going to great pains in order to attain financial freedom. I was going to great pains in order to understand what they were doing and eventually write a book about them. There were radically different things at stake for me and for my research participants.

Many ethnographers conduct research about worlds that are already familiar to them: an institution they know, a world they had belonged to or still belong to, a community in which they have been involved as activists, or a setting in which they have spent some time until they became aware of its potential as a research site. Several ethnographers also conduct research about people they like or with whom they politically sympathize.[5] I did none of those things. From the outset of this project, I knew that I was not entering a world of people with whom I would particularly share moral, political, or economic values. I was also entering a world about which I knew very little. I always thought that this approach—studying a world about which the researcher initially knows very little, made up of people whose ideas may be quite different from the researcher's—was an effective, although often more difficult, way of doing ethnography. The fact that I did not already understand the ideas and practices that I was studying pushed me to try harder to comprehend the meanings shared by my subjects. Those ideas may have been different from my own, but my job was not to contrast them with mine (although sometimes it was hard not to do so). My task was to understand the internal coherence of those ideas and practices. My approach to financial self-help was open; I simply tried to learn as much as I could. As sociologist Eva Illouz (2008:4) states, "the point of cultural analysis is not to measure cultural practices against what they ought to be or ought to have been but rather to understand how they have come to be what they are and why, in being what they are, they 'accomplish things.'"

But the fact that I tried to remain agnostic does not mean that I disappeared. It was still me who was trying to understand a world that differed substantially from my own. Instead of pretending to be a receptive blank slate, which is impossible, I used my own subjective reactions to the advantage of comprehending the meanings that those in this world give to their interactions. For example, in Chapter 4 ("Creating a World of Abundance"), I could only discover the general organization of interest and disinterest as noncontradictory and the compelling power of network marketing after examining my own reactions to what I observed. I realized that my feeling offended by the organizers' attitudes (who pitched their company while teaching) was based on a different way of organizing one's interest and disinterest. In ethnography and interviewing, the researcher learns from his or her own encounter with the world under scrutiny. There is no point in neglecting the fact that it is a social relation between researcher and subjects. Knowledge is the product of the analysis of that encounter and that relationship. During my fieldwork, I learned to understand the internal logic of discourses and practices of financial self-help, and my interactions in the field allowed me to understand it even better.

However, I should not exaggerate the distance between myself and financial self-help. Although I personally reject many of the ideas espoused by financial gurus, the concerns of participants of financial self-help were about issues that are not exclusive to that world. Participants shared ideas, performed practices, and constituted groups devoted to things that we all are somewhat forced to think about in capitalist societies: our personal finances, our money, our jobs, our retirement, and our freedom. Although the groups themselves are unique in that they actively dedicate themselves to advancing their financial position by following specific theories and practices, their concerns are not foreign to those who do not take it so seriously or do not make them so central to their lives.

I learned a lot from presenting this research formally and informally to several audiences. Often people asked me questions that had more to do with their own lives than with the lives of my respondents. In a few occasions, although it was not at all my intention, members of audiences told me that while they were listening to my presentation, they started to think about their own personal finances. Some started to wonder if they were managing their own finances correctly. Other listeners indirectly questioned participants and readers of financial self-help, thereby reaffirming their own financial behavior. When discussing my own research with friends and acquaintances who had never heard the name of a financial success best-seller, let alone read one, they voiced their own repertoires of ideas and practices in order to justify their own choices in their financial lives, thereby resisting the mandate to acquire "financial intelligence." These friends of mine seemed to vitally need to believe that making money was not as important as participants of financial self-help made it seem to be. After months of fieldwork, I saw myself sharing my research subjects' ideas with my own acquaintances, and somewhat defending them from outside attacks. These informal discussions with "outsiders" helped me assess how much I understood the world of financial self-help in its own logic. I must confess I found some guilty pleasure in this task.

I enjoyed the way an informal conversation about my research quickly turned into a conversation about the ethics of money and investing and about the moral and financial choices of those in front of me. As a sociologist and especially as a teacher, I have been trained to present ideas and theories that I do not necessarily share but which I consider worth understanding and analyzing in their own coherence. In these discussions, I usually felt as I feel in my classes, where I defend theories I do not particularly share, just to show that they do make sense and they are not as easy to debunk as they may seem at first sight. Why did many of my conversations with outsiders turn out this way? Because, whether we like it or not, we are all forced (today more than ever) to think about money and finances and deal with the anxieties they produce, whether or not wealth is a goal of our own. We all acquire and develop values that give money an imagined role in our lives. Talking about money and recognizing its importance (or lack of importance) is not a trivial matter. It affects the way we consciously or unconsciously see ourselves as free human beings.

During my fieldwork, I participated in activities designed to make people carefully examine their relationship with money and finances. Like the rest of the participants, I was asked to write about or narrate what I do with money. Coaches suggested during these activities that the way we handle money every day (something people do not dwell on very often) reveals a lot about how we *are* in relation to money. During one Cashflow game, all players had to bring up statements we heard about money at home when we were growing up. The goal was to discover how those ideas still carry weight within us today. My responses were not very different from those of other players. Like many others, I grew up hearing that money does not grow on trees, that it is limited, and that you have to work hard for it. In many ways, I was no different from other people there. I have never owned a "real" investment in my life. I never had a "financial education" more specific than just knowing that I cannot spend more than what my income is, and to be careful about debt. As of today, my banking activities are limited to checking accounts, secure low-rate savings accounts, and occasionally a certificate of deposit. I am not financially sophisticated whatsoever. I do not have "passive income," and I prefer not to think a lot about my personal finances. I have never been anything other than a salaried employee (both in the public or private sector) or a student on fellowship, and I never received any significant income from investments of any kind. As Robert Kiyosaki and his fans would put it, I have always worked for money and I never had money working for me. Luckily, and unlike a majority of Americans, I have never had significant debt (thanks partly to the availability of free public universities in Argentina, which did not force me to acquire a student loan for my education). I did not know much about investment or personal finance before I started this project and, coming from a working-class family, I was taught the value of education and job stability (something my own parents did not have) and wariness of financial risks. Thus, in many ways I fit very well the broad target of financial self-help.

I knew from the beginning of my fieldwork that reading a book or playing a game with the goal of becoming rich (or more accurately, achieving financial freedom) was radically different from doing those things with the goal of writing about the experience (Schutz 1944). Thus, I never expected or desired to feel the same way as others with whom I shared activities. But on the other hand, it is quite impossible, even as protected as I was thanks to my role as researcher, not to feel some of the same anxieties and think the same reflections that practices and discourses of financial self-help produce in genuine practitioners. Financial self-help offers powerful narratives about who we are and who we should be. It is not easy to approach them without considering their application in one's own life.

Financial self-help's first step is to question one's own financial upbringing and one's attraction to security over risk. Why did I choose to devote myself to an academic career? I obviously think, like most scholars, that the reasons have to do with passion, trying to contribute to knowledge, being recognized, or improving the world (I recognize that there must be a lot of variation among different scholars on the reasons people pursue this career). But academia is an activity that in many ways is "shielded" from the market. After all, academia is one of the few strongholds resisting the advance of flexible labor (although it seems to be falling, too). As Gerald Davis puts it, "The employment practices of large manufacturers and other bureaucratic firms, which once set the standard for middle-class life in America, are irrelevant for most of the population, and the idea of an organization providing a career of stable employment has been banished to civil servants and that sliver of academics with tenure" (2009:3). While there are risks involved in an academic career, they are different from the financial risks that financial self-help prompts us to embrace.

Throughout my fieldwork, I was occasionally seen as an example of the "poor" mindset imagined by Kiyosaki. In 2009, Sonny (the New York Cashflow organizer) asked me what I was planning to do after finishing my research, and I told him that my goal was to become a professor. "So you're staying in the E [employee] quadrant," he replied. I had never seen my goal in such bleak terms. I had to agree and tell Sonny that my goal was indeed to stay in the E quadrant. So he proposed that we plan seminars on how to become rich. I told Sonny that I did not feel qualified to do that, to which he replied that I was just thinking negatively. I told him that I did not have any financial success to demonstrate. He said that if I write a book about the Cashflow clubs and have a few investments, it should be enough to give workshops. A few months later, as I was in the process of finding a job, I had a phone conversation with Sonny and told him about my tribulations with the academic job market. Sonny told me, "I can't believe that after all this time you are still thinking like an employee! You have gone through all this learning now, but you're still thinking about jobs. When are you going to become an entrepreneur? Jobs will disappear. And the tenure thing that professors have, that's gonna be over! You gotta start thinking from the I and B quadrant, you're still seeing the world from the E and S quadrants." Sonny knew from the day we met that I was solely writing about financial self-help groups, not embarking on the path to financial freedom like my respondents. He usually called me "the professor" in front of other people, often asked me how my "paper" was going, and made sure others knew that my research was legitimate. I saw Sonny on several occasions outside the activities he organized or participated in. He was always nice to me and told me that for him interacting with someone from outside his trade and from another country was also very interesting. But he never gave up on the idea that my immersion should have an impact on me. He often pointed at my limitations as a potential entrepreneur or investor. Once, during a Cashflow game, I made a decision on an investment that Sonny judged to be fairly bold. He said that it was not crazy, but it was on the edge—too risky. I jokingly replied, "That's who I am!" Sonny looked at me and promptly, solemnly answered, "No, that's not who you are." My interactions with Sonny had helped him profile me in terms of my future goals and my risk tolerance. He knew me. A few months after that exchange, he told me that one of his goals was to get the poor person out of me.

That was not the first time financial self-help participants professed being invested in my own learning as a financial being and not as a researcher. Since my first visit to his Saturday meetings in New York, Steve insisted that, even though he understood that I was there to conduct research, I should both take advantage of the learning and con-tribute to the group by bringing information about deals that I might run into. He often asked if I did my homework (which most times consisted of taking small steps toward buying rental property or setting up a business). Several players and interviewees asked me if what I was learning was changing me, and wondered when I was going to start taking action and apply the philosophies that I was absorbing. I always answered the truth: that I was learning a lot, and that all my energy needed to go into my research. Starting a journey like the one they were undertaking (whether it was desirable or not) would have been impossible for me at the time. Eventually, I said, after I was done with my book, I would perhaps consider applying what I had learned in so many Cashflow sessions and other activities.

I would like to emphasize how frightening and overwhelming it felt during my field-work to come face to face daily with a set of cultural resources that insisted emphatically that I (and everyone else not on the path to financial freedom) was doing everything wrong financially, and that I might regret all my silly decisions in the future, for example when I find myself with no job, or with no money in retirement. Regardless of my personal rejection of the idea that "money works," the thought of having an income without working is highly appealing. And I cannot stress enough how it often doesn't seem so difficult to achieve when one is immersed so deeply in financial self-help circles. After coming home from fieldwork, I often found myself allured by all these opportunities. Whether it was joining Vacation Express, purchasing software to start trading online, or getting a business line of credit to be in a position to acquire real estate property, all these activities and the idea of financial freedom made more sense to me the closer I was to the field.

Leaving the field and going back to the academic world (with a different system of rewards and recognition) would modify my view of the vital need to get involved in any of these activities.[6] In fact, informal interactions and formal introductions at the beginnings of workshops provided several opportunities for me to explain not just what I was doing there but also my source of income. Especially in Argentina, I had a hard time explaining to people that I received a fellowship from an American university, that I was actually being paid to perform ethnographic research, and that I did not really have a boss or, technically, an employer. When I explained all this, I realized that attending a seminar or a game session with the goal of becoming rich made far more sense than conducting fieldwork in order to write a book that would surely not make me rich. While immersed in the financial self-help world, I occasionally found myself thinking that the strange subculture that required an explanation about its counterintuitive principles was not financial self-help, but the academic world. "Perhaps they should be studying me," I thought to myself several times. One Cashflow player in Argentina concluded as we were playing that given that I had a fellowship while doing fieldwork, I was technically receiving "passive income" and therefore temporarily out of the rat race.[7]

Another challenge that came up during fieldwork was the question of how deeply I should involve myself in these groups. This is a serious issue that every ethnographer faces, with deep consequences for the ethics of their research. I was tempted, for example, to purchase a franchise of Vacation Express so that I could participate more in the company, have more access to people and their practices, or perhaps share their feelings more deeply. Several ethnographers have described gaining more knowledge of the worlds in question by getting more involved (most notably Loic Wacquant, for whom training alongside Chicago boxers and actually becoming one made a difference in his understanding of boxing, and in the boxers' relation with him and regard for him).

Unsurprisingly, I received repeated proposals to become a member of Vacation Express. I attended company events and the Financial Freedom Argentina workshops in which new members were recruited, I spent time with members, and I understood how the system worked, so for some people it did not make much sense that I did not become a member myself. Various participants were surprised to see me at all these events, and they never lost hope that at some point I would realize how good a business it was. Fernando, an enthusiastic member, implored me after a presentation, "Are you sure, Daniel? People are making money!" When I showed up (once again) at a huge company event, Alejandro said jokingly to other members around him: "I'm going to put him upside-down and squeeze the 4,000 pesos out of him [to enter the network]."

While getting into the network might possibly have gotten me more privileged access to certain activities and people, I chose not to (and not just because it was very expensive). First of all, if I had invested in a franchise of a network marketing company, I would have needed to recruit people, not only in order to recover my investment but also simply because that is what members do. One is recruited to recruit others, and not doing so would have affected my recruiters negatively. Accepting a membership would have posed a host of ethical dilemmas, since I would have been directly making money out of research subjects while presumably getting others involved in a business I had many doubts about. Second, it would probably have changed the way other people saw me. My status as a member of the network would surely have become more important than my status as a researcher. It would have opened some doors but closed others because I would have had an interest in recommending Vacation Express to others, regardless of my ethical commitment as a researcher. While there was indeed something to be lost in terms of access, I chose not to become a member.

By staying away from further involvement, my "outsider" status as a university researcher resulted in some people seeing me as a sort of authoritative voice with regard to business opportunities such as Vacation Express. I decided not to offer any strong opinions about Vacation Express when I was asked. Because I was at the time trying to understand the structure of the network marketing system and the logic of their activity, I did not have a firm or well-developed opinion. I never assumed that I knew more than my participants. After all, they were deciding to spend money on it or not, so they were the experts. If I recommended that others join, this meant siding with Financial Freedom Argentina members and their interests, while a clear recommendation against it seemed like an awkward course of action too, given that they were helping me considerably with my fieldwork. When I was asked for an opinion, I answered that I did not know enough because I had never participated in network marketing, but it seemed to be an interesting organization. I added that it did not look like it was for everyone—it seemed that in order to do well people had to devote a significant amount of time and effort, something that was not always stressed enough in invitations to join. Finally, I said that, like in every industry, there must be variations between companies.

For the most part, I believe participants perceived me as a curiosity. In the first Cashflow event I attended in Buenos Aires in July 2007, I told Financial Freedom organizer Alejandro casually during the game who I was and what I was doing there. "How long are you staying?" he said. "If you want, you can join us. We're doing events throughout the country every weekend." I thanked him and said that would be fantastic—truly a great research opportunity. Alejandro suggested, "Let's coordinate, because what you're doing is cool, and also you are skilled at this [*estás canchero*], so you can participate in the events." He called Ramiro, who was advising another table, and told him, "You know what, Ramiro? He's studying in the United States, and he's doing research for a book on all this." Ramiro interrupted, "He should be with us!" Alejandro continued, "That's what I'm saying, he's staying until February, so I told him that he can join us and participate with us in all the events he wants." Thus, after much worry about how difficult it would be to gain access to financial self-help circles, I was offered virtually free and unlimited access to the formal events of the Financial Freedom Argentina group. Although Alejandro did not ask for anything in exchange, I helped the group as needed in preparing and disassembling game tables, and in what was probably most helpful for them: answering questions about the game in the sessions with many tables. As I explained in Chapter 3, at the beginning of the game it can be very hard to understand its mechanics, and the three or four leaders who went around the tables answering questions were often overwhelmed. So I often joined them as a volunteer coordinator and moved between tables answering questions, although at other times I was just one more player in the room.

Most workshops had a moment of introductions in which everyone said what they did and what their goals were. In those occasions I always had the chance to introduce myself (and publicly thank the organizers for letting me participate). Sometimes Financial Freedom Argentina organizers introduced me when they presented their staff, and mentioned with pride that they were being studied by someone from a university in the United States. They also joked about me studying participants like guinea pigs (yes, people still have those "laboratory" images about social researchers). Usually a few people showed interest about what I was doing, especially the fact that I was living and studying in the United States. They asked me about the university, about life in New York, and about financial self-help groups and financial opportunities in the United States. In general, my insider-outsider status as a researcher did not seem problematic. I imagine most event participants simply saw that I was some sort of academic attachment to the group, and that I enjoyed answering questions about Cashflow (which gave me more opportunities to observe different tables and the kinds of questions people asked). However, on one occasion Matías asked me to wear their distinctive t-shirt (with the name of the group and a Cashflow Quadrant logo). While in some circumstances the privilege of being a member of the staff might be desirable for an ethnographer, I thought that wearing the t-shirt was not a good idea. In this case, I believed that my outsider status was preferable, since the group offered business opportunities like Vacation Express, and I was afraid that people would think that I was a member and I might have had some financial interest at stake. I never knew who I was going to meet down the road in different activities of various groups that might have disliked each other, so I preferred to maintain a neutral status. In Argentina, saying that one "wears the jersey" [*ponerse la camiseta*] of a company or a group means that one is a committed representative, so I was concerned about the symbolic significance of my wearing the group t-shirt. This incident illustrates the problematic status of the researcher as insider-outsider. Sometimes it is desirable to remain an outsider. The group had been quite generous to me in giving me access to their events, but I nevertheless disappointed the person who was offering help. When he offered me a signal of inclusion, it was me who highlighted my outsider status.

For confidentiality reasons and research ethics I promised to change in my writing the names of the persons I met in the field or interviewed, as well as their organizations. But I found that oftentimes I was more concerned about protecting identities than participants themselves were. When Matías casually heard that I was not using real names in my writing, he was disappointed. He actually expected the name of his group to appear, and he told me (half joking) that he thought that I would write that his group was the best financial club. He joked that when he heard that the name of the group would not be featured, he lost interest in me (although luckily nothing really changed after that). I chose to protect identities anyway, as it is standard ethnographic practice. Most important, Matías's words made me realize that he thought that I would write "good" things about them. While I did not necessarily plan to write "bad" things, his comment made me realize that we probably had different ideas of the purposes of my research.

This was not the only occasion in which I felt that people I met in the field had a different idea of what an appropriate research project about them should say. I have always been thankful for the people who let me participate in their activities for my research. Participating in other people's worlds is a privilege, not a right. I owe this project's success to the good will of those who kindly accepted my presence observing or interviewing them. However, the results of my research might not have the practical implications they may have hoped for: how to succeed financially. In informal conversations with group leaders both in New York and Buenos Aires, they sometimes hinted implicitly or explicitly about what they thought my contribution should be. Their suggestions always had to do with effectiveness. Once as we walked back to the subway from a Cashflow game, Steve told me that the goal of my research should be to make a difference. He was interested in understanding what makes some groups more successful than others. He suggested that I could make my research profitable by selling it to Robert Kiyosaki, who would be very interested in knowing about my findings in order to be more successful with his products. "You could make a difference," Steve said, "if you know why one person is successful and the other one is not." He suggested research designs aimed at isolating the one variable that would explain individual success using financial self-help. He wanted to know why some people in his group "take action" while others don't, and suggested what he thought the main reason was: motivation. Both his question and his answer were in line with the main tenets of financial self-help—individualizing the responsibility for "taking action." Steve's interest in knowing what makes one person succeed and another fail and his immediate attention to motivation was for me once again revealing of the power of financial self-help and its appeal.

Financial self-help users may or may not find in this book the answers to their most urgent questions, particularly not one about effectiveness. But I hope that this study might show them their own world and their own activities in a different light, and perhaps encourage them to take another look at why they are asking the question of what makes some succeed while others fail. After all, that is what sociology is all about.

Notes

Introduction

1. See Brady (2014:16). In a study of the various scholarly uses of neoliberalism, Boas and Gans-Morse (2009) identified four uses of the term in social science literature. First, neoliberalism has been used to describe various economic reform policies, including privatization of public services, deregulation of markets, fiscal austerity, and in general the reduction of the role of the state in the economy since the 1970s. Second, it has also been used to describe a comprehensive and coherent development strategy (as opposed to specific policy recommendations) contrasted with state-led development models. Third, it is often used to describe "normative ideas about the proper role of individuals versus collectivities and a particular conception of freedom as an overarching social value" (144). Finally, neoliberalism has been employed to characterize the economic paradigm of neoclassical economic theory, which assumes the perfect functioning of markets. Terry Flew (2014) identifies six ways of using the term *neoliberalism*: "(1) an all-purpose denunciatory category; (2) 'the way things are'; (3) an institutional framework characterizing particular forms of national capitalism, most notably the Anglo-American ones; (4) a dominant ideology of global capitalism; (5) a form of governmentality and hegemony; and (6) a variant within the broad framework of liberalism as both theory and policy discourse." See also Davies (2014).

2. Treating neoliberalism as governmentality does not mean disregarding its policy and ideological elements, but rather understanding that they are not always consistent because they are subjected to and motivated by a governmentality. Anthropologist James Ferguson (2010:172) argues that while using the term *neoliberalism* with more precision is undoubtedly good, there is still some utility in words that "bring together more than one meaning. As long as we can avoid the mistake of simply confusing the different meanings, the word can be an occasion for reflecting on how the rather different things to which it refers may be related."

3. Under this human capital framework, anything people do can be considered an investment in their human capital (Read 2009:30).

4. It is important to highlight that while the term *self* has been used in several theoretical traditions, I use the term throughout this book within the tradition of gov-

ernmentality studies initiated by Foucault in his later work. This means considering subjects "not simply as passive victims of social practices of power and social domination" but rather as creative agents (Elliott 2008:91). Foucault's shift of focus from technologies of domination to technologies of the self around the late 1970s and early 1980s has been the subject of considerable scholarship. Scholars have debated about what exactly changed in Foucault's approach from the years of *Discipline and Punish* to his later work on care of the self in Greco-Roman cultures and in Christianity. Analyses range from significant methodological breaks to continuity (Brady 2014; Collier 2009; Dilts 2011; Koopman 2013). According to Stephen Collier, there is indeed a methodological shift in Foucault's abandonment of "epochal and totalizing diagnoses" that characterized some of his earlier work and his preference for a "fuzzy history" approach, in which different forms of power cohabitate and are linked "in a topological space" (Collier 2009:89–90). It seems clear that Foucault decreased his emphasis on practices of crude subjugation and discipline (such as the practices typically analyzed in the *Discipline and Punish* period) and moved into an exploration of practices of the self that may or may not involve self-domination, or at least in which domination is not the main feature (Foucault 1997b:282). The lectures on neoliberal governmentality (Foucault 2008) seem to be a hinge that connects Foucault's earlier concern with discipline with his later historical exploration of ethics and care of the self (Foucault 2005:252). Throughout this period, Foucault became increasingly interested in how subjects fashioned themselves and less concerned with more coercive forms of subjectification.

5. For an analysis of the place of economic performativity in the larger field of economic sociology, see Fourcade (2007) and Zelizer (2007).

6. Subject formation and the self has been a consistent focus of governmentality, while economic performativity concentrates on the technical aspects that make action possible, with no consideration for things like self, self-conception, motivation, or desire. Yet there are important affinities between these two theories. Research on governmentality has consistently highlighted the significance of technical aspects of government, although with more specific attention than economic performativity to the intersections between the technical and the political (Callon and Muniesa 2005:1232; Miller 2001). For example, Miller and Rose (1990, 2008) formulated the idea of governing "from a distance" in neoliberalism, borrowing the concept of "action at a distance" from actor-network theorist Bruno Latour. Both were talking about the mediations of nonhumans, but Rose and Miller mobilized Latour's concept to emphasize how it facilitates a form of government in which the ruler does not directly impose on the ruled. Fourcade (2007:1026) also suggested points of contact between the two theories. She says that economic performativity could be thought of as a theory of modernity, given that it offers an account of the centrality of market technologies in modern society and their capacity to transform the lives and social relations of market actors. For Fourcade, this means that "performative analysis in the sociology of markets is a natural rejoinder to a neofoucauldian tradition that focuses on calculability as the primary technology of neoliberal governmentality."

7. It is important to distinguish the terms I use analytically from the native terms from the world of financial self-help. I refer throughout this book to concepts such as self, technologies of the self, autonomy, neoliberalism, calculative tools, and inertia even though these are not used by financial self-help fans or authors. The most commonly used terms by fans are financial freedom, financial intelligence, financial education, and rat race.

8. Many of Robert Kiyosaki's books were written with the collaboration of his business partner until 2008, Sharon L. Lechter. The book covers show Lechter's name only in smaller font than Kiyosaki's and after the word *with*.

9. I discovered throughout my research that it is virtually impossible to find reliable numbers for best-selling book sales. I gathered these estimates from several media sources. The most optimistic number (twenty-eight million) comes from Kiyosaki's own promotional materials.

10. In spite of the recent turmoil in the American financial system, in Argentina the United States is usually seen as the pinnacle of financial certainty and stability.

11. This book is not organized around a comparison of the two countries. To understand consistently the ideas, techniques, and practices of financial self-help enthusiasts, I draw on material from both places throughout this book, except for Chapter 5, in which I focus on the specific challenges of Argentine users. The goal is not to compare the economies in the United States and in Argentina, or how neoliberalism has had an impact in each country, or how Argentines and Americans in general feel about financial self-help. As anthropologist Clifford Geertz (1973:22) said, ethnographers don't study villages, they study *in* villages. The goal of using two cases is to examine how similar tools and practices of financial self-help (originated in the United States) are adopted across national contexts and how they are understood by users exposed to different conditions in regard to financial stability.

12. In *Pound Foolish: Exposing the Dark Side of the Personal Finance Industry*, journalist Helaine Olen (2013) offered this kind of exposé of the myths of American financial gurus.

13. All names of participants, organizers, and locations have been altered to ensure confidentiality.

14. I also attended Cashflow meetings held by two other New York meetup groups. These groups were not as consistent as Sonny in organizing games.

Chapter 1

1. In her study of contemporary self-improvement books, sociologist Micki McGee acknowledges the difficulties of defining clear-cut boundaries for the self-help genre. Many books that authors did not consider self-help have made it onto lists of self-help titles or have been shelved in self-improvement sections of bookstores (see McGee 2005:193–96). My approach is different from studies of the self-help genre that draw a sample from best-selling titles. My study starts from Robert Kiyosaki and his followers, and includes other authors and resources that arose during my fieldwork.

2. Kiyosaki's books, for example, are ignored by the authors of the list of the one hundred best business books of all time (Covert and Sattersten 2009).

3. Financial self-help has received much less attention than such other topics within the realm of self-improvement as gender, family, work, and childrearing (Brown 2003; Coyle and Grodin 1993; Hazleden 2004; Kieken 1997; Krafchick, Zimmerman, Haddock, and Banning 2005; McGee 2005; Rapping 1996; Shields, Steinke, and Koster 1995; Simonds 1992; Travis 2009; Woods 1996; Zimmerman, Holm, and Starrels 2001). The wider world of self-help has received some attention by scholars, especially in the fields of psychology and women's studies. Most analyses, from the left to the right of the political spectrum, have been critical of self-help for different reasons. Conservative authors such as Salerno (2005) and Sommers and Satel (2005) question self-help and psychology for producing weak subjects that undermine the American spirit of autonomy and entrepreneurship. Just accepting that we need help expresses doubts about this spirit. To a certain extent, they see the expansion (and failure) of self-help not just as a problem for individuals, but rather as a danger to national strength. From a more progressive position, Micki McGee, in her critical approach to "makeover culture," challenges the idea of individual agency put forward by self-help: "the idea that one can make oneself, invent oneself, is not only fundamentally mistaken but also a profoundly alienating one that implies estrangement from the social position of one's origins as well as from those individuals who fostered one's development" (McGee 2005:8). Part of the available work on self-help has analyzed it using the concepts of governmentality and technologies of the self (Binkley 2009; Eisler 2004; Hazleden 2003; Papalini 2007; Rimke 2000). Although most do not examine financial self-help specifically, as I do, these studies stress the individualistic and ultimately oppressive effects of self-help.

4. For two recent reviews of the growing literature on the financialization of the economy and its effects, see Davis and Kim (2015) and van der Zwan (2014). While the popularization of finance as part of the larger process of financialization is a fairly recent development (Harrington 2008; Davidson 2012), it also has a longer (and slower) history dating back to the nineteenth century (Aitken 2007; Preda 2001).

5. A thorough historical recounting of success manuals since the nineteenth century would be out of the scope of this book and already has been done by various authors. The point of this historical detour is to show that, although connections with previous manuals are evident, the contemporary financial self-help genre represented by Kiyosaki emerged and grew as a response to changes in the last quarter of the twentieth century (Baida 1990; Burns 1976; Cawelti 1965; Ehrenreich 2009; Huber 1971). For historical analyses of success manuals, see McGee (2005), Rischin (1965), Starker (2002), Weiss (1969), and Wyllie (1954).

6. Biggart found four major varieties of self-help between 1950 and 1980: (1) success-through-striving books; (2) displacement books; (3) manipulation manuals; and (4) entrepreneurial scheme books. These categories to a great extent matched three possible strategies that workers could develop to cope with their working environment. *Success-through-striving books*, such as Peale's *The Power of Positive Thinking* [published in 1952], served those who decided to climb up the corporate ladder to improve their job positions. But there were other options. The second alternative, what Biggart calls *displacement books*, vouched for an alternative structure of goals and an escape from

the pressures of the modern corporation in tune with the counterculture that emerged in the 1960s. Books such as *The Peter Principle* [1969] or *Your Erroneous Zones* [1976] advocated a retreat from dominant values about work, success, and competition; the avoidance of stress and pressure; and the pursuit of gratification through alternative rewards, rejecting institutionalized definitions of approval (Biggart 1983:302–5). For those with hopes of "making it," a third variety of self-help was *manipulation manuals*, with titles such as *Winning Through Intimidation* [1973] and *Power! How to Get it, How to Use it* [1975]. These books, like the success-through-striving variety, offered advice for the in-the-corporation strategy. But they also offered an appealing narrative for those who tried to make it independently, decidedly outside of the formal organizational environment of corporations. Finally, the fourth variety resembled current financial self-help in terms of the strategy for which it advocated: *entrepreneurial scheme books*, as Biggart calls them, were the main option for the out-of-the-corporation strategy. Books such as *How I Made $2,000,000 in the Stock Market* [1960] anticipated current resources that advocate the use of the financial system for enrichment.

7. There are countless scholarly accounts of the demise of the welfare and industrial society and the rise of neoliberalism and finances since the 1970s (see, for example, Bell 1976; Boltanski and Chiapello 2005; Davis 2009; Hacker 2006; Harvey 2007).

8. As I mentioned earlier, Kiyosaki's description largely fits scholarly macro descriptions of the shift from the "society of organizations" to post-industrial or "financialized" society. However, he does not delve into differences among workers (both white collar and blue collar) born before 1935. Although job stability and the role of corporations and government in workers' social security was indeed stronger in that era, it was not so for everyone equally, particularly considering race and gender discrimination in the labor market.

9. This praise for the trait of extreme adaptability to changes in the economy is also famously advocated in the widely popular book *Who Moved My Cheese?* (see also Brown 2003; Johnson 1998; McGee 2005:73–76).

10. I must add that since the emergence of the Internet, financial self-help practitioners have been able to access a wealth of scattered information, training, and services online. This accessible and practical information competes with formal higher education in terms of providing "real life" expertise that can be used to pursue financial freedom.

11. Unlike in the United States, Argentina offers public higher education for free. Private universities are not free, but students usually do not have to take out huge loans as in the U.S. As a result, the decision to pursue higher education does not have the personal financial implications in Argentina that it has in the U.S.

12. Although this idea runs throughout Kiyosaki's materials, in 2013 he published a guide to financial education aimed at parents called *Why "A" Students Work for "C" Students and "B" Students Work for the Government* (Kiyosaki 2013).

13. In Argentina, partial privatization of the social security system in the 1990s did not give individuals much control over their accounts like in the United States. However, the poor performances of both the public and private retirement systems support the argument that individuals ought to take care of their retirement and cannot be content

with emaciated public pensions. In a dramatic reversal of the retirement policies of the previous decade, the Argentine government re-nationalized all retirement accounts in 2008 (Barrionuevo 2008; see Golbert 2000; Madrid 2003).

14. Two books published by Kiyosaki after I finished fieldwork are called *Rich Dad's Conspiracy of the Rich* and *Unfair Advantage*. That advantage is, according to Kiyosaki, financial intelligence. The conspiracy refers to the deficient distribution not of wealth itself, but of financial intelligence. Kiyosaki presents himself as a sort of modern-day Robin Hood: someone who is leveling the playing field by promoting and distributing financial intelligence so that people can overcome their unfair disadvantages and beat the conspiracy to keep them poor (see Kiyosaki 2009, 2011).

15. $N = 4,713$. 499 cases had no information in this field.

Chapter 2

1. The term *libertarian* usually leads to confusion, not only because it has been used differently in different countries and at different points in history, but also because there are left and right libertarian philosophies, which, to make matters worse, coincide on some issues. What I am referring to by *libertarianism* is the radical forms that right-wing liberalism took roughly in the second half of the twentieth century, particularly in the United States (see Doherty 2007).

2. Ayn Rand published several fiction and nonfiction books promoting her philosophy. Her novels are the most popular (see, for example, Rand 1943, 1959, 2007).

3. The users of financial self-help I met during my fieldwork were not particularly attracted to doctrinal or explicitly ideological texts. Consuming financial self-help products was mostly a practical activity. As Foucault and others have shown, it is precisely in these "practical texts" (and in what readers do with them) where we can find "rules, opinions, and advice on how to behave as one should" (Foucault 1990:12; see also Giraudeau 2012). The practicality of these texts does not mean, however, that they are disconnected from certain intellectual roots. Libertarian writings were rarely a direct influence on readers or a presence in the field, but the ethical orientation to financial freedom can be traced back to some ideas of libertarianism.

4. David's presentation was in many ways an attempt to identify some of the four aspects Foucault defines as constitutive of ethics, of the relationship one ought to have with oneself (Foucault 1990:25–32; 1997a:263–68). According to Foucault, the ethical substance is the part of oneself that is determined as in need of ethical work, the material to be worked on. In this case, it is what David calls the "operating system," a term imported from informatics but yet compelling because it identifies something that is at the core of the self yet modifiable (with great effort). Unlike unchangeable DNA, it is material amenable to being worked on through practices of the self. The "operating system" was slowly crafted through home upbringing and represents one's conformist attitudes with one's financial situation, which are indicative of a larger inclination for fear and dependence.

5. Several online forums and websites have had endless discussions about the truth of the tale of the two dads. For example, John T. Reed, an investor who opposes Kiyo-

saki and his ideas, devotes a whole section of his website (http://www.johntreed.com/ Kiyosaki.html) to debunking the myth of the two dads. As I discuss in Chapter 4, most fans do not really care.

6. For a discussion of security and freedom in relation to family, see Godbout and Caille (2000:34–35). Their argument is that the family is a shelter from the choice and freedom that are supposed to reign in modern societies. One is not free in the family (in the sense that one cannot walk out of relationships so easily), but one receives security in exchange for membership. It is not surprising, then, that family is problematized in the financial self-help discourse, since it restricts autonomy. It is, however, at least ironic that many fans say that they would like to have financial freedom in order to be able to spend time with their families.

7. Before they can identify what Foucault called the ethical substance, individuals have to recognize the need for it through the *mode d'assujettissement*, the way in which a subject is invited to recognize oneself as in need of ethical work (Foucault 1990:27, 1997a:264). The latter quote is illustrative in this regard. Whereas at first participants' struggles with money, dissatisfaction with their financial situation, or boredom with employment appear as motivators for ethical work on the self, through participation in financial self-help activities they reinterpret instances of their lives in which not dis-satisfaction but their *satisfaction* with work arrangements indicates the need to work on the self. They need to work on the self not just when they have failed financially but, more important, when they have grown too comfortable with their non-entrepreneurial selves. Money is not really the goal but rather a vehicle for ethical work on the self.

8. The work of sociologist Nikolas Rose is particularly helpful in tracing the shifts in the use of various forms of expertise with the advent of neoliberalism: "The very powers which the technologies of welfare accorded to those who possessed knowledge and could speak the truth enabled expertise to establish enclosures within which its author-ity could not be challenged, effectively insulating itself from external political attempts to govern it. In contrast, advanced liberal modes of rule have a certain 'formal' charac-ter. The calculative regimes of positive knowledge of human conduct are to be replaced by the calculative regimes of accounting and financial management" (see Rose 1993:295).

9. On the show, Serin said that he thought of writing a "what not to do" book as a warning. But he said he would wait until he recovered from his financial crisis, be-cause he knew that anyone could screw up and write about it, and that overcoming his setbacks would give him credibility. Optimism is built in to financial self-help; no one would publish a book about failure unless it could be interpreted as success. After his sudden fame, Serin faded from the public eye.

10. Although I conducted a great proportion of my New York fieldwork in groups in which African Americans and Latinos were the majority, I rarely heard any explicit ref-erence to race or ethnicity in their discourse. There is a great deal of scholarly literature about the impact of race and ethnicity on the way people think about mobility (Lacy 2007; see, for example, Pattillo 1999, 2007). But I found that it did not have a discursive presence in the settings in which I participated, perhaps because Kiyosaki's dominant narratives do not include any reference to race or ethnicity. There are a few financial

self-help books explicitly written by African Americans for African Americans, for example, *Think and Grow Rich: A Black Choice* (Kimbro 1991); *Why Should White Guys Have All the Fun? How Reginald Lewis Created a Billion-Dollar Business Empire* (Lewis 1995); and *How to Succeed in Business Without Being White: Straight Talk on Making It in America* (Graves 1997). But I never heard anyone mentioning or saw anyone using any of these books. Books for women, on the other hand, were more visible.

11. While there are investment clubs and other informal collective organizations for women only (Harrington 2008), they were not the focus of my fieldwork. Jean Chatzky, for example, encourages her readers to start women's *money groups*, just to have the possibility of talking about finances with other women (Chatzky 2006:10–11; see also Lieber 2008).

12. The widespread myth that women do stupid things with money—or that women do stupid things at a higher rate than men—is increasingly criticized in media commentary about financial self-help (see Seligson 2010).

Chapter 3

1. Since Sonny is involved in several groups, attendants frequently do not know (or care) to which club a given session belongs. In the last few months of my research, one of the clubs became largely inactive. However, the frequency of games did not change, because Sonny kept organizing games with other clubs or meetups.

2. I noticed that Sonny stopped charging players the symbolic five dollar fee but did not pay much attention to it. When I asked why he changed the policy, Sonny told me that Steve, the leader of the New York group, asked him to keep all the activities associated with the group free of charge.

3. For a more detailed account of my participation in game sessions, see the Methodological Appendix.

4. There is a more advanced version of the game, called Cashflow 202, which includes the same board but a different set of cards, including the possibility of buying options. However, I do not consider it here because I never saw anyone playing it in any of the groups in which I participated.

5. Dreams are located in the squares of the fast track, identified by a pink color and a price. Having to choose a dream reminds players that not everything is about money and accounting, but also about an imagined fictional future (Beckert 2013). "You won't be able to achieve financial freedom if you don't have a big dream that drives you," said Matías during a game. Available dreams are diverse and allow players to make a comfortable choice. Examples of dreams are dinner with the president, a cabin at a Montana lake, playing golf around the world, or funding a research center for cancer and AIDS.

6. During games with new players, landing on the "baby" square often leads to jokes, because of the dissonance between the happiness a player should feel if it was a real event, and the fact that the baby creates a new monthly expense. Cashflow prompts people to bluntly consider life events like having a child in terms of its implications for financial freedom.

7. Also, beginners usually read the whole text of each opportunity card that comes

up. After a while, players learn to disentangle the numbers from the accompanying text, which is irrelevant to their calculations.

8. This praise of consumer frugality in favor of investment echoes Benjamin Franklin's *Necessary Hints to Those That Would Be Rich*, famously regarded by Max Weber as the ideal type of the spirit of capitalism (Weber 2002b:48–50). However, as I discussed in Chapter 2, frugality has limited significance in Kiyosaki's world: he maintains that frugal people are selling their souls to money. Frugality does not bring genuine success, but financial intelligence does. In this sense, spending without recording and classifying correctly is the most serious sin. Calculative tools, Kiyosaki argues, make all the difference.

9. This scene is similar to the behavioral experiment usually called "The Ultimatum Game," in which people turn down free money just because other experimental subjects are getting more. The ultimatum game points to factors other than individual maximization of benefit that play a role in people's economic decisions (Kiser and Bauldry 2005:179).

10. I address more generally the issue of adapting American tools in the Argentine context in Chapter 5.

11. On several occasions, I thanked the group organizers who let me do fieldwork at their events by helping players and answering their questions. In these sessions, I tried as much as possible to stick to the rules and procedures and to avoid engaging in translations into "real life." First, as the researcher, I did not want to be the person introducing this connection. Second, how could I translate the game into the world of investing and financial freedom if that was not my "real life"? I discovered that keeping the game at the game level demanded a great deal of effort. Translation is an integral part of the game. Meanings, accounting, work on the self, and translation are integrated in such a way that it is difficult to separate them in practice.

12. Sonny eventually decided to return to the original rule of using one die in New York games. He said that he did so because the game is also about learning patience—another virtue espoused by financial self-help gurus.

Chapter 4

1. Zelizer calls these practices meant to set or maintain boundaries "relational work."

2. These are classic financial self-help books from the 1920s and 1930s (Clason 2002; Hill 2007).

3. These organizations are popular throughout the world, with some of the largest companies such as Herbalife, Tupperware, and Amway having a strong global presence. The World Federation of Direct Selling Associations (WFDSA) estimates that direct selling was a $168 billion industry globally in 2012, with over eighty-nine million participants worldwide and fifteen million in Latin America and the Caribbean. The direct-selling industry in the United States represents a market of over $33 billion, while sixteen million people belong to the direct-selling community. The retail sales of direct selling in Argentina alone were estimated at $1.66 billion, with six hundred fifty thousand participants (WFDSA 2013b). Although it was not the case of Vacation Express, the

MLM organization in Argentina that I analyze in this chapter, the majority of direct-selling distributors in every country are women (Biggart 1989; Casanova 2011), with 75 percent of female distributors in the United States and 96 percent in Argentina (WFDSA 2013b). When they started to flourish in the 1950s, direct-selling companies provided middle-class women with a novel way to enter the labor market without leaving the home, benefitting from their local social networks to sell products mainly tailored for housewives (such as Tupperware and beauty products) (Biggart 1989; Clarke 1999; Vidas 2008). Vacation Express did not offer a good or service that was clearly understood to be oriented toward women, and therefore both men and women participated in it.

4. While in the following pages I describe in some detail the first workshop that I attended, the basic structure was similar to the other workshops I attended by this group in the following months.

5. For the sake of clarity, my description is simpler than the actual system. There is, for example, an "advanced binary," in which members can open multiple nodes, as if they were multiplying themselves in the network.

6. This point is important methodologically, and will be developed further in the methodological appendix. I used my own subjective reactions to help comprehend the meanings that those in this world give to their interactions. My own feeling of offense by the attitude of organizers was based on a different way of symbolically organizing interest and disinterest.

7. As I will discuss in the methodological appendix, while Omar and others knew my interest as a researcher, some people never lost hope that I would become interested in the business, or at least treated me like any other of their invitees or potential recruits.

8. The words in Spanish may not have an accurate translation in English. The word *manejar* could be translated as handling, managing, or even manipulating. It implies, in Weberian terms, power without belief in its legitimacy. The word *dirigir* is closer to lead, direct, conduct. It suggests willful acceptance and consensus. The idea is that in network marketing people do not lose their autonomy, and if they follow someone else, it is due to leadership and not sheer power as in the employee-boss relationship.

Chapter 5

1. Some recent examples of the narrative of Argentine decadence at home and abroad are Vargas Llosa (2008), Aguinis (2009), Petit (2014), and *The Economist* (2014).

2. On the Americanization of culture in Latin America and elsewhere, see Joseph, LeGrand, and Salvatore (1998), Wagnleitner and May (2000), De Grazia (2005), Canclini (2001), and Moreno (2003).

3. See, for example, Stratta (2004), Campanario (2005, 2006a, 2006b, 2007), La Nación (2004, 2007), El Día (2007, 2009).

4. For a description of consumer practices when faced with hyperinflation in the case of Brazil (which was remarkably similar to Argentina), see O'Dougherty (2002:51–76).

5. It was only at the end of 2003 that all provincial currencies had been taken out of circulation.

6. There are several works chronicling the events of those days. See, for example, Bonasso (2002), Camarasa (2002), Vilas (2006), and Nabot (2011).

7. According to D'Avella (2014), this wariness explains the use of real estate in Argentina more as a refuge for value than an attempt to obtain a profit. Unlike dollars in a bank or under the mattress, "bricks" (as Argentines call real estate) have a materiality that makes them less likely to disappear in a crisis or be stolen if kept at home. Also, since real estate is valued in dollars, it maintains its real value over time. In 2012, balance of payment problems led the government to restrict the purchase of foreign currency, which in turn opened up a parallel market of dollars with a much higher price than official transactions. The government tax agency established how many dollars each individual could acquire based on his or her income. Argentina is one of the countries with the highest amount of (undeclared) dollar bills outside the United States (Greeley 2013; Judson 2012). For more on the cultural role of the dollar in the Argentine economy, see Bercovich and Rebossio (2013), Grimson (2012), and the essays collected in Kaufman (2013).

8. As noted in chapter 1, besides having a different retirement system, in 2008 the Argentine government re-nationalized retirement funds, which had been mostly private since the mid-1990s. Even in the privatized social security system that Argentina had from 1994 to 2008, investment decisions of retirement funds were not made by the workers themselves, but by funds administrators. The level of control that a worker has of his or her retirement account in the United States is much higher than that of Argentine employees on their mandatory retirement accounts.

9. See, for example, the work of Elaine de Silveira Leite (2011, 2013) on financial self-help in Brazil.

10. See, for example, Ibañez Padilla (2005). Andy Freire writes about entrepreneurship more generally, and he is also one of the few local references (Freire 2004). Unlike American books and authors, these local books were very rarely mentioned, even after I asked interviewees to think of Argentine authors. Websites, blogs, financial sections of newspapers, online forums, and local magazines like *Inversor Global* also came up in interviews when I inquired about local resources, but not published authors.

11. I do not provide a reference entry for this book to protect the anonymity of research subject Matías (a pseudonym). "Rafael Agüero" is also a pseudonym.

12. Raúl Alfonsín was the president of Argentina from 1983 to 1989. He resigned during the hyperinflation crisis of 1989.

13. Here Luciano seems to be pointing at privileged information for those particularly well connected, which seems to contradict the notion that financial knowledge is within anyone's reach. However, Luciano is stressing a larger point Matías made about preparedness: those who acquired financial intelligence and took seriously expanding their networks to include those with more knowledge could easily predict the crash that was coming.

14. For a description of these operations, see Auguste, Dominguez, Kamil, and Tesar (2006).

Conclusion

1. See, for example, Babb (2001), Dezalay and Garth (2002), Harvey (2007), and Mirowski and Plehwe (2009).

2. For an analysis of Junior Achievement's educational ideas, see Imen (2012).

3. Although there is not enough research yet on these efforts outside the field of economics, several sociologists and anthropologists are currently conducting research on this growing field. For example, see the ongoing work of Jeanne Lazarus (2013, 2015) in France, Lúcia Müller (2014, 2015) and collaborators in Brazil, Donncha Marron (2013) and Chris Clarke (2015) in the UK, and Chris Arthur (2012) in Canada.

4. For a debate on this point, see Miller (2002) and Holm (2007).

Methodological Appendix

1. Although I formally ended my fieldwork in mid-2009, I still sporadically attended activities in New York for another year after that.

2. I provide more details on the Cashflow groups and my fieldwork in games in Chapter 3.

3. On the uses of online communities in qualitative research, see Bargh, McKenna, and Fitzsimons (2002), Gatson and Zweerink (2004), and Robinson and Schulz (2009).

4. There is, of course, the notion of activist research, which advocates for an embrace of dual loyalties, in terms of producing knowledge for academic purposes but also to be an organic part of the activist struggles of the organizations under study. See for example, Hale (2006, 2007).

5. Some examples of recent ethnographies in which the researcher was previously involved with the world under study are Desmond (2007), Juris (2008), Mears (2011), Ríos (2011), Benzecry (2011), Anteby (2013), and Contreras (2013).

6. Loic Wacquant describes a similar feeling, of the attraction of boxing the closer he was to the gym (Wacquant 2003).

7. Although only one person reached this conclusion about my income, the fact that a player framed my fellowship in terms of *passive income* suggests that people often frame the researcher's activities using their own categories of understanding (or in this case, the categories they are learning at the time of fieldwork). This fits Venkatesh's (2002) description of how people in the housing project he studied framed his fieldwork as "doin' the hustle," that is, applying the categories with which they framed their own activities in the projects. Several participants understood better when I explained my activity using their concepts. For example, I often explained that I was focused on my research and writing, just like they were focused on acquiring financial freedom. By making those two goals comparable, I managed to bridge modes of work and income that appeared incommensurable.

References

Abelin, Mireille. 2012. "Fiscal Sovereignty: Reconfigurations of Value and Citizenship in Post-Financial Crisis Argentina." PhD Dissertation, Columbia University, New York.

Aguinis, Marcos. 2009. *¡Pobre patria mía!* Buenos Aires: Sudamericana.

Ailon, Galit. 2015. "Rethinking Calculation: The Popularization of Financial Trading Outside the Global Centres of Finance." *Economy and Society* 44(4):592–615.

Aitken, Rob. 2007. *Performing Capital: Toward a Cultural Economy of Popular and Global Finance.* New York: Palgrave Macmillan.

Al Jazeera English. 2009. "'Rich Dad, Poor Dad'—Riz Khan." *Aljazeera.com.* Retrieved December 2, 2014 (http://www.aljazeera.com/programmes/rizkhan/2009/11/2009112 495221673225.html).

Anteby, Michel. 2013. *Manufacturing Morals: The Values of Silence in Business School Education.* Chicago: University of Chicago Press.

Arthur, Chris. 2012. *Financial Literacy Education: Neoliberalism, the Consumer and the Citizen.* Rotterdam; Boston: Sense Publishers.

Auguste, Sebastian, Kathryn Dominguez, Herman Kamil, and Linda Tesar. 2006. "Cross-Border Trading as a Mechanism for Implicit Capital Flight: ADRs and the Argentine Crisis." *Journal of Monetary Economics* 53(7):1259–95.

Auyero, Javier. 2007. *Routine Politics and Violence in Argentina: The Gray Zone of State Power.* Cambridge; New York: Cambridge University Press.

Babb, Sarah L. 2001. *Managing Mexico: Economists from Nationalism to Neoliberalism.* Princeton, NJ: Princeton University Press.

Bach, David. 2004. *The Automatic Millionaire: A Powerful One-Step Plan to Live and Finish Rich.* New York: Broadway Books.

Baida, Peter. 1990. *Poor Richard's Legacy: American Business Values from Benjamin Franklin to Donald Trump.* New York: W. Morrow.

Bargh, John A., Katelyn Y. A. McKenna, and Grainne M. Fitzsimons. 2002. "Can You See the Real Me? Activation and Expression of the 'True Self' on the Internet." *Journal of Social Issues* 58(1):33–48.

Barrionuevo, Alexei. 2008. "Argentina Nationalizes $30 Billion in Private Pensions." *The*

New York Times, October 22. Retrieved December 12, 2014 (http://www.nytimes.com /2008/10/22/business/worldbusiness/22argentina.html).

Barry, Andrew, Thomas Osborne, and Nikolas Rose. 1996. *Foucault and Political Reason: Liberalism, Neo-Liberalism, and Rationalities of Government.* Chicago: University of Chicago Press.

Basualdo, Eduardo. 2001. *Sistema político y modelo de acumulación en la Argentina: Notas sobre el transformismo argentino durante la valorización financiera, 1946–2001.* Buenos Aires: Universidad Nacional de Quilmes Ediciones.

BBC News. 2011. "'Anyone Can Make Money from a Crash.'" *BBC*, September 26. Retrieved December 16, 2014 (http://www.bbc.co.uk/news/business-15059135).

Becker, Howard S. 2009. "How to Find Out How to Do Qualitative Research." *International Journal of Communication* 3:545–53.

Beckert, Jens. 2013. "Imagined Futures: Fictional Expectations in the Economy." *Theory and Society* 42(3):219–40.

Bell, Daniel. 1976. *The Coming of Post-Industrial Society.* New York: Basic Books.

Benzecry, Claudio E. 2011. *The Opera Fanatic: Ethnography of an Obsession.* Chicago: University of Chicago Press.

Bercovich, Alejandro, and Alejandro Rebossio. 2013. *Estoy verde: Dólar. Una pasión argentina.* Buenos Aires: Aguilar.

Bermudez, Ismael. 2002. "Los 20 puntos clave del nuevo paquete." *Clarín*, February 4. Retrieved May 2, 2014 (http://edant.clarin.com/diario/2002/02/04/e-00602.htm).

Bernard, Tara Siegel. 2010. "Financial Advice by Women for Women." *The New York Times*, April 23. Retrieved December 11, 2014 (http://www.nytimes.com/2010/04/24/ your-money/24money.html).

Bernheim, B. Douglas, Daniel M. Garrett, and Dean M. Maki. 2001. "Education and Saving: The Long-Term Effects of High School Financial Curriculum Mandates." *Journal of Public Economics* 80(3):435–65.

Biggart, Nicole Woolsey. 1983. "Rationality, Meaning, and Self-Management: Success Manuals, 1950–1980." *Social Problems* 30(3):298–311.

———. 1989. *Charismatic Capitalism: Direct Selling Organizations in America.* Chicago: University of Chicago Press.

Binkley, Sam. 2009. "The Work of Neoliberal Governmentality: Temporality and Ethical Substance in the Tale of Two Dads." *Foucault Studies* 6:60–78.

Boas, Taylor C., and Jordan Gans-Morse. 2009. "Neoliberalism: From New Liberal Philosophy to Anti-Liberal Slogan." *Studies in Comparative International Development* 44(2):137–61.

Boltanski, Luc, and Eve Chiapello. 2005. *The New Spirit of Capitalism.* London; New York: Verso.

Bonasso, Miguel. 2002. *El palacio y la calle: Crónicas de insurgentes y conspiradores.* Buenos Aires: Planeta.

Bourdieu, Pierre. 1983. "The Field of Cultural Production, or: The Economic World Reversed." *Poetics* 12(4):311–56.

———. 1990. *The Logic of Practice.* Stanford: Stanford University Press.

———. 1998. *Practical Reason: On the Theory of Action*. Stanford: Stanford University Press.

Brady, Michelle. 2014. "Ethnographies of Neoliberal Governmentalities: From the Neoliberal Apparatus to Neoliberalism and Governmental Assemblages." *Foucault Studies* 18:11–33.

Brown, Megan. 2003. "Survival at Work: Flexibility and Adaptability in American Corporate Culture." *Cultural Studies* 17(5):713–33.

Burchell, Graham. 1996. "Liberal Government and Techniques of the Self." In *Foucault and Political Reason: Liberalism, Neo-Liberalism, and Rationalities of Government*, ed. A. Barry, T. Osborne, and N. Rose, 19–36. Chicago: University of Chicago Press.

Burns, Jennifer. 2009. *Goddess of the Market: Ayn Rand and the American Right*. Oxford, UK: Oxford University Press.

Burns, Rex. 1976. *Success in America: The Yeoman Dream and the Industrial Revolution*. Amherst: University of Massachusetts Press.

Byrne, Rhonda. 2006. *The Secret*. New York; Hillsboro: Atria Books; Beyond Words.

Cahn, Peter S. 2011. *Direct Sales and Direct Faith in Latin America*. New York: Palgrave Macmillan.

Callon, Michel. 1998. "The Embeddedness of Economic Markets in Economics." In *The Laws of the Markets*, ed. Michel Callon, 1–57. Oxford; Malden, MA: Blackwell/ Sociological Review.

———. 2007. "What Does It Mean to Say That Economics Is Performative?" In *Do Economists Make Markets? On the Performativity of Economics*, ed. D. MacKenzie, F. Muniesa, and L. Siu, 311–57. Princeton, NJ: Princeton University Press.

Callon, Michel, and Fabian Muniesa. 2005. "Peripheral Vision: Economic Markets as Calculative Collective Devices." *Organization Studies* 26(8):1229–50.

Camarasa, Jorge A. 2002. *Días de furia*. Buenos Aires: Editorial Sudamericana.

Campanario, Sebastián. 2005. "Padre rico y rendidor." *Clarín*, January 9. Retrieved September 9, 2014 (http://edant.clarin.com/suplementos/economico /2005/01/09/ n-00501.htm).

———. 2006a. "La 'biblia del cuentapropismo' que bate récords de ventas." *Clarín*, April 20. Retrieved September 9, 2014 (http://old.clarin.com/diario/2006/04/20/el pais/p-01603.htm).

———. 2006b. "Las ediciones del 2006." *Clarín*, February 26. Retrieved September 9, 2014 (http://old.clarin.com/suplementos/economico/2006/02/26/n-00501.htm).

———. 2007. "Nadie puede destronar al 'padre rico.'" *Clarín*, July 12. Retrieved September 9, 2014 (http://old.clarin.com/diario/2007/07/12/elpais/p-02101.htm).

Canclini, Nestor García. 2001. *Consumers and Citizens: Globalization and Multicultural Conflicts*. Minneapolis: University Of Minnesota Press.

Casanova, Erynn Masi de. 2011. *Making up the Difference: Women, Beauty, and Direct Selling in Ecuador*. Austin: University of Texas Press.

Castells, Manuel. 1996. *The Rise of the Network Society*. Malden, MA: Blackwell.

Cawelti, John. 1965. *Apostles of the Self-Made Man*. Chicago: University of Chicago Press.

Chatzky, Jean Sherman. 2006. *Make Money, Not Excuses: Wake Up, Take Charge, and Overcome Your Financial Fears Forever*. New York: Crown Business.

Chiapello, Eve. 2015. "Financialisation of Valuation." *Human Studies* 38(1):13–35.

Clarke, Alison J. 1999. *Tupperware: The Promise of Plastic in 1950s America*. Washington, DC: Smithsonian Institution Press.

Clarke, Chris. 2015. "Learning to Fail: Resilience and the Empty Promise of Financial Literacy Education." *Consumption Markets & Culture* 18(3): 257–76.

Clason, George S. 2002. *The Richest Man in Babylon*. New York: Signet.

Collier, Stephen J. 2009. "Topologies of Power: Foucault's Analysis of Political Government Beyond 'Governmentality.'" *Theory, Culture & Society* 26(6):78–108.

Competition Bureau of Canada. 2009. "Multi-Level Marketing Plans and Schemes of Pyramid Selling." Retrieved December 2, 2014 (http://www.competitionbureau.gc.ca /eic/site/cb-bc.nsf/eng/03035.html).

Contreras, Randol. 2013. *The Stickup Kids: Race, Drugs, Violence, and the American Dream*. Berkeley: University of California Press.

Covert, Jack, and Todd Sattersten. 2009. *The 100 Best Business Books of All Time: What They Say, Why They Matter, and How They Can Help You*. New York: Portfolio.

Coyle, Kelly, and Debra Grodin. 1993. "Self-Help Books and the Construction of Reading: Readers and Reading in Textual Representation." *Text and Performance Quarterly* 13:61–78.

Criminal. Directed by Gregory Jacobs. 2004. Burbank, CA: Warner Home Video, 2005. DVD.

Dardot, Pierre, and Christian Laval. 2014. *The New Way of the World: On Neoliberal Society*. London; New York: Verso.

D'Avella, Nicholas. 2014. "Ecologies of Investment: Crisis Histories and Brick Futures in Argentina." *Cultural Anthropology* 29(1):173–99.

Davidson, Roei. 2012. "The Emergence of Popular Personal Finance Magazines and the Risk Shift in American Society." *Media, Culture & Society* 34(1):3–20.

Davies, William. 2014. "Neoliberalism: A Bibliographic Review." *Theory, Culture & Society* 31(7–8):309–17.

Davis, Gerald F. 2009. *Managed by the Markets: How Finance Re-Shaped America*. Oxford; New York: Oxford University Press.

Davis, Gerald F., and Suntae Kim. 2015. "Financialization of the Economy." *Annual Review of Sociology* 41(1):203–21.

Defensoria del Pueblo de la Ciudad de Buenos Aires. 2010. *RESOLUCIÓN No. 3546/10. Cuestionan actividad por incentivación del consumo en la Escuela No. 13*. Buenos Aires. Retrieved December 2, 2014 (http://www.defensoria.org.ar/institucional/ resoluciones10.php).

de Certeau, Michel. 1984. *The Practice of Everyday Life*. Berkeley: University of California Press.

De Grazia, Victoria. 2005. *Irresistible Empire: America's Advance Through Twentieth-Century Europe*. Cambridge, MA: Belknap Press of Harvard University Press.

Dean, Mitchell. 1999. *Governmentality: Power and Rule in Modern Society*. London; Thousand Oaks, CA: Sage.

Desmond, Matthew. 2007. *On the Fireline: Living and Dying with Wildland Firefighters*. Chicago: University Of Chicago Press.

Dezalay, Yves, and Bryant G. Garth. 2002. *The Internationalization of Palace Wars: Lawyers, Economists, and the Contest to Transform Latin American States*. Chicago: University Of Chicago Press.

Dilts, Andrew. 2011. "From 'Entrepreneur of the Self' to 'Care of the Self': Neo-Liberal Governmentality and Foucault's Ethics." *Foucault Studies* 12:130–46.

DiMaggio, Paul. 2002. "Endogenizing 'Animal Spirits': Toward a Sociology of Collective Response to Uncertainty and Risk." In *The New Economic Sociology: Developments in an Emerging Field*, ed. Mauro F. Guillén, Randall Collins, Paula England, and Marshall Meyer, 79–100. New York: Russell Sage.

Doherty, Brian. 2007. *Radicals for Capitalism: A Freewheeling History of the Modern American Libertarian Movement*. New York: Public Affairs.

Duneier, Mitchell. 2001. *Sidewalk*. New York: Farrar, Straus and Giroux.

The Economist. 2014. "A Century of Decline: The Tragedy of Argentina." February 15. Retrieved September 3, 2014 (http://www.economist.com/news/briefing/21596582 -one-hundred-years-ago-argentina-was-future-what-went-wrong-century-decline).

Ehrenreich, Barbara. 2009. *Bright-Sided: How the Relentless Promotion of Positive Thinking Has Undermined America*. New York: Metropolitan Books.

Eisler, Karyn L. 2004. "'Health, Wealth and Happiness': Self-Help, Personal Empowerment, and the Makings of the Neo-Liberal Citizen." PhD Dissertation, The University of British Columbia, Vancouver, B.C., Canada.

Elbaum, Marcelo. 2008. *Hombre rico, hombre pobre: El arte de aumentar la riqueza personal*. Buenos Aires: Planeta.

El Día. 2007. "'Padre Rico', un boom que trasciende lo editorial." July 15. Retrieved September 10, 2014 (http://www.eldia.com.ar/catalogo/20070715/informaciongeneral18.htm).

———. 2009. "Los más vendidos." October 11. Retrieved September 10, 2014 (http://www.eldia.com.ar/catalogo/20091011/revistadomingo54.htm).

Elliott, Anthony. 2008. *Concepts of the Self*. 2nd ed. Cambridge; Malden, MA: Polity Press.

Ferguson, James. 2010. "The Uses of Neoliberalism." *Antipode* 41(S1):166–84.

Fine, Gary Alan. 1983. *Shared Fantasy: Role-Playing Games as Social Worlds*. Chicago: University of Chicago Press.

Flew, Terry. 2014. "Six Theories of Neoliberalism." *Thesis Eleven* 122(1):49–71.

Fligstein, Neil, and Adam Goldstein. 2015. "The Emergence of a Finance Culture in American Households, 1989–2007." *Socio-Economic Review* 13(3):575–601.

Foucault, Michel. 1982. "The Subject and Power." *Critical Inquiry* 8(4):777–95.

———. 1988. *Technologies of the Self: A Seminar with Michel Foucault*. Amherst: University of Massachusetts Press.

———. 1990. *The History of Sexuality, Vol. 2: The Use of Pleasure*. New York: Vintage Books.

——. 1997a. "On the Genealogy of Ethics: An Overview of Work in Progress." In *Ethics: Subjectivity and Truth*, ed. P. Rabinow, 253–80. New York: New Press.

——. 1997b. "The Ethics of the Concern for Self as a Practice of Freedom." In *Ethics: Subjectivity and Truth*, ed. P. Rabinow, 281–302. New York: New Press.

——. 2005. *The Hermeneutics of the Subject: Lectures at the Collège de France 1981–1982.* New York: Picador.

——. 2008. *The Birth of Biopolitics: Lectures at the Collège de France, 1978–79.* Basingstoke, England; New York: Palgrave Macmillan.

Fourcade, Marion. 2007. "Theories of Markets and Theories of Society." *American Behavioral Scientist* 50(8):1015–34.

Fourcade, Marion, and Kieran Healy. 2007. "Moral Views of Market Society." *Annual Review of Sociology* 33(1):285–311.

Fraile, Lydia. 2009. "La experiencia neoliberal de América Latina. Políticas sociales y laborales desde el decenio de 1980." *Revista Internacional del Trabajo* 128(3):235–55.

Freire, Andy. 2004. *Pasión por emprender: De la idea a la cruda realidad.* Barcelona: Granica.

Frenkel, Roberto, and Jaime Ros. 2004. "Desempleo, políticas macroeconómicas y flexibilidad del mercado laboral. Argentina y México en los noventa." *Desarrollo Económico* 44(173):33–56.

Fridman, Daniel. 2010. "A New Mentality for a New Economy: Performing the Homo Economicus in Argentina (1976–1983)." *Economy and Society* 39(2):271–302.

Gatson, Sarah N., and Amanda Zweerink. 2004. "Ethnography Online: 'Natives' Practising and Inscribing Community." *Qualitative Research* 4(2):179–200.

Gatto, John. 1992. *Dumbing Us Down: The Hidden Curriculum of Compulsory Schooling.* Philadelphia: New Society Publishers.

Geertz, Clifford. 1973. "Deep Play: Notes on the Balinese Cockfight." In *The Interpretation of Cultures; Selected Essays*, 412–54. New York: Basic Books.

Gerchunoff, Pablo, and Lucas Llach. 2003. *El ciclo de la ilusión y el desencanto: Un siglo de políticas económicas argentinas.* Buenos Aires: Ariel.

Giraudeau, Martin. 2012. "Remembering the Future: Entrepreneurship Guidebooks in the US, from Meditation to Method (1945–1975)." *Foucault Studies* 13: 40–66.

Godbout, Jacques T., and Alain C. Caille. 2000. *The World of the Gift.* Montreal: McGill-Queen's University Press.

Goffman, Erving. 1961. "Fun in Games." In *Encounters: Two Studies in the Sociology of Interaction*, 17–81. Indianapolis: Bobbs-Merrill.

Golbert, Laura. 2000. "The Social Agenda in Argentina: A Review of Retirement and Employment Policies." In *Social Development in Latin America: The Politics of Reform*, ed. J. S. Tulchin and A. M. Garland, 227–42. Boulder, CO: Lynne Rienner.

González Bombal, Inés, and Mariana Luzzi. 2006. "Middle-Class Use of Barter Clubs: A Real Alternative or Just Survival?" In *Broken Promises?: The Argentine Crisis and Argentine Democracy*, ed. E. Epstein and D. Pion-Berlin, 141–60. Lanham: Lexington Books.

Gordon, Colin. 1987. "The Soul of the Citizen: Max Weber and Michel Foucault on Rationality and Government." In *Max Weber, Rationality and Modernity*, ed. S. Lash and S. Whimster, 293–316. London: Allen & Unwin.

Graves, Earl. 1997. *How to Succeed in Business Without Being White: Straight Talk on Making It in America*. New York: HarperBusiness.

Greeley, Brendan. 2013. "Argentines Hold More Than $50 Billion in U.S. Currency. Here's How We Know." *BusinessWeek: Global_economics*, May 15. Retrieved September 16, 2014 (http://www.businessweek.com/articles/2013-05-15/argentines-hold-more-than -50-billion-in-u-dot-s-dot-currency-dot-heres-how-we-know).

Grimson, Alejandro. 2012. "Dólar y memoria: Un trauma cultural." *Le Monde Diplomatique (Spanish Edition)* 157, July.

Hacker, Jacob S. 2006. *The Great Risk Shift: The Assault on American Jobs, Families, Health Care, and Retirement—And How You Can Fight Back*. New York; Oxford: Oxford University Press.

Hale, Charles R. 2006. "Activist Research v. Cultural Critique: Indigenous Land Rights and the Contradictions of Politically Engaged Anthropology." *Cultural Anthropology* 21(1):96–120.

———. 2007. *Engaging Contradictions: Theory, Politics, and Methods of Activist Scholarship*. Berkeley; London: University of California Press.

Hamann, Trent H. 2009. "Neoliberalism, Governmentality, and Ethics." *Foucault Studies* 6:37–59.

Harrington, Brooke. 2008. *Pop Finance: Investment Clubs and the New Investor Populism*. Princeton, NJ: Princeton University Press.

Harrison, Steve, and Bradley Communications Corp. 2006. "Want to Make It Big as an Author?" Retrieved November 22, 2014 (http://www.yourquantumleap.com/Kiyosaki Video.html).

Harvey, David. 2007. *A Brief History of Neoliberalism*. Oxford; New York: Oxford University Press.

Hazleden, Rebecca. 2003. "Love Yourself: The Relationship of the Self with Itself in Popular Self-Help Texts." *Journal of Sociology* 39(4):413–28.

———. 2004. "The Pathology of Love in Contemporary Relationship Manuals." *The Sociological Review* 52(2):201–17.

Henricks, Thomas S. 2006. *Play Reconsidered: Sociological Perspectives on Human Expression*. Urbana: University of Illinois Press.

Hill, Napoleon. 2007. *Think and Grow Rich*. Columbia, MD: Marketplace Books.

Hira, Tahira K., and Cäzilia Loibl. 2008. "Gender Differences in Investment Behavior." In *Handbook of Consumer Finance Research*, ed. J. J. Xiao, 253–70. New York: Springer.

Hoffman, Steve G. 2006. "How to Punch Someone and Stay Friends: An Inductive Theory of Simulation." *Sociological Theory* 24(2):170–93.

Holm, Petter. 2007. "Which Way Is Up on Callon?" In *Do Economists Make Markets? On the Performativity of Economics*, ed. D. MacKenzie, F. Muniesa, and L. Siu, 225–43. Princeton, NJ: Princeton University Press.

Huber, Richard. 1971. *The American Idea of Success*. New York: McGraw-Hill.

Ibañez Padilla, Gustavo. 2005. *Manual de economía personal—Cómo potenciar sus ingresos e inversiones*. Buenos Aires: Dunken.

Illouz, Eva. 2008. *Saving the Modern Soul: Therapy, Emotions, and the Culture of Self-Help*. Berkeley: University of California Press.

Imen, Pablo. 2012. "Junior Achievement o la pedagogía del capital." *Realidad Económica* 271:79–95.

Johnson, Spencer. 1998. *Who Moved My Cheese?: An Amazing Way to Deal with Change in Your Work and in Your Life*. New York: Putnam.

Joseph, G. M., Catherine LeGrand, and Ricardo Donato Salvatore. 1998. *Close Encounters of Empire: Writing the Cultural History of U.S.-Latin American Relations*. Durham, NC: Duke University Press.

Judson, Ruth. 2012. *Crisis and Calm: Demand for U.S. Currency at Home and Abroad from the Fall of the Berlin Wall to 2011*. Rochester, NY: Board of Governors of the Federal Reserve System. Retrieved September 16, 2014 (http://www.federalreserve .gov/pubs/ifdp/2012/1058/ifdp1058.pdf).

Juris, Jeffrey S. 2008. *Networking Futures: The Movements Against Corporate Globalization*. Durham, NC: Duke University Press.

Kalleberg, Arne L. 2011. *Good Jobs, Bad Jobs: The Rise of Polarized and Precarious Employment Systems in the United States, 1970s to 2000s*. New York: Russell Sage Foundation.

Kaufman, Alejandro, ed. 2013. *Cultura social del dólar*. Buenos Aires: UBA Sociales.

Kennedy, Diane. 2001. *Loop-Holes of the Rich: How the Rich Legally Make More Money & Pay Less Tax*. New York: Warner Books.

Kieken, Anna Carroll. 1997. "Women Readers of Self-Help Books: The Role of Interpersonal Factors in Behavior Change." PhD Dissertation, California Institute of Integral Studies, San Francisco.

Kimbro, Dennis. 1991. *Think and Grow Rich: A Black Choice*. New York: Fawcett Columbine.

King, Charles, and James W. Robinson. 2000. *The New Professionals: The Rise of Network Marketing as the Next Major Profession*. Roseville, CA: Prima Soho.

Kiser, Edgar, and Shawn Bauldry. 2005. "Rational Choice Theories in Political Sociology." In *The Handbook of Political Sociology*, ed. T. Janoski, R. Alford, A. Hicks, and M. A. Schwartz, 172–86. New York: Cambridge University Press.

Kiyosaki, Kim. 2006. *Rich Woman: A Book on Investing for Women—Because I Hate Being Told What to Do!* Scottsdale, AZ: Rich Press.

Kiyosaki, Robert. 1993. *If You Want to Be Rich & Happy, Don't Go to School: Ensuring Lifetime Security for Yourself and Your Children*. Rev. ed. Lower Lake, CA: Aslan Pub.

———. 1999. *The Cashflow Quadrant: Rich Dad's Guide to Financial Freedom*. Paradise Valley, AZ: TechPress.

———. 2000a. *Rich Dad Secrets to Money, Business and Investing—and How You Can Profit from Them*. Niles, IL: Nightingale-Conant.

———. 2000b. *Rich Dad's Guide to Investing: What the Rich Invest In That the Poor and Middle Class Do Not!* New York: Warner Business Books.

———. 2002. *Rich Dad's Prophecy: Why the Biggest Stock Market Crash in History Is Still*

Coming—and How You Can Prepare Yourself and Profit from It! New York: Warner Books.

———. 2005a. *Rich Dad's The Business School—For People Who Like Helping People.* Scottsdale, AZ: TechPress.

———. 2005b. *You Can Choose to Be Rich: Rich Dad's 3-Step Guide to Wealth.* Scottsdale, AZ: Cashflow Technologies.

———. 2009. *Rich Dad's Conspiracy of the Rich: The 8 New Rules of Money.* New York: Business Plus.

———. 2011. *Unfair Advantage: The Power of Financial Education.* Scottsdale, AZ: Plata.

———. 2013. *Why "A" Students Work for "C" Students and "B" Students Work for the Government.* Scottsdale, AZ: Plata.

Kiyosaki, Robert, and Sharon L. Lechter. 1998. *Rich Dad, Poor Dad: What the Rich Teach Their Kids About Money That the Poor and Middle Class Do Not!* Paradise Valley, AZ: TechPress.

Knox, Noelle. 2006. "10 Mistakes That Made Flipping a Flop; 24-Year-Old Got in Over His Head in the Real Estate Biz." *USA Today*, October 23, B1.

Koopman, Colin. 2013. "The Formation and Self-Transformation of the Subject in Foucault's Ethics." In *A Companion to Foucault*, ed. C. Falzon, T. O'Leary, and J. Sawicki, 526–43. Malden, MA: Wiley.

Krafchick, Jennifer L., Toni Schindler Zimmerman, Shelley A. Haddock, and James H. Banning. 2005. "Best-Selling Books Advising Parents About Gender: A Feminist Analysis." *Family Relations* 54(1):84.

Krippner, Greta R. 2011. *Capitalizing on Crisis: The Political Origins of the Rise of Finance.* Cambridge, MA: Harvard University Press.

Lacy, Karyn. 2007. *Blue-Chip Black: Race, Class, and Status in the New Black Middle Class.* Berkeley: University of California Press.

Lakoff, George, and Mark Johnson. 1980. *Metaphors We Live By.* Chicago: University of Chicago Press.

La Nación. 2004. "Best sellers." May 30. Retrieved September 9, 2014 (http://www.lanacion.com.ar/605633-best-sellers).

———. 2007. "Best sellers." July 22. Retrieved September 9, 2014 (http://www.lanacion.com.ar/927554-best-sellers).

———. 2012. "La Cámpora y su confusión entre adoctrinar y capacitar." September 13, 30.

Langley, Paul. 2008. *The Everyday Life of Global Finance: Saving and Borrowing in Anglo-America.* Oxford, UK: Oxford University Press.

Larner, Wendy. 2000. "Neo-Liberalism: Policy, Ideology, Governmentality." *Studies in Political Economy* 63:5–25.

Latour, Bruno (as Jim Johnson). 1988. "Mixing Humans and Nonhumans Together: The Sociology of a Door-Closer." *Social Problems* 35(3):298–310.

Latour, Bruno. 2007. *Reassembling the Social: An Introduction to Actor-Network-Theory.* New York: Oxford University Press.

Lazarus, Jeanne. 2013. "De l'aide à la responsabilisation. L'espace social de l'éducation financière en France." *Genèses* 93:76–97.

———. 2015. "Gouverner les conduites économiques par l'éducation financière. L'ascension de la financial literacy." In *Gouverner les conduites*, ed. S. Dubuisson-Quellier. Paris: Presses de Sciences Po.

Leite, Elaine da Silveira. 2011. "Reconversão de habitus: O advento do ideário de investimento no Brasil." PhD Dissertation, Universidade Federal de Sao Carlos, Sao Carlos, SP. Retrieved December 18, 2014 (http://www.bdtd.ufscar.br/htdocs/tedeSimplificado/tde_arquivos/24/TDE-2012-02-28T155012Z-4205/Publico/4111.pdf).

———. 2013. "Financialization, Crisis, and a New Mania in Brazil." In *The Brazilian State: Debate and Agenda, Bildner Western Hemisphere Studies*, ed. M. A. Font and L. Randall, 297–315. Lanham, MD: Lexington Books.

Lemke, Thomas. 2001. "'The Birth of Bio-Politics': Michel Foucault's Lecture at the Collège de France on Neo-Liberal Governmentality." *Economy and Society* 30(2):190–207.

Levit, Cecilia, and Ricardo Ortiz. 1999. "La hiperinflación argentina: Prehistoria de los noventa." *Revista Época* 1(1):53–69.

Lewis, Reginald. 1995. *Why Should White Guys Have All the Fun? How Reginald Lewis Created a Billion-Dollar Business Empire*. New York: Wiley.

Leyshon, Andrew, and Shaun French. 2009. "'We All Live in a Robbie Fowler House': The Geographies of the Buy to Let Market in the UK." *The British Journal of Politics & International Relations* 11(3):438–60.

Leyshon, Andrew, and Nigel Thrift. 2007. "The Capitalization of Almost Everything: The Future of Finance and Capitalism." *Theory, Culture & Society* 24(7–8):97–115.

Lieber, Ron. 2008. "Forming a Club to Share Financial Wisdom." *The New York Times*, November 1. Retrieved December 1, 2014 (http://www.nytimes.com/2008/11/01/business/yourmoney/01money.html).

Lin, Ken-Hou, and Donald Tomaskovic-Devey. 2013. "Financialization and U.S. Income Inequality, 1970–2008." *American Journal of Sociology* 118(5):1284–1329.

Lusardi, Annamaria, and Olivia S. Mitchell. 2007a. "Baby Boomer Retirement Security: The Roles of Planning, Financial Literacy, and Housing Wealth." *Journal of Monetary Economics* 54(1):205–24.

———. 2007b. "Financial Literacy and Retirement Preparedness: Evidence and Implications for Financial Education." *Business Economics* 42(1):35–44.

———. 2008. "Planning and Financial Literacy: How Do Women Fare?" *American Economic Review* 98(2):413–17.

———. 2011. "Financial Literacy Around the World: An Overview." *Journal of Pension Economics and Finance* 10(4):497–508.

Luzzi, Mariana. 2008. "La institución bancaria cuestionada. Actitudes y representaciones de los ahorristas frente a los bancos en el contexto de la crisis de 2001 en Argentina." *Crítica en Desarrollo* 2:173–90.

———. 2010a. "Las monedas de la crisis. Pluralidad monetaria en la Argentina de 2001." *Revista de Ciencias Sociales de la Universidad Nacional de Quilmes* 17:205–21.

————. 2010b. "¿Qué significa ahorrar?: Transformaciones de las prácticas monetarias durante la última crisis argentina." In *Trabajo, conflictos y dinero en un mundo globalizado, investigaciones y ensayos*, ed. V. A. Hernandez, 109–24. Buenos Aires: Biblos.

————. 2012. "La monnaie en question: pratiques et conflits à propos de l'argent lors de la crise de 2001 en Argentine." PhD Dissertation, École des Hautes Études en Sciences Sociales, Paris.

Lyons, Angela C., Yunhee Chang, and Erik M. Scherpf. 2006. "Translating Financial Education into Behavior Change for Low-Income Populations." *Financial Counseling and Planning* 17(2):27–45.

Lyons, Angela C., Lance Palmer, Koralalage S. Jayaratne, and Erik Scherpf. 2006. "Are We Making the Grade? A National Overview of Financial Education and Program Evaluation." *Journal of Consumer Affairs* 40(2):208–35.

MacKenzie, Donald. 2009. *Material Markets: How Economic Agents Are Constructed*. Oxford, UK: Oxford University Press.

MacKenzie, Donald A., Fabian Muniesa, and Lucia Siu. 2007. *Do Economists Make Markets? On the Performativity of Economics*. Princeton, NJ: Princeton University Press.

Madrid, Raúl L. 2003. *Retiring the State: The Politics of Pension Privatization in Latin America and Beyond*. Stanford, CA: Stanford University Press.

Mandell, Lewis. 2008. "Financial Education in High School." In *Overcoming the Saving Slump: How to Increase the Effectiveness of Financial Education and Saving Programs*, ed. Annamaria Lusardi, 257–79. Chicago: University of Chicago Press.

Marron, Donncha. 2014. "'Informed, Educated and More Confident': Financial Capability and the Problematization of Personal Finance Consumption." *Consumption Markets & Culture* 17(5): 491–511.

Martin, Randy. 2002. *Financialization of Daily Life*. Philadelphia: Temple University Press.

McGee, Micki. 2005. *Self-Help, Inc.: Makeover Culture in American Life*. Oxford; New York: Oxford University Press.

————. 2007. "The Secret's Success." *The Nation* 284(22):4–6.

Mears, Ashley. 2011. *Pricing Beauty: The Making of a Fashion Model*. Berkeley: University of California Press.

Mennicken, Andrea, and Peter Miller. 2014. "Michel Foucault and the Administering of Lives." In *Oxford Handbook of Sociology, Social Theory and Organization Studies: Contemporary Currents*, ed. P. S. Adler, P. du Gay, G. Morgan, and M. Reed, 11–38. Oxford, UK: Oxford University Press.

Miller, Daniel. 2002. "Turning Callon the Right Way Up." *Economy and Society* 31(2):218–33.

Miller, Peter. 2001. "Governing by Numbers: Why Calculative Practices Matters." *Social Research* 68(2):379.

————. 2008. "Calculating Economic Life." *Journal of Cultural Economy* 1(1):51–64.

Miller, Peter, and Nikolas Rose. 1990. "Governing Economic Life." *Economy and Society* 19(1):1–31.

———. 2008. *Governing the Present: Administering Economic, Social and Personal Life.* Cambridge, MA: Polity Press.

Mirowski, Philip, and Dieter Plehwe. 2009. *The Road from Mont Pelerin: The Making of the Neoliberal Thought Collective.* Cambridge, MA: Harvard University Press.

Mitchell, Timothy. 2005. "The Work of Economics: How a Discipline Makes Its World." *European Journal of Sociology / Archives Européennes de Sociologie* 46(02):297–320.

Moreno, Julio. 2003. *Yankee Don't Go Home! Mexican Nationalism, American Business Culture, and the Shaping of Modern Mexico, 1920–1950.* Chapel Hill: University of North Carolina Press.

Müller, Lúcia. 2014. "Negotiating Debts and Gifts: Financialization Policies and the Economic Experiences of Low-Income Social Groups in Brazil." *Vibrant: Virtual Brazilian Anthropology* 11(1):191–221.

———. 2015. "Las finanzas en lo cotidiano: Consideraciones sobre las políticas de inclusión y educación financiera en el Brasil contemporáneo." In *El laberinto de las finanzas. Estudios sociales de la economía contemporánea,* ed. A. Wilkis and A. Roig, 211–26. Buenos Aires: Biblos.

Muniesa, Fabian. 2014. *The Provoked Economy: Economic Reality and the Performative Turn.* London: Routledge.

Nabot, Damián. 2011. *Dos semanas, cinco presidentes: Diciembre de 2001: La historia secreta.* Buenos Aires: Aguilar.

Neiburg, Federico. 2010. "Sick Currencies and Public Numbers." *Anthropological Theory* 10(1-2):96–102.

Nine Queens (Nueve Reinas). Directed by Fabián Bielinsky. 2000. Culver City, CA: Columbia TriStar Home Entertainment, 2002. DVD.

Norwood, Robin. 1997. *Women Who Love Too Much: When You Keep Wishing and Hoping He'll Change.* New York: Pocket Books.

Novick, Marta, Miguel Lengyel, and Marianela Sarabia. 2009. "De la protección laboral a la vulnerabilidad social. Reformas neoliberales en la Argentina." *Revista Internacional del Trabajo* 128(3):257–75.

Obradovich, Gabriel. 2006. "Cuando muere el peso: Los intercambios cotidianos con los bonos provinciales de Entre Ríos." *Apuntes de Investigación del CECYP* 11:113–40.

O'Dougherty, Maureen. 2002. *Consumption Intensified: The Politics of Middle-Class Daily Life in Brazil.* Durham, NC: Duke University Press.

Olen, Helaine. 2013. *Pound Foolish: Exposing the Dark Side of the Personal Finance Industry.* New York: Portfolio/Penguin.

O'Malley, Pat. 1996. "Risk and Responsibility." In *Foucault and Political Reason: Liberalism, Neo-Liberalism, and Rationalities of Government,* ed. A. Barry, T. Osborne, and N. Rose, 189–207. Chicago: University of Chicago Press.

Orman, Suze. 1997. *The 9 Steps to Financial Freedom.* New York: Crown.

———. 2007a. *Women & Money: Owning the Power to Control Your Destiny.* New York: Spiegel & Grau.

———. 2007b. *Women & Money: Owning the Power to Control Your Destiny.* Arlington, VA: PBS Home Video.

Otálora, Mariano. 2011. *Del colchón a la inversión: Guía para ahorrar e invertir en la Argentina*. Buenos Aires: Planeta.

Papalini, Vanina. 2007. "La domesticación de los cuerpos." *Enlace* 4(1):39–53.

Pattillo, Mary. 1999. *Black Picket Fences: Privilege and Peril Among the Black Middle Class*. Chicago: University of Chicago Press.

———. 2007. *Black on the Block: The Politics of Race and Class in the City*. Chicago: University of Chicago Press.

Pedroso Neto, Antonio J. 2010. "A dinâmica do marketing de rede: Relações sociais e expectativas de um novo estilo de vida." *Horizontes Antropológicos* 16(33):93–120.

———. 2014. *A construção e a dinâmica do mercado em rede: O caso da Amway do Brasil*. Palmas, Tocatins: EDUFT.

Petit, Jean-Pierre. 2014. "Leçons argentines." *Le Monde.fr*. Retrieved September 2, 2014 (http://www.lemonde.fr/economie/article/2014/08/25/lecons-argentines_4476134 _3234.html).

Plata Dulce. Directed by Fernando Ayala. 1982 Buenos Aires: Aries Cinematográfica Argentina; Editorial Perfil, 2000. DVD.

Power, Michael. 2011. "Foucault and Sociology." *Annual Review of Sociology* 37(1):35–56.

Pratt, Michael G. 2000. "The Good, the Bad, and the Ambivalent: Managing Identification Among Amway Distributors." *Administrative Science Quarterly* 45(3):456.

Pratt, Michael G., and José Antonio Rosa. 2003. "Transforming Work-Family Conflict into Commitment in Network Marketing Organizations." *The Academy of Management Journal* 46(4):395–418.

Preda, Alex. 1999. "The Turn to Things: Arguments for a Sociological Theory of Things." *Sociological Quarterly* 40(2):347–66.

———. 2001. "The Rise of the Popular Investor: Financial Knowledge and Investing in England and France, 1840–1880." *Sociological Quarterly* 42(2):205–32.

Pucciarelli, Alfredo R., ed. 2006. *Los años de Alfonsín: El poder de la democracia o la democracia del poder?* Buenos Aires: Siglo XXI.

Rand, Ayn. 1943. *The Fountainhead*. Indianapolis: Bobbs-Merrill.

———. 1959. *We the Living*. New York: Random House.

———. 2007. *Atlas Shrugged*. 2nd Rev. ed. New York: Signet.

Ranney, David. 2003. *Global Decisions, Local Collisions: Urban Life in the New World Order*. Philadelphia: Temple University Press.

Rapping, Elayne. 1996. *The Culture of Recovery: Making Sense of the Self-Help Movement in Women's Lives*. Boston: Beacon Press.

Read, Jason. 2009. "A Genealogy of Homo-Economicus: Neoliberalism and the Production of Subjectivity." *Foucault Studies* 6:25–36.

Rimke, Heidi Marie. 2000. "Governing Citizens Through Self-Help Literature." *Cultural Studies* 14(1):61–78.

Rios, Victor M. 2011. *Punished: Policing the Lives of Black and Latino Boys*. New York: New York University Press.

Rischin, Moses. 1965. *The American Gospel of Success*. Chicago: Quadrangle Books.

Ritzer, George. 2004. *The McDonaldization of Society*. Thousand Oaks, CA: Pine Forge Press.

Robinson, Laura, and Jeremy Schulz. 2009. "New Avenues for Sociological Inquiry Evolving Forms of Ethnographic Practice." *Sociology* 43(4):685–98.

Rose, Nikolas. 1993. "Government, Authority and Expertise in Advanced Liberalism." *Economy and Society* 22(3):283.

———. 1996. "Governing 'Advanced' Liberal Democracies." In *Foucault and Political Reason: Liberalism, Neo-Liberalism, and Rationalities of Government*, ed. A. Barry, T. Osborne, and N. Rose, 37–64. Chicago: University of Chicago Press.

———. 1999. *Powers of Freedom: Reframing Political Thought*. Cambridge; New York: Cambridge University Press.

Rose, Nikolas, Pat O'Malley, and Mariana Valverde. 2006. "Governmentality." *Annual Review of Law and Social Science* 2(1):83–104.

Salerno, Steve. 2005. *SHAM: How the Self-Help Movement Made America Helpless*. New York: Crown.

Sallaz, Jeffrey J. 2008. "Deep Plays: A Comparative Ethnography of Gambling Contests in Two Post-Colonies." *Ethnography* 9(1):5–33.

Sassatelli, Roberta. 2007. *Consumer Culture: History, Theory and Politics*. Los Angeles: Sage.

Schutz, Alfred. 1944. "The Stranger: An Essay in Social Psychology." *American Journal of Sociology* 49(6):499–507.

Schvarzer, Jorge, and Hernán Finkelstein. 2003. "Bonos, cuasi monedas y política económica." *Realidad Económica* 193:79–95.

The Secret. Directed by Drew Heriot. 2006. Chicago: TS Production. DVD.

Seligson, Hannah. 2010. "Why So Many Financial Advice Books Perpetuate the False Notion That Women Are Bad with Money." *Slate*, November 10. Retrieved December 12, 2014 (http://www.slate.com/id/2274416/).

Shields, Stephanie A., Pamela Steinke, and Beth A. Koster. 1995. "The Double Bind of Caregiving: Representation of Gendered Emotion in American Advice Literature." *Sex Roles* 33(7):467–88.

Sigal, Silvia, and Gabriel Kessler. 1997. "La hiperinflación en Argentina: Comportamientos y representaciones sociales." In *La investigación social hoy: A cuarenta años de la recreación del Instituto de Sociología (UBA)*, ed. D. Canton and J. R. Jorrat, 155–87. Buenos Aires: Instituto de Investigaciones Gino Germani & Oficina de Publicaciones del CBC, UBA.

Simonds, Wendy. 1992. *Women and Self-Help Culture: Reading Between the Lines*. New Brunswick, NJ: Rutgers University Press.

Smith, Tara. 2003. "Money Can Buy Happiness." *Reason Papers* 26(Summer):7–19.

———. 2007. *Ayn Rand's Normative Ethics: The Virtuous Egoist*. Cambridge, MA: Cambridge University Press.

Sommers, Christina Hoff, and Sally L. Satel. 2005. *One Nation Under Therapy: How the Helping Culture Is Eroding Self-Reliance*. New York: St. Martin's Press.

Starker, Steven. 2002. *Oracle at the Supermarket: The American Preoccupation with Self-Help Books*. New Brunswick, NJ: Transaction.

Steiner, Philippe. 2008. "Foucault, Weber and the History of the Economic Subject." *The European Journal of the History of Economic Thought* 15(3):503–27.

Stratta, Isabel. 2004. "Libros de negocios: La receta para cocinar un best seller." *Clarín*, May 23. Retrieved September 9, 2014 (http://edant.clarin.com/suplementos/economico/2004/05/23/n-00311.htm).

Szakolczai, Arpad. 1998. "Reappraising Foucault." *American Journal of Sociology* 103(5):1402–10.

Tiempo Argentino. 2011. "Una fundación enseña valores del libre mercado en escuelas públicas." November 27. Retrieved November 5, 2014 (http://tiempo.infonews.com/nota/93477).

Travis, Trysh. 2009. *The Language of the Heart: A Cultural History of the Recovery Movement from Alcoholics Anonymous to Oprah Winfrey*. Chapel Hill: University of North Carolina Press.

Trump, Donald, and Robert Kiyosaki. 2006. *Why We Want You to Be Rich: Two Men, One Message*. Scottsdale, AZ: Rich Press.

Valentine, Debra A. 1998. "Pyramid Schemes." Prepared statement of the General Counsel for the U.S. Federal Trade Commission on pyramid schemes, presented at the International Monetary Fund's Seminar on Current Legal Issues Affecting Central Banks. Retrieved December 11, 2014 (http://www.ftc.gov/public-statements/1998/05/pyramid-schemes).

Valverde, Mariana. 1998. *Diseases of the Will: Alcohol and the Dilemmas of Freedom*. Cambridge; New York: Cambridge University press.

van der Zwan, Natascha. 2014. "Making Sense of Financialization." *Socio-Economic Review* 12(1):99–129.

Van Maanen, John. 1988. *Tales of the Field: On Writing Ethnography*. Chicago: University of Chicago Press.

Vargas Llosa, Mario. 2008. "Borges y los piqueteros." *El País*, April 6. Retrieved June 1, 2014 (http://elpais.com/diario/2008/04/06/opinion/1207432812_850215.html).

Venkatesh, Sudhir. 2002. "'Doin' the Hustle': Constructing the Ethnographer in the American Ghetto." *Ethnography* 3(1):91–111.

Verdery, Katherine. 1995a. "'Caritas': And the Reconceptualization of Money in Romania." *Anthropology Today* 11(1):3–7.

———. 1995b. "Faith, Hope, and Caritas in the Land of the Pyramids: Romania, 1990 to 1994." *Comparative Studies in Society and History* 37(4):625–69.

Vidas, Anath Ariel De. 2008. "Containing Modernity: The Social Life of Tupperware in a Mexican Indigenous Village." *Ethnography* 9(2):257–84.

Videla, Eduardo. 2012. "Escuela y adoctrinamiento." *Página/12*, September 17. Retrieved November 6, 2014 (http://www.pagina12.com.ar/diario/sociedad/3-203535-2012-09-17.html).

Vilas, Carlos M. 2006. "Neoliberal Meltdown and Social Protest: Argentina 2001–2002." *Critical Sociology* 32(1):163–86.

Villarreal, Juan. 1985. "Los hilos sociales del poder." In *Crisis de la dictadura argentina: Política económica y cambio social, 1976–1983*, ed. P. Paz, E. Jozami, and J. Villarreal, 197–283. Mexico City: Siglo XXI Editores.

Visacovsky, Sergio. 2010. *"Hasta la próxima crisis": Historia cíclica, virtudes genealógicas y la identidad de clase media entre los afectados por la debacle financiera en la Argentina, 2001–2002*. Mexico City: Centro de Investigación y Docencia Económicas (CIDE), División de Historia.

Wacquant, Loïc. 2003. *Body & Soul: Notebooks of an Apprentice Boxer*. Oxford; New York: Oxford University Press.

Wagnleitner, Reinhold, and Elaine Tyler May. 2000. *Here, There, and Everywhere: The Foreign Politics of American Popular Culture*. Hanover, NH: University Press of New England.

Weber, Max. 2002a. "Prefatory Remarks to Collected Essays in the Sociology of Religion." In *The Protestant Ethic and the Spirit of Capitalism: And Other Writings*, 356–72. New York: Penguin Classics.

———. 2002b. *The Protestant Ethic and the Spirit of Capitalism: And Other Writings*. New York: Penguin Classics.

Weiss, Richard. 1969. *The American Myth of Success from Horatio Alger to Norman Vincent Peale*. New York: Basic Books.

WFDSA. 2013a. "Avoiding Illegitimate Schemes." Retrieved October 26, 2014 (http://www.wfdsa.org/about_dir_sell/?fa=schemes1).

———. 2013b. "Global Statistics." Retrieved October 19, 2014 (http://www.wfdsa.org/about_wfdsa/?fa=globalStats).

Wherry, Frederick F. 2008. "The Social Characterizations of Price: The Fool, the Faithful, the Frivolous, and the Frugal." *Sociological Theory* 26(4):363–79.

———. 2014. "Analyzing the Culture of Markets." *Theory and Society* 43(3–4):421–36.

Whitford, Josh. 2005. *The New Old Economy: Networks, Institutions, and the Organizational Transformation of American Manufacturing*. Oxford; New York: Oxford University Press.

Wilson, Ara. 1998. "Decentralization and the Avon Lady in Bangkok, Thailand." *PoLAR: Political and Legal Anthropology Review* 21(1):77–83.

———. 1999. "The Empire of Direct Sales and the Making of Thai Entrepreneurs." *Critique of Anthropology* 19(4):401–22.

———. 2004. *The Intimate Economies of Bangkok*. Berkeley: University of California Press.

Woods, Nina Elina. 1996. "Women's Self-Help: A Feminist Critique." PhD Dissertation, Queen's University at Kingston, Canada.

World Economic Forum. 2011. *Global Education Initiative. Latin America Roundtable on Entrepreneurship Education*. Rio de Janeiro: World Economic Forum. Retrieved December 10, 2014 (http://www3.weforum.org/docs/WEF_GEI_LAEntrepreneurship Education_Report_2011.pdf).

Wyllie, Irvin. 1954. *The Self-Made Man in America: The Myth of Rags to Riches*. New Brunswick, NJ: Rutgers University Press.

Zelizer, Viviana. 2005. *The Purchase of Intimacy*. Princeton, NJ: Princeton University Press.

———. 2007. "Pasts and Futures of Economic Sociology." *American Behavioral Scientist* 50(8):1056–69.

Zimmerman, Toni Schindler, Kristen E. Holm, and Marjorie E. Starrels. 2001. "A Feminist Analysis of Self-Help Bestsellers for Improving Relationships: A Decade Review." *Journal of Marital and Family Therapy* 27(2):165.

Index